Preparing for

Reflective Teaching

Preparing for
Reflective Teaching

Carl A. Grant
University of Wisconsin–Madison

Allyn and Bacon, Inc.
Boston • London • Sydney • Toronto

Library of Congress Cataloging in Publication Data
Main entry under title:
    Preparing for reflective teaching.
    1. Teaching—Addresses, essays, lectures. 2. Teachers—
Self-rating of—United States—Addresses, essays,
lectures. I. Grant. Carl A.
LB1025.2.P656 1984 371.1'02 83-25790
ISBN 0-205-08092-8

Printed in the United States of America
10 9 8 7 6 5 4 3 2 1
88 87 86 85 84

Contents

Chapter 1. The Teacher

Chapter 2. Schools and Society

Chapter 3. Curriculum and Materials

Chapter 4. Instruction and Classroom Management

Chapter 5. Kids

Preface

It would be ideal if we could meet each week in a different school throughout the United States — even the world — to discuss teaching and talk to enthusiastic professional educators and community people who support and respect our profession. Since I don't have the money, however, to finance such a provocative learning experience, allow me to use this book to chat with you about reflective teaching.

Reflective teaching (as you will discover in the first article) occurs when you question and clarify why you have chosen your classroom methods, procedures, and content. It also includes studying the school environment in relationship to those choices to determine how the environment encourages or hinders reflective teaching. Reflective teaching is an ongoing process that involves careful re-examination of what you have done and the social context in which it was done in order to help you do what you wanted to do better. It is thinking analytically about your goals, your teaching actions, and your teaching environment, and using those thoughts to improve your future teaching.

It is important for you to understand that the journey from the student's desk to the teacher's desk is a tough and challenging one. In fact, teaching has become a much more difficult job in the last twenty-five years, and there doesn't seem to be any indication that the hard work that accompanies it is going to diminish in the near future. The recent reports describing the need for improvement in education represent a call for reflective teaching.

Although I work at a university, I spend a great deal of my time in schools, talking with students and teachers, and studying the process of schooling. I firmly believe the most important thing that you can do for yourself and the teaching profession is to think reflectively and critically about what you are doing. This reflective thinking is crucial to your becoming a terrific teacher.

This book, I hope, will help you think reflectively and critically about teaching. Each of the articles in the book raises questions about teaching that you should work through; questions are also raised before and after several articles. Many of the articles were written especially for the book in response to the invitation: "If you had only five or ten minutes to talk with a group of prospective teachers about your area of interest, what would you say? Be provocative, informative, and straight-forward." The remainder of the articles is the fruit of month of searching for materials that would meet the same criteria.

Preparing for Reflective Teaching is divided into five chapters: The Teacher, School and Society, Curriculum, Instruction and Classroom Management, and Kids. I would strongly urge you to read the first chapter first. After that the choice is yours.

Chapter 1

The Teacher

From the title, you will have gathered that this book has been designed to help you become a reflective teacher. You are probably wondering what a reflective teacher is, whether that is the kind of teacher you wish to become, and how this book can help you become one. Anticipating your questions, Ken Zeichner and I have written an article to clarify what reflective teaching means and to provide you with suggestions to help you on your way to becoming a reflective teacher. As you read the rest of this book, use these suggestions to analyze what the authors of the remaining papers are saying and to evaluate their arguments in relation to your own values and beliefs about teaching.

On Becoming a Reflective Teacher

Carl A. Grant and Kenneth M. Zeichner
University of Wisconsin

If teachers today are to initiate young people into an ethical existence, they themselves must attend more fully than they normally have to their own lives and its requirements; they have to break with the mechanical life, to overcome their own submergence in the habitual, even in what they conceive to be virtuous, and to ask the "why" with which all moral reasoning begins.[1]

Maxine Greene
Teacher as Stranger

As you proceed with your professional education, you will continually be confronted with numerous choices about the kind of teacher to become. Recent literature in education has clearly shown that teachers differ substantially according to their goals and priorities and to the instructional and classroom management strategies that they employ.

Written expressly for *Preparing for Reflective Teaching*.

These differences among teachers have usually been portrayed as contrasting "types." For example, much has been written in recent years about the differences between teachers who are "open or traditional," "child-centered or subject-centered," "direct or indirect," and "humanistic or custodial." These dichotomies attempt to differentiate teachers who hold different views about what is important for children to learn, preferred instructional and management strategies, and types of curricular materials, and about the kinds of school and classroom organizational structures within which they want to work. The kind of teacher you wish to become, the stands you take on educational issues, and the knowledge and skills you need for putting your beliefs into action all represent decisions you as a prospective teacher need to make.

Over a hundred years of educational research has yet to discover the most effective instructional methods and school and classroom organizational structures for all students. This, together with the fact that "rules for practice" cannot now and probably never will be easily derived from either college coursework or practical school experience, makes your choices regarding these issues and the manner in which you determine them of great importance.

With regard to instructional strategies and methods, you will literally be bombarded in your courses and practicums with suggestions and advice regarding the numerous techniques and strategies that are now available for the instruction of children in the various content areas. For example, you will be taught various strategies for leading discussions, managing small groups, designing learning centers, administering diagnostic and evaluative procedures, and teaching concepts and skills.

Furthermore, in each of the content areas there are choices to be made about a general approach or orientation to instruction over and above the choice of specific instructional techniques and procedures. You, ultimately, must make decisions about which approach or combination of approaches to employ amid competing claims by advocates that their approach offers the best solution to problems of instruction.

Undoubtedly, there is a great deal of debate in education today over how to go about teaching agreed upon content and skills and about the ways to manage classrooms and children. However, the question of *what* to teach, and to whom, precedes the question of *how* to teach. The selection of content to be taught to a particular group of children and of the types of instructional materials and resources to support this process are issues of great importance despite the fact that any school in which you are likely to work will have some set of policies. Although there are limits placed upon teachers regarding curricular content and materials, teachers usually have some latitude in the selection of specific content and materials within broad curricular guidelines.

For example, in the state of Wisconsin it is required that teachers teach the history of their state as part of the 4th grade social studies curriculum. Within these guidelines, individual teachers usually have some degree of choice about what to teach or emphasize about Wisconsin history and about what materials to use. This holds true in most curricular areas; even where schools have adopted particular instructional approaches and programs, such as in reading and math, teachers are still permitted some degree of personal discretion in the selection of content and materials.

You will also face a set of options about the kinds of school organizational structures in which you will work, and you will need to be aware that not all structures are compatible with all positions on issues of curriculum and instruction. At the elementary school level, for example, do you prefer to work in a self-contained classroom with one group of children or do you prefer to work closely with colleagues in a departmentalized context, such as is found in many individually guided education schools? Furthermore, you must begin to form positions about the kinds of school and classroom structures that will support the kind of teaching you want to do.

In addition to these numerous choices and issues, there is another and more basic choice facing you. This choice concerns the way in which you go about formulating positions with regard to the issues mentioned above. To what degree will you consciously direct this process of decision-making in pursuit of desired ends and in light of educational and ethical principles? On the other hand, to what degree will your decisions be mechanically directed by others; by impulse, tradition, and authority? An important distinction is made between being a reflective or an unreflective teacher, and it necessarily involves every prospective teacher no matter what your orientation and regardless of the specific positions that you eventually adopt on the issues of curriculum and instruction.

You may be wondering what we mean by being a reflective teacher. In the early part of this century, John Dewey made an important distinction between human action that is reflective and that which is routine. Much of what Dewey had to say on this matter was directed specifically to teachers and prospective teachers, and his remarks remain very relevant for those in the process of becoming teachers in the 1980s. According to Dewey,[2] *routine action* is behavior that is guided by impulse, tradition, and authority. In any social setting, and the school is no exception, there exists a taken-for-granted definition of everyday reality in which problems, goals, and the means for their solution become defined in particular ways. As long as everyday life continues without major interruption, this reality is perceived to be unproblematic. Furthermore, this dominant world view is only one of the many views of reality that would theoretically be possible, and it serves as a barrier to recognizing and experimenting with alternative viewpoints.

Teachers who are unreflective about their work uncritically accept this everyday reality in schools and concentrate their efforts on finding the most effective and efficient means to achieve ends and to solve problems that have largely been defined for them by others. These teachers lose sight of the fact that their everyday reality is only one of many possible alternatives. They tend to forget the purposes and ends toward which they are working.

Dewey defines *reflective action*,[3] on the other hand, as behavior which involves active, persistent, and careful consideration of any belief or practice in light of the grounds that support it and the further consequences to which it leads. According to Dewey, reflection involves a way of meeting and responding to problems. Reflective teachers actively reflect upon their teaching and upon the educational, social and political contexts in which their teaching is embedded.

There are three attitudes that Dewey defines as prerequisites for reflective action.[4] First, *openmindedness* refers to an active desire to listen to more sides than one, to give full attention to alternate possibilities, and to recognize the possibility of error even in the beliefs that are dearest to us. Prospective teachers who are openminded are continually examining the rationales (educational or otherwise) that underlie what is taken to be natural and right and take pains to seek out conflicting evidence on issues of educational practice.

Second, an attitude of *responsibility* involves careful consideration of the consequences to which an action leads. Responsible student teachers ask themselves why they are doing what they are doing in the classroom in a way that transcends questions of immediate utility and in light of educational purposes of which they are aware. If all that is taught in schools were imparted through the formally sanctioned academic curriculum and if all of the consequences of teachers' actions could be anticipated in advance, the problem here would be much simpler than it is in actuality. However, there is a great deal of agreement among educators of various ideological persuasions that much of what children learn in school is imparted through the covert processes of the so called "hidden curriculum" and that many consequences of the actions of educators are unanticipated outcomes that often contradict formally stated educational goals. Given the powerful impact of the hidden curriculum on the actual outcomes of schooling and the frequently unanticipated consequences of our actions, reflection about the potential impact of our actions in the classroom is extremely important.

The third and final attitude of the reflective teacher is one of *wholeheartedness*. This refers to the fact that openmindedness and responsibility must be central components in the life of the reflective teacher and implies that prospective teachers who are reflective must take active control over their education as teachers. A great deal of research demonstrates that prospective teachers very quickly adopt beliefs and practices of those university and school instructors with whom they work. Many prospective teachers seem to become primarily concerned with meeting the oftentimes conflicting expectations of university professors and cooperating teachers, and with presenting a favorable image to them in the hope of securing favorable evaluations. This impression management is understandable and is a natural consequence of existing power relationships in teacher education, but the divided interest that results tends to divert students' attention from a critical analysis of their work and the context in which it is performed. If reflectiveness is to be part of the lives of prospective teachers, students will have to seek actively to be openminded and responsible or else the pressure of the taken-for-granted institutional realities will force them back into routine behavior.

Possession of these attitudes of openmindedness, responsibility, and wholeheartedness, together with a command of technical skills of inquiry (for example observation) and problem solving define for Dewey a teacher who is reflective. Reflection, according to Dewey,

> emancipates us from merely impulsive and routine activity . . . enables us to direct our actions with foresight and to plan according to ends in view of purposes of which we are aware. It enables us to know what we are about when we act.[5]

On the other hand, according to Dewey, to cultivate unreflective activity is "to further enslavement for it leaves the person at the mercy of appetite, sense and circumstance."[6]

Choosing between becoming a reflective teacher or an unreflective teacher is one of the most important decisions that you will have to make. The quality of all of your decisions regarding curriculum and instruction rests upon this choice.

You are probably saying to yourself, "Of course I want to be a reflective teacher, who wouldn't. But, you need to tell me more." The following sections of the paper discuss the three characteristics of reflective thinking in relation to classroom teaching, analyze whether reflective teaching is a realistic and/or desirable goal, and offer suggestions for how you can begin to become a reflective teacher.

Further Insight

We have pointed out that openmindedness, responsibility, and wholeheartedness are the characteristics of reflective thinking. Let us now discuss each characteristic in relation to classroom teaching.

Openmindedness

When you begin to teach, both as a student teacher and as a licensed teacher, you will most likely be asked to accept teaching procedures and strategies that are already being used in that school or classroom. Will you accept these without question, or will you explore alternative ways of looking at existing teaching practices? For example, celebrating holidays like Thanksgiving and Columbus Day helps to affirm the prevailing historical accounts of these days as well as the customs and traditions associated with them. As a teacher, would you be willing to reevaluate what and how you teach about holidays if some of the students in your class hold a different point of view about them? Would you modify your teaching to take into account their views and beliefs? Being a reflective teacher means that you keep an open mind about the content, methods, and procedures used in your classroom. You constantly reevaluate their worth in relation to the students currently enrolled and to the circumstances. You not only ask why things are the way that they are, but also how they can be made better.

The reflective teacher understands that school practices are not accepted because they are clothed in tradition. If, for example, most of the boys but only a few of the girls are being assigned to Industrial Arts, you should inquire as to why this is happening. You could then begin to formulate teaching and counseling plans (for example, career opportunities, workshops) that would allow students regardless of gender to benefit from the training that is available in those courses.

Responsibility

Teaching involves moral and responsible action. Teachers make moral choices when they make voluntary decisions to have students attain one educational objective instead of another. These decisions are conscious actions that result in certain consequences. These actions can be observed when teachers develop curriculum and choose instructional materials. For example, until recently a textbook company had two basal readers in its reading series. One basal reader was somewhat racially integrated and the other had all white characters. When teachers consciously chose one basal reader over the other or did not modify the all white reader to correct the racial bias, they made a decision that affected not only their students' racial attitudes and understanding about different groups of people, but also their attitudes about themselves. In other words, teachers can encourage ethnocentric attitudes as well as teach an unrealistic view of the world community beyond the school community by failing to provide knowledge about other groups.

As a reflective teacher you are aware of your actions and their consequences. You are aware that your teaching behavior should not be conditioned merely by the immediate utility of an action. For example, it may be much easier to have your students answer questions or work problems on conveniently prepared ditto sheets than to have them do small group projects or hold classroom debates. It may also be much easier if you use one textbook to teach a unit on the Mexican American War than if you use multiple textbooks and other historical documents that would represent both governments' points of view. But immediate utility cannot become the sole justification for your actions and cannot excuse you from the consequences of your actions. Your actions must have a definite and responsibly selected purpose. You have an obligation to consider their consequences in relation to the lives of the students you have accepted the responsibility to teach.

Wholeheartedness

A reflective teacher is not openminded and responsible merely when it is convenient. Openmindedness and responsibility are integral, vital dimensions of your teaching philosophy and behavior. For example, we have seen teachers publicly advocate a belief in integrating handicapped students into the regular class; however, when observing in their classrooms, we saw the handicapped students treated in isolation because the curriculum and the instructional strategies had not been modified to capitalize upon the students' strengths or to acknowledge the students' individual differences. The teachers often left handicapped students to sit in the outer boundaries of the classroom instead of changing the physical environment of the classroom—desk arrangements—to allow them to move about freely as other students would. As a reflective teacher, you do not hesitate or forget to fight for your beliefs and for a quality education for all.

The reflective teacher is dedicated and committed to teaching *all students*, not just certain students. Many of your peers say they want to teach because they love and enjoy working with kids. Are they *really* saying *any* and *all* kids, or are they saying kids that are just like them? The story of Mary Smith will help to illustrate our point. During a job interview with a rural school system, Mary Smith, a graduate from a large urban university, was composed and fluent in discussing teaching methods and curriculum. She also stressed her genuine love for and enjoyment of children and her desire to help them. Her "performance" was so compelling that she was invited to accept a teaching position. Mary Smith, we must point out, believed what she said in the interview and eagerly looked forward to her teaching assignment. Her assignment was to a six room rural school, where the majority of the students spoke with a heavy regional dialect that she had never before heard. The students' reading and mathematics achievement according to standardized tests was three to four years below grade level. Their behavior and attitudes toward school were different from what she had been accustomed to. They regarded the schools as boring and irrelevant to their life style and their future, and they demonstrated their disregard for the school and the teacher by disobeying many instructional and behavioral "requests." Mary tried diligently for three months to get the students to cooperate and follow her instructions. At the beginning of the fourth month, however, she resigned her position. In her letter of resignation she stated that "these kids are not ready to accept what I have been trained to give them. Therefore, I will seek teaching employment where the students want to learn."

There are many teachers like Mary Smith, but the reflective teacher is not one of them. The reflective teacher is wholehearted in accepting *all* students and is willing to learn about and affirm the uniqueness of each student for whom he or she accepts responsibility. If you are a reflective teacher, your teaching behavior is a manifestation of your teaching philosophy and you are unswerving in your desire to make certain that the two become one and the same.

Is Reflective Teaching a Realistic and/or Desirable Goal?

Throughout this century many educators have argued that teachers need to be more reflective about their work. The argument is often made that schools and society are constantly changing and that teachers must be reflective in order to cope effectively with changing circumstances. By uncritically accepting what is customary and by engaging in fixed and patterned behaviors, teachers make it more unlikely that they will be able to change and grow as situations inevitably change. Furthermore, it is commonly accepted that no teacher education program, whatever its focus, can prepare teachers to work effectively in all kinds of classroom settings. Therefore, it becomes important for you to be reflective in order that you may intelligently apply the knowledge and skills gained in your formal preparation for teaching to situations that may be very different from those you experienced during your training.

At the same time many questions have been raised about whether reflective teaching is a realistic or even necessary goal to set before prospective teachers. The purpose of this section is to examine briefly three of the most common objections that have been raised about the goal of reflective teaching and to demonstrate how, despite these doubts, it is still possible and desirable for teachers to work toward a more reflective orientation to both their work and their workplace.

Is It Possible to Take the Time to Reflect?

Many have argued that the nature of teaching and the ecology of classrooms make reflective teaching unrealistic and even undesirable. For example, it is frequently pointed out that classrooms are fast-paced and unpredictable environments where teachers are often required to make spontaneous decisions in response to childrens' ongoing reactions to an instructional program. Phillip Jackson has estimated that teachers engage in approximately 1,000 interpersonal interactions on any given day and there is no way to describe life in the classroom as anything but extremely complex.[7]

Furthermore, institutional constraints such as high pupil-teacher ratios, the lack of released time for reflection, and pressures to cover a required curriculum with diverse groups of children who are compelled to come to school shape and limit the range of possible teacher actions. The point is made that teachers do not have the time to reflect given the necessity of quick action and the press of institutional demands. According to this view, intuitiveness (as opposed to reflectiveness) is an adaptive response and a natural consequence of the fast-paced and unpredictable nature of classroom life and is necessary for teachers to be able to negotiate classroom demands.

Phillip Jackson expresses serious doubts about whether teachers could even function at all in classrooms if they spent more time reflecting about the purposes and consequences of their work.

> If teachers sought a more thorough understanding of their world, insisted on greater rationality in their actions, were completely openminded in their consideration of pedagogical choices and profound in their view of the human condition, they might well receive greater applause from intellectuals, but it is doubtful that they would perform with greater efficiency in the classroom. On the contrary, it is quite possible that such paragons of virtue, if they could be found to exist, would actually have a deuce of a time coping in any sustained way with a class of third graders or a play yard full of nursery school tots.[8]

While classrooms are indeed fast-paced and complex environments, it does not automatically follow that reflective teaching is incompatible with this reality and that teachers by necessity must rely primarily upon intuition and unreflective actions. Several studies[9] have convincingly shown that the quality of teacher deliberations *outside* of the classroom (for example, during planning periods or team meetings) affects the quality of their future actions *within* the classroom. As Dewey points out, "To reflect is to look back on what has been done to extract the meanings which are the capital stock for dealing with further experience."[10] Reflection which is directed toward the improvement of classroom practice does not necessarily need to take place within the classroom to have an impact on classroom practice. Despite the fact that reflection as has been defined in this paper does not occur in many schools even when there has been time set aside for that purpose,[11] the possibility still exists.

Furthermore, the fast pace of classroom life does not preclude a certain amount of reflection within its boundaries. Those who have written about reflective teaching have never argued for "complete openness of mind." On the contrary, reflective teaching involves a balance between thought and action; a balance between the arrogance that blindly rejects what is commonly accepted as truth and the servility that blindly receives this "truth." There is clearly such a thing as too much thinking, as when a person finds it difficult to reach any definite conclusion and wanders helplessly among the multitude of choices presented by a situation, but to imply that reflection necessarily paralyzes one from action is to distort the true meaning of reflective teaching.

Is It Possible to Act on the Results of Reflection?

Another objection that has frequently been raised is that even if teachers do reflect on the purposes and consequences of their actions, they are not able to act on the results of their inquiries if the desired course of action is in conflict with the dominant institutional norms of their school. According to this view, teachers are basically functionaries within a bureaucratic system; they have prescribed roles and responsibilities, and in order to survive in that system they must always give way to institutional demands. In other words, why bother with reflection if you always have to do what you are told to do anyway? Encouraging prospective teachers to reflect about their work is viewed as a hopeless endeavor, because whatever habits of reflectiveness are developed during preservice training will inevitably be "washed out" by inservice school experience as teachers are forced into standardized patterns of behavior and into conformity with bureaucratic norms of obedience and loyalty to those in authority. As Wayne Hoy and William Rees[12] point out, the forces of bureaucratic socialization in schools are strong and efficient.

As was mentioned earlier, there is little doubt that schools as institutions and the societal contexts in which they are embedded exert numerous pressures on teachers to conform to certain behavioral norms, to cover certain curricular content and to use particular methods of instruction and classroom management. However, while they are necessarily constrained by these institutional pressures and by their own individual biases and predispositions, teachers do to varying degrees play active roles in shaping their own occupational identities. If, for example, you were to survey the teachers within a given school, it would probably be fairly easy to identify a dominant "teacher culture" in that school, which defines a set of viewpoints about curriculum, instruction, classroom management and organization. Yet, at the same time, you will inevitably find differences and conflicts among teachers in that school in terms of their beliefs, their instructional methods, and the ways in which they have organized their classrooms. Not all teachers in a given school are alike, and the very existence of these differences within the same institutional conditions is evidence of the potential for teachers to act upon their beliefs even if they conflict with the dominant viewpoints in a given setting.

In reality, the habits of mind and pedagogical skills that you develop now in your formal education for teaching will not necessarily be "washed out" by school experience. The world of teaching necessarily involves a constant interplay between choice and constraint. No matter how prescribed the curriculum and whatever the degree of consensus over behavioral norms for teachers in the settings in which you will work, there will always be some degree of conflict over what is natural and right and some amount of space for you to act alone or with others to reshape the nature of the school in which you work. There are more than a few teachers who do not fit the bureaucratic mold that is frequently portrayed in educational literature, and there is potentially enough room for most teachers within their prescribed roles for some degree of reflection to take place.

Is It Necessary to Reflect?

A third objection that has been raised about reflective teaching is that it is not necessary to be reflective in order to be an effective teacher. Advocates of this position point to the many highly regarded teachers in our schools who succeed without apparently reflecting on the purposes and consequences of their work. For example, Phillip Jackson studied fifty teachers who were identified by their principals and by general reputation as being outstanding teachers, and he concluded that these exemplars of educational practice approached their work in classrooms largely through intuition rather than through any process of rational analysis.

This conclusion has been confirmed by much of the recent research on teacher thinking[13] by studies of teacher-pupil interactions[14] and by

Dan Lortie's[15] study of the "ethos" of the teaching profession. According to many education researchers, teachers for the most part, including good teachers, do not seem to be especially reflective or analytic about their work. On the contrary, a substantial number of teachers seem to accept uncritically what is currently fashionable. As a result, the position is often taken that it is unnecessary to be reflective because one can be a good teacher without being so.

There are several responses that one could make to this objection. First, there are numerous problems with the conclusions that many researchers have drawn about the predominance of intuitive behavior. Specifically, while it may be true that many teachers rely primarily on instinct and feeling while in the classroom, there is no basis for concluding that good teachers do not put a lot of thought into their work both before and after instruction. Many of these researchers have failed to study what teachers actually do in their classes and how they construct and justify specific activities. What actually goes on in the minds of good teachers —when it is studied—is still not well understood. Furthermore, there are some real problems with the view that university scholars are as a group more reflective than teachers, especially when these conclusions are drawn by those who identify themselves as being most reflective. In our view there is no convincing evidence that those in universities are any more or less likely as a group to be reflective or analytic about their work than teachers are.

Our own experience in talking with teachers has convinced us that the really good ones do reflect upon their work and that educational researchers have failed to capture much of what goes on in the minds of teachers. In fact, studies of attempted school reform provide some evidence that teachers *do* reflect. For example, those who have studied the processes of change in schools have generally concluded that teachers are very selective about what they will incorporate into their classrooms, and in our view this selectivity refutes the position that there is little thought and judgment underlying teacher's work.[16]

There is one further reason for rejecting the view that reflective teaching is not necessary. Scheffler clearly summarizes this view:

> Justification for reflection is not . . . simply a matter of minimal necessity. It is rather a matter of desirability, and a thing may be desirable, not because it is something that we could not do without, but because it transforms and enhances the quality of what we do and how we live.[17]

As Scheffler's statement points out, you may be able to get by, by putting little thought into your work, but if you want to strive to be the best teacher that you possibly can, then there is in reality no alternative to reflective teaching. Many teachers profess that they want their students to be thoughtful about the work that they do in school so that they will eventually develop an independence of mind that will enable them to be active participants in a democratic society. If we hold these goals for our children, the place to begin is with ourselves. If the schools of today were all that they could be, one could safely ignore our arguments. But if there is more that we can do to make our schools and our society more enriching, humane and just, then we need reflective teachers to play an integral role in this process.

How to Begin

You may be asking, "How can I become reflective, especially given the fact that I haven't started teaching yet?" The suggestions that we will now offer will help you get started. Remember, becoming a reflective teacher is a continual process of growth.

Many educators have correctly pointed out that even before you enter a formal program of teacher preparation you have already been socialized to some extent by the twelve years or more you have spent as a student. You have spent literally thousands of hours assessing schools and classrooms and have by now internalized (largely unconsciously) conceptions of children, learning, the roles of teacher and student, curriculum, beliefs and assumptions concerning almost every issue related to schooling. From our point of view, a good place to begin the process of reflective teaching is to examine these numerous predispositions that you bring with you into formal preparation for teaching. Consciously or not, these will affect how you will perceive what will be presented to you in your teacher education program and how you will interpret your own and others' actions in the classroom.

It is important for you to begin to discriminate between beliefs and assumptions that rest upon tested evidence and those that do not, and to be cautious about putting confidence into beliefs that are not well justified. Some of our ideas have, in fact, been picked up from other people merely because they are widely accepted views, not because we have examined them carefully. Because of the nature of teaching, we may often be compelled to act without full confidence in a point of view or an approach to a problem. This is unavoidable. However, if we remain tentative about our beliefs, the possibility will remain that we may revise our thinking if future evidence warrants it. On the other hand, if we are dogmatic about our beliefs and refuse to entertain the possibility that we may be in error, the avenues for further growth are closed off. There are no greater errors that prospective teachers can make than those that stem from an unbending certainty in one's beliefs.

In *Dilemmas of Schooling*, Ann and Harold Berlak propose several specific steps for proceeding with a reflective analysis of the assumptions and beliefs regarding schooling that one brings into one's teacher preparation.[18] The first step is to begin to articulate your current beliefs regarding a host of specific issues and to examine the assumptions that underlie these beliefs. For example, what knowledge and skills should be taught to different groups of children? How much control should a teacher exert over childrens' learning and behavior? To what extent should teachers transmit a common core of values and beliefs to all children, and to what extent should the curriculum attend to the cultural knowledge and background experiences of children? The issues here are endless. The above examples are only intended as illustrations of the kinds of questions that can be considered.

The next step is to compare your own beliefs with the beliefs of others. It is important for you to seek actively to understand the beliefs of others (peers, instructors, friends,) within your formal courses and, more generally, by reading, observing, and talking to others in both professional and nonprofessional settings. Prospective teachers who are sensitive to the tentative nature of their beliefs take pains to examine any issue from more than one perspective.

Once you have begun to identify the substance of your own beliefs and have become more conscious of alternatives that exist or could be created, it is important for you to do some thinking about the origins and consequences of these beliefs. For example, how has your own biographical history (for example, unique factors in your upbringing, your school experience as a pupil) affected the way in which you currently think about issues of schooling? Which of your current beliefs have you examined carefully through weighing and then rejecting alternative points of view, and which do you hold merely because they are widely accepted by those with whom you associate? Also, which of your current beliefs are the result of outside forces over which you have no control, and which beliefs are merely rationalizations masking an unwillingness to risk the difficulties and/or the possible displeasure of others that would result from their implementation?

Along with doing this analysis of the origin of your beliefs, you should begin to consider the possible consequences for yourself and others of holding particular beliefs. For example, what meanings (intended and unintended) are children likely to take from particular beliefs if they were actually implemented in the classroom? In considering the likely consequences of various courses of action it is important to consider more than the immediate utility of an action. The costs associated with what works in the short run to help you get through a lesson smoothly at times may outweigh the benefits to be gained.

Because of the intimate relationship that exists between the school and society, any consideration of the consequences of an educational action must inevitably take one beyond the boundaries of the classroom and even the school itself. There is no such thing as a neutral educational activity. Any action that one takes in the classroom is necessarily linked to the external economic, political and social order in either a primarily integrative or a creative fashion. Either a teaching activity serves to integrate children into the current social order or it provides children with the knowledge, attitudes or skills to deal critically and creatively with that reality in order to improve it. In any case, all teaching is embedded in an ideological background, and one cannot fully understand the significance or consequences of an activity unless one also considers that activity in light of the more general issues of social continuity and change.

For example, what are the likely consequences for the life chances of various groups of children if you present school knowledge as certain and objective to some groups of children and stress the tentativeness of knowledge to others? In other words, if you teach some students to accept what they are told and others to question and make their own decisions, how will this affect the social roles they hold later, and which group of children will you be preparing for which social roles? This example is cited to make the point that one can at least begin to identify the connections between everyday classroom practices and issues of social continuity and change. Because of the numerous forces acting upon children over a period of many years, we can never be certain of the effect that any given course of action by one teacher has in the long run, but it is certain that, despite the complexity, linkages do exist. It is important at least to attempt to think about the consequences of our actions in a way that transcends questions of immediate utility.

Finally, once you have begun to think about the origins and consequences of the beliefs that you bring into your formal education, the issue of "craft" also needs to be considered. What knowledge and skills will you need to gain in order to implement successfully the kind of teaching that follows from your educational beliefs? If you as a prospective teacher are reflective, you do not passively absorb any and all of the skills and knowledge that others have decided are necessary for your education as a teacher. The craft knowledge and skills for teaching that you will gain during your formal preparation will originate from two major sources: your university instructors and supervisors, and the teachers and administrators with whom you will work during your practicum experiences in schools. If you are reflective about your own education for teaching, you will give some direction to the craft knowledge and skills that you learn in your training.

Within the university your socialization for teaching is much more than the learning of "appropriate" content and procedures for teaching.

The knowledge and skills that will be communicated to you through your university courses are not neutral descriptions of how things are; in reality, they are *value governed selections* from a much larger universe of possibilities. Selections that reflect the educational ideologies of the instructors with whom you come into contact. Some things have been selected for your pursuance while other things have been deemphasized or even ignored. These selections reflect at least implicitly answers to normative questions about the nature of schooling, the appropriate roles for teachers and students, how to classify, arrange and evaluate educational knowledge, and how to think about educational problems and their solutions. But just as you will find diversity in the educational perspectives of a group of teachers in any given school, within any university program different university instructors will emphasize, deemphasize and ignore difficult points of view. As a result, it often becomes necessary for you to make decisions about the relevance of conflicting positions on an issue and to seek out information that supports views that may have been selected out by your instructors.

Therefore, if you want to give some direction to your education and to play an active role in shaping your own occupational identity, it becomes important for you to be constantly critical and reflective about that which is presented to you and that which has been omitted. That which is presented to you may or may not be the most appropriate craft knowledge and skill to help you get where you want to go. You need to filter all that is offered to you through your own set of priorities. At the same time, identify and use the instructors' stances about educational issues as alternatives that can help you develop your own beliefs. Generally, the same critical orientation that we have encouraged you to bring to bear upon your own prior experiences and beliefs should also be applied to that which is imparted to you by university instructors. Specifically, what are the origins and consequences of the viewpoints presented, and of the alternatives that are available or could be created?

Finally, one important part of your education for teaching will be the time you spend observing and working with teachers and administrators in school practicums. When you participate in a practicum you come into a setting (someone else's classroom) after certain patterns have been established and after certain ways of organizing time, space, instruction and so forth have become routine. Cooperating teachers, who make many of these decisions, will often not take the time to explain to you how and why these decisions have been made, partly because the routines are by then part of the taken-for-granted reality of their classrooms. Consequently, prospective teachers often fail to grasp how what they see came to be in the first place and are often incapable of creating certain structures on their own once they have their own classrooms. This is a serious lapse in an education student's learning because it is difficult to understand any setting adequately without understanding how it was produced. If you want to understand the settings in which you will work, you will need to question your teachers about the reasons underlying what exists and is presently taken for granted. The following questions illustrate the things you should seek to understand: Why is the school day organized as it is? Why is math taught every day but science taught only once per week? How and why was it decided to teach this particular unit on pollution? How are children placed into groups for reading and what opportunities exist for movement among groups? These regularities exist for particular reasons and it is up to you to seek an understanding of how what is, came to be.

You will also need to ask your cooperating teachers about the ways in which particular decisions are being made while you are there. Although many of the basic patterns of classrooms will be established before you arrive, others will still be developing. The basic problem here is for you to gain an understanding of the thought processes that underlie your cooperating teacher's current actions. Importantly, many researchers have discovered that unless education students initiate these kinds of discussions with their mentors, the logic behind classroom decisions is often missed by prospective teachers.[19] Experienced teachers may take many important factors for granted, and unless you actively probe for what underlies their behavior you will miss much of what is significant about the nature of teacher decision-making.

Seymour Sarason proposes that two basic questions be asked of any educational setting. One is what is the rationale underlying the setting? And the other is what is the universe of alternatives that could be considered?[20] We strongly feel that asking these questions is necessary in order for you to gain the maximum benefit from your practical experience in schools. If you choose not to follow our advice but to take a primarily passive role as a student teacher, your learning will be limited to that which you happen upon by chance. If you want to be a certain kind of teacher and to have a particular quality of impact on children, you will need to insure that your education for teaching will help you get where you want to go and that where you want to go is worth the effort. As you gain more experience you may frequently change your mind about the kind of teacher you want to become, but taking an active part in your own professional preparation will at least give you some control over determining the direction in which you are headed.

We have attempted to alert you to some of the numerous issues that you will have to confront during the next few years of your education for teaching. We have argued that there is a fundamental choice for you to make: whether you will give some direction to your training or let others direct it for you. In doing so, we have argued that reflective teaching is both possible and desirable. If the teachers of tomorrow are to contribute to the revitalization and renewal of our schools, there is no alternative. However, as in all decisions, the final choice is up to you.

Notes

[1] Maxine Greene, *Teacher as Stranger* (Belmont, CA: Wadsworth Publishing Co, 1973), p. 46.

[2] John Dewey, *How We Think: A Restatement of the Relation of Reflective Thinking to the Educative Process* (Chicago: Henry Regnery and Co., 1933).

[3] *Ibid.*

[4] *Ibid.*

[5] *Ibid.*, p. 17.

[6] *Ibid.*, p. 89.

[7] Phillip Jackson, *Life in Classrooms* (New York: Holt, Rinehart and Winston, 1968).

[8] *Ibid.*, p. 151.

[9] For example, see John Eliott, "Developing Hypotheses about Classrooms From Teachers' Personal Constructs," *Interchange* 7:2 (1976-1977) 1-22.

[10] Dewey, *How We Think*, p. 87.

[11] Frequently, discussions that occur among teachers during planning sessions, team meetings, etc., focus almost entirely on procedural issues (for example, *How* will we teach what has already been decided to teach?) to the neglect of curricular questions, such as "What should we be teaching and why?" See Thomas Popkewitz, B. Robert Tabachnick, and Gary Wehlage, *The Myth of Educational Reform* (Madison: University of Wisconsin Press, 1982) for an example of how this occurs in exemplary "individually guided education" schools.

[12] Wayne Hoy and William Rees, "The Bureaucratic Socialization of Student Teachers," *Journal of Teacher Education*, 28 (January-February, 1977) 23-26.

[13] Christopher Clark and Robert Yinger, "Research on Teacher Thinking," *Curriculum Inquiry*, 7 (Winter, 1977): 279-304.

[14] Jere Brophy and Thomas Good, *Teacher-Pupil Relationships: Causes and Consequences* (New York: Holt, Rinehart and Winston, 1974).

[15] Dan Lortie, *School Teacher* (Chicago: University of Chicago Press, 1975).

[16] John Goodlad and M. Frances Klein, *Behind the Classroom Door* (Washington, Ohio: Jones Publishers, 1970).

[17] Israel Scheffler, "University Scholarship and the Education of Teachers," *Teachers College Record* 70 (October, 1968) 1-12.

[18] Ann Berlak and Harold Berlak, *Dilemmas of Schooling* (London: Methuen, 1981).

[19] B. Robert Tabachnick, Thomas Popkewitz, and Kenneth Zeichner, "Teacher Education and the Professional Perspectives of Student Teachers," *Interchange* 10:4 (1979-80) 12-29.

[20] Seymour Sarason, *The Culture of the School and the Problem of Change* (Boston: Allyn and Bacon, 1971).

Do you like your job? We all know people who are in occupations they do not like, and yet they remain in them because they have to put bacon and eggs on the table. To help you choose a career that you will still like fifteen years from now, the following papers may be very useful. Read them, and then ask yourself some hard questions.

Why do I really want to become a teacher?
What do I think teaching will really be like?
How do I think that I, as a teacher, can improve upon the educa-
tion I received while growing up?
Do I think teaching will be a career that I will love after I have been
doing it fifteen years? Why? Why not?

Why I Decided to Become a Teacher . . .
or How I Was Educated Into Submission

Eric H. Arnold
Producer of Hole in the Sock Productions

I joined the educational system
at a very early age.

Quite embryonic in the
development of my mind (and
everything else), I believed everything.
The first day was the worst—
leaving home early in the morning,
warned to keep my clothes clean and
being crossed by the established students
of the school (proudly wielding their
safety flags in my direction).
Kindergarten was a time to
learn to play with other children, to
"interact meaningfully." We would sit
crosslegged in the auditorium. We were
told to be quiet while watching a film,
Hemo the Magnificent.
That whole year I concentrated
on how to pronounce the word
kindergarten.
The meaning would come
later.

It is fortunate that I learned to talk before I entered school. At least I didn't pronounce my "S's" like "Sh's."

And that was luck.

Noise was important.

Don't make any.

And do not make messes. Be sure to put your toys in the proper cubby hole. Imagine one's *own* cubby hole with one's toys in it.

The cubbies were inspected each week to be sure they were tidy.

I have never heard or used the word *tidy* anywhere else but in school.

Tidiness was important.

Teachers had definite phobias about tidiness but rarely was I to comprehend their earnestness.

I knew at five years of age that I was destined to have a messy desk for the rest of my life.

I accepted it.

The anguish I went through every Friday afternoon for the official "cleanup" and "inspection" before we were allowed to go home was irksome.

I knew where everything went.

My attitude toward my desk was my earliest remembered character trait.

I was really in for trouble.

Tidiness meant control.

Especially to an observing administrator.

"Scotty—S.O.S.!"

"Scotty—S.O.S.!"

This is the cry a teacher would make when things were getting out of control.

Ensuing messiness.

Scotty was always quick to
respond to calls for help.

"Throw-Up Sally" was a clear
case of the need for "Scotty—S.O.S.!"
Whenever Sally couldn't make it to the
bathroom in time, Scotty was
summoned.

The teacher would say that
Sally had an accident.

No messes were tolerated.
Not even for a second.
Human mess, play mess, art
mess, homework mess, Sally's mess.
All were the same.

Learning the difference
between play clothes and school clothes
was basic. It helped us distinguish
between "school life" and "life."

We learned our school
behavior. We learned the "This is how
we do this."

When to speak, when to use
the bathroom, when to play.

We had to "unlearn" them
when we got home. And that meant we
didn't learn anything in school.

School gave structure to our
lives.

Before that we were
prepubescent anarchists.

Learning to sit "Indian-style"
was an important basic concept the first
year. Cross your legs with the option of
the right or left leg on top. When there
was a school assembly, we would be
seated in the first three rows—on the
floor, Indian-style and no noise, please.

We would look toward the

back of the room at the third graders
and beyond.

They all had chairs and they
knew it.

The sixth graders were
pompously sitting in the back of the
auditorium, right in front of the school
clerks and the assistant principal.

The assistant principal was
always standing, arms folded across his
chest, making sure the kids were quiet
while he chatted with the other adults.

Even the librarian was talking
to the other librarian.

The *silence!* look of the
principal was commanding. But his
actions spoke louder—the sounds of
adult footsteps coming from behind.
Then, a cold, clammy hand at the back
of your neck.

You were caught making
"children-chatter" to your neighbor.

Not the person sitting next to
you, but your *neighbor.*

"And stand at the back of the
auditorium! We'll discuss this later!"
You wonder if the pain of the moment
will ever go away. Your friends assume
angelic postures and attitudes and sigh
with relief at their reprieve.

Years later, a situation like
that acquires humor and irony.

It's something you laugh
about.

If you remember it.

If you're treating someone else
the same way when you're an adult, it
means you didn't remember.

A trip to the principal.
You stand strong—silently—
not wanting to implicate others. The

watery feeling comes to your eyes and you can see your friends through the windows of the office. They are having running races between telephone poles.

It is like watching a drive-in movie from a road and you can't hear the voices.

Are your friends thinking about you now?

Are they concerned about the big trouble you're in?

It's just a regular school day for them.

A note home follows.

Your scarlet letter.

Very quickly, the matter is taken "in hand" by your parents. They act immediately. Punishment.

You thought you were safe at home.

You want to react.

You can't. You're too small. They don't understand. You didn't do anything that bad.

But you could have.

You're not going to do that to *your* kid.

If you remember.

Things will get better.

There is always next year to look forward to.

First grade, second grade, and on up to sixth grade.

Graduation.

Then it's junior high and eventually the pinnacle—high school!

Unless, of course, you might plan to go on to college.

But it is in grade school where the early seeds are sown.

You begin to acquire school graces which are unlike those you have

practiced in life. Soon you can no longer
tell the difference between the two.
   You quickly learn not to
disrupt school order.
   And order is everywhere.

   Bells ring to signal the events
of the day.
   I had thought before I went to
school that the sound of bells ringing
was beautiful.
   In school bells prevent you
from hearing the question you're
listening for.

   And the P.A.
   Public Address System.
   The class finally settles into a
quiet reading time.
   "Students caught making
snowballs, iceballs, and so forth on school
grounds will be sent to my office
immediately."
   You lose your concentration.

   Older me.
   I survived it all.
   Kindergarten.
   First grade.
   Elementary school, junior high,
senior high, college and graduate school.
   The total graduate.
   With a short memory.

   I am a teacher.
   My concerns are class size,
discipline, supplies, parents,
administrators, and other teachers.
   And the students.
   And me.
   And my loss of memory.

Career Should Be Labor of Love

Sydney J. Harris
"Strictly Personal"

I had returned home from a lecture tour, tired and not feeling very well, and here I was tapping away at my typewriter, sipping a cup of hot tea and humming to myself.

The lady I live with said, "If you don't feel so good, why don't you go up to bed?" and I replied, quite truthfully, "It makes me feel better to sit here working."

This is the beauty of doing work you enjoy, so that while it is a chore in one respect, it is a pleasure in another. And I earnestly urge all young people contemplating their careers to keep in mind that nothing in work is finally rewarding unless it is work you would be willing to do for nothing if you could afford to.

This is the ultimate test for lifelong congeniality in a career, of no matter what sort. Money is not the most important thing; fame is fleeting and uncertain; even status is irksome and uncomforting after a time. All that remains at the end is satisfaction and occasionally delight in the performance itself.

Do not do what does not please you; it does not pay, no matter how beguiling the material rewards may seem to be. The pot of gold that appears to be gleaming at the end of the rainbow is less gratifying than the rainbow itself.

The best recipe for a long and happy life is to be able to approach each new morning with anticipation and zest for the job, whatever it may be. This does not mean, of course, that we are not sometimes disgruntled or frustrated or bored; but, during the long haul, these disaffecting moments are washed away by the tide of contentment, the swell of gratification, at doing well what one does best.

If you are engaged in work you like, the drudgery and tedium involved in it seem worthwhile. The talented wood-carver who works patiently for hours, and whistles at his work, is getting more out of life and of himself than the affluent stockbroker who needs three martinis to get through the afternoon.

The people I have known who seem to rest most easily within themselves are those who have found, by design or lucky accident, the niche made just for them, in whatever field it may be, lofty or humble, so long as it gives them a sense of being needed, of being purposeful, and of doing it a little better than most others can.

And those who seemed most unhappy, whatever their degree of external success, were the ones to whom the job was a *means*, not an end, a way of earning a living rather than a way of living. All they can look forward to is retirement, as boring, in a different way, as their jobs are. When the heart goes, the hands should still be tapping away happily.

An Open Letter to Prospective Teachers

Lavinia Mancuso
Principal, PS155, New York City

Choosing a career these days is much more complicated than it used to be, especially for women. When I graduated from college in 1964, there were few jobs available for semi-educated women, and all of them required typing, teaching or wearing a uniform. Elementary education was considered the most ladylike: you could get home in time to prepare supper; you could "always go back to it;" and the banks would give you a mortgage. In those days, teaching was also a good career choice for minorities (perhaps because governesses and tutors historically were included in the servant class), and for ambitious men who wanted to advance easily through the ranks of the housewives.

Thanks to advances by the civil and women's rights movements, the field of education is no longer the only haven for the downtrodden. At least women and minorities have access to equal opportunity or the illusion of it. However, education still remains a viable career alternative for people who want to be productive without joining the corporate rat race. It is certainly the most positive of the helping professions, because the vast majority of the clients are physically, emotionally, and intellectually sound. Furthermore, when a teacher makes a breakthrough with a difficult student, the teacher can continue to enjoy the benefits, instead of having to pronounce the student cured and send him or her on his or her way, as do social workers, nurses and psychologists.

In any case, choosing a career is still a major life decision and should not be undertaken capriciously or to satisfy one's mother. All prospective workers should analyze their talents and interests, and the emo-

Written expressly for *Preparing for Reflective Teaching.*

tional, financial and societal rewards of each career possibility. An important consideration, especially for prospective teachers, is the extracurricular life-style that accompanies each career. Will you be able to live the way you want on a teacher's salary? Will you feel put upon if you spend your evenings grading papers or writing plans? Is a long summer vacation really important to you? If you live in a small town, can you accept your role as a quasi-public person? The answers to these questions have as much to do with long term happiness as attitudes about the job itself.

One consideration which has no importance unless you are a senior citizen is previous expenditure of time and effort. Fond memories of baby sitting and two semesters of foundations of education should not lock you into a career in teaching. Liking school is also a poor indicator of vocation; the roles of teacher and student are very different. You would be better off trying to project what will satisfy you five years from now, rather than relying on what pleased you in the past. It is seldom too late to move either into or out of a career in education. The skills and information acquired in the pursuit of an education degree can be used in any number of fields and vice versa. (I am sure that a random survey of forty-five year olds would find very few of them working in the exact area of their undergraduate preparation.) There is no harm and great good in working at a variety of jobs before going into education. In addition to the obvious benefit of being better able to make students aware of career possibilities, the teacher with outside work experience has a clearer view of the differences between teaching and other jobs. Several teachers I know are sure that if they weren't doing penance in their classrooms they would be in the boardroom of IBM, but if they had spent some time in the business world, they would know that IBM has thousands of jobs below the top level which pay less and are far less interesting than teaching.

Before you consider teaching as a career, you should understand clearly that teaching is a job and not a divine mission. Martyrs usually do not have the sense of humor needed to deal with generation upon generation of children and adolescents. Being a teacher is more like being a salesperson, except that the product is algebra instead of vacuum cleaners, and the customers deserve full disclosure and an airtight guarantee. Contrary to popular opinion, teaching is not an escape, nor is it a career for shrinking violets or people whose egos are easily bruised. Unfortunately, while sales is the more lucrative profession, teaching is one of the least, and teachers must take solace in the intrinsic value of the product and the neediness of the clients.

It is an open secret that teachers are losing ground economically, as starting salaries and raises fail to keep up with inflation. The union movement of ten years ago made tremendous gains, but membership is down, morale is low, and even the larger organizations are losing their clout. Unfortunately, education's long history of subsistence pay has conditioned the public to expect something for nothing, and even some teachers seem to feel guilty about being able to eat regularly. Militancy is one of the required attitudes of teachers if this trend is to be reversed. Only teachers themselves can do it, and young teachers have the energy and the risk-taking capacity necessary to rejuvenate the movement. Remember the United States is not the third world, and teaching is not the Peace Corps; living in genteel poverty is not at all pleasant in the midst of the American dream.

As an arm of organized society, education is tremendously influenced by politics, economics, and popular culture. You should carefully consider current trends and how they affect teaching. On the practical side, a look at economics reveals that shrinking birthrates and educational budgets have closed schools, increased class size, and made creative programming more and more more difficult. The birthrate/ budget problem is a matter of attitudes as well as numbers. Adults without school-aged children are not eager to have their tax dollars spent on the education of others, and parents of only children are not sympathetic to teachers who see their unique offspring as members of a group. Public regard for teaching seems to be at an all time low, with the media, parent advocacy groups, and even the university establishment engaged in a public vendetta against teachers and public school officials.

Internal and external educational policies follow philosophical trends, and the pendulum swings regularly between conservative and liberal ideology. There are debates about the role of schools (for example, should schools prepare workers, or should the young engage in apprenticeships on the job?), and the appropriate content and presentation of the curriculum (for example, should teachers use phonics or sight words in teaching reading?).

As our nation becomes more conservative politically, the role of the school is again being redefined, but we have yet to see what affect this redefinition will have on curriculum and methodology. Until recently, the school was becoming more and more of a comprehensive service institution. In addition to teaching the three Rs, schools were given the responsibility for providing meals, after-hours child care, psychological and medical services, and parental training. The academic manifestations of these humanistic concerns were nongraded classrooms, child and interest centered curricula, and individualized instruction. While all this was very fine from a humanitarian point of view, occasionally the essential business of education was forgotten.

The reaction is now full upon us. The new watchwords are "back to basics," "minimum standards," and "testing," and curricula are being designed to reflect the priorities of the educational establishment rather than of the learner. In many school systems, the work of each grade is packaged and homogenized, and those children who do not internalize the package repeat the grade until they do. The latest teacher's guides look like play scripts, and supplementary materials take the form of practice sheets and "assessment tools."

As a veteran of the humanistic period and a self-styled liberal educator, I am amazed to find myself applauding this change. "Minimum standards," if they are clearly spelled out, give both students and teachers an exact idea of their goals and progress. It has always been the mission of the schools to equip students with the skills and concepts essential for functioning in the adult world. In the name of innovation, during the pendulum swing to the left, this simple vocational goal was thrown out of focus. Curriculum was designed to meet the needs of the learner rather than the larger society, and social adjustment was sometimes given more priority than skill development. Everyone was allowed to travel at his or her own pace, even though some students missed the boat entirely. Unfortunately, children from lower class homes are often hurt by this liberalizing process; they have traditionally attended school in the hope of becoming middle class, and the liberalized school was insisting that they were fine just the way they were. "Minimum standards" are now being set to ensure that every student ends up with a more or less equal education, and that each grade's work will be some commonly accepted body of knowledge rather than a series of projects based on the teacher's or students' current interest.

Unfortunately, good and bad ideas are often linked, so that we find "minimum standards" and "back to basics" together in the same campaign rhetoric, as if eliminating music will automatically raise standards for student literacy. Eliminating such "frills" as music and art simply eliminates a key element of our culture and a creative avenue for self-expression and vocational success. A basics program once again penalizes the poor, as they are not in the habit of taking private lessons.

Uniformity of curriculum does not guarantee high quality, just consistency and reliability. It is the content of the curriculum that determines its quality. One of the scariest aspects of the basics movement is its low regard for such key elements of modern education as technology and real mastery of foreign languages, and its yearning to return to another generation's curriculum, one which was racist and sexist, and often intellectually empty. With its simplistic approach to reading and writing and the kind of math that is done on one's fingers, a strictly basics curriculum will prepare the students for instant obsolescence in a world of calculators, computers and grand opera on television. Unfortunately, thinking also seems to have a low priority in the basics curriculum, as if good grammar and great thoughts could not coexist in the same composition. Conservative educators are forgetting that the purpose of reading and writing and accurate mathematics is to facilitate and clarify the communication of ideas, both new and old. It will be the task of the new teachers to reconcile these philosophical differences and distill the best from both movements so that the students can experience both intellectual and technical excellence.

On the personal side, you must analyze the job on a task-by-task basis to be sure that reading is the activity in which you want to spend your most productive hours. Once you have reasonable mastery of the job and the students, teaching can offer real personal satisfaction. It is still a profession, an honorable endeavor and a real chance to be your own boss. You do not have to climb the administrative ladder or engage in educational politics in order to be appreciated and effective; you do not even have to get along very well with your supervisors and peers. Excellent classroom teachers are truly priceless, and when you reach that level of competence, you can practically write your own ticket about style and methodology.

Unfortunately, too many new teachers do not have a clear idea of the job at hand. They have illusions about the nature of education and their role in it, and they become frustrated and less productive than they could be. First, many prospective teachers share the same negative opinion as the general public about those teachers already on the job, and they make unrealistic plans for setting the establishment straight. But, after finding that they spend their first year of teaching keeping their heads above water, dealing with discipline, paperwork, preparation and fatigue, their idealistic energy sometimes turns into cynicism or apathy. Second, new teachers come with wonderfully creative ideas, but they usually lack the confidence and skill to implement them effectively. For survival, they resort to the tried methodology of their older colleagues and sometimes give up on experimentation altogether. Ideally, new teachers should tuck away those creative ideas and bring them out one by one as they and their students are ready to handle them. The best classroom is an eclectic one, where there is a mix of innovative and traditional techniques.

The prospective teacher should know what to expect from the job. Teaching is never dull, but it is often difficult. Students who joyfully do their homework and listen in rapt attention are rare and, perhaps, abnormal.[1] It is a myth that such things as reading or French or calculus are learned naturally. They must all be taught systematically—at home, in school, or in France. (If reading or writing, for example, were as natural as speaking or walking, there would be no preliterate societies, just as there are no speechless or nonambulatory ones, and, of course, there would be no need for teachers to teach those subjects.) Good teaching is a constant struggle to push children to the limits of their ability, to fill them with the information required by our culture and our times, and to prod them into some form of independent thought. At most levels of elementary and high school, teachers must seek challenge in the process of teaching, not the content. It is not basic phonics that is interesting about teaching first grade but the discovery of the connections and the sequence of instruction that make phonics meaningful to first graders. In teaching, one learns a great deal about how people learn, how people think, and how they store and retrieve information.

As a prospective teacher, you should not look to teaching as your major source of intellectual stimulation in the academic areas without losing enthusiasm and desire for new insights. Teachers have many after-school hours for their own research and intellectual fulfillment, and they should learn to use these hours to best advantage. Teaching is a physically and an emotionally taxing job, the intensity of which is unequalled in most business situations, and teachers must cherish and exploit their afternoons and vacations. No one should ever feel guilty about leaving at three o'clock.

One of the things that few new teachers are prepared to handle is paperwork. Some of it is essential for the proper management of a class or a school; some of it is just fodder for idle computers. New teachers must learn to handle paper so that it will not exhaust their time and prevent their teaching. They must learn to analyze, prioritize, and dispose of it in the most efficient way possible. Under no circumstances should teachers themselves create additional paperwork, such as pupil profiles or checklists, unless such data provokes a quantum leap in the quality of the children's learning. Spending one's time teaching children to read is more effective than charting their failure in elaborate detail.

Prospective teachers and everyone else are hearing a great deal about teacher burnout, the flames of which are probably kindled in excessive paperwork. Burnout happens to any intelligent person who does the same thing year after year without change or advancement. Dentists, housewives, and stockbrokers get burned out too, but they take up golf or commit suicide. Teaching is less mechanical than most jobs; the burned out worker is less able to function at half strength, and the problem is more apparent. Large companies keep their executives constantly on the move with job changes, new locations, travel, and special projects. Teachers can do the same for themselves by changing grades, subjects, schools, and students, and by taking courses, sabbaticals, and long faraway vacations. If you find yourself heading for a rut, make an immediate change in the classroom, by trying out new teaching strategies and routines, and by initiating or volunteering to participate in experimental projects. (Such experiments keep you on your toes, and they also bring you to the attention of the powers that be, in case you are interested in a promotion.) When all else fails, a job change may be the only solution, and teaching never pays so much that one cannot afford to leave. As people live longer and longer, one career may not be sufficient for a working life that may span fifty years.

The group of teachers that seems to be experiencing the most frustration is the group that works with those children who are linguistically, culturally and/or economically "different" from the mainstream. A cycle of blame has arisen, where the media blame the teachers, the teachers blame the children, and so on. Since many of you will begin your careers in poor and/or minority neighborhoods, it is important for you to understand the dynamics of educating "different" children.

Schools in poor neighborhoods play a very important role in the relationship between their students and the larger society. In fact, the school may be the single most important community institution. The students need and expect a good education, and they do not have other options. Before making any more assumptions about these students and what constitutes high quality education for them, educators have to take another look at the interaction between these "different students" and the mainstream school society.

School is a mini-society unto itself. It reflects the larger society just as the mirrors in the fun house reflect the onlooker; the general outline is there, but some parts are magnified and others are blurred beyond recognition. For instance, verbal skills are highly prized in school, as are neatness and conforming behavior. Educators themselves tend to be successful products of this mini-society, so successful that they choose to remain in it. They excel at school skills, and they share school values, but they may have little firsthand knowledge of the outside world and the people who run it. The problem with education today is not so much the skills being taught or the people doing the teaching. Even the most radical mudslinger would not advocate a society of illiterate slobs running amok. The problem is that school people see school as the total society, and they have little regard for the skills or people not reached by the standard curriculum.

The truth is that, while basic literacy and good manners can easily be taught in school, entrepreneurship and technical intuition cannot, and, while some personalities thrive in the atmosphere of the classroom, others do not. It is the duty of the school system to provide the maximum number of students with the widest possible array of skills and information, and it is also incumbent on school officials to be honest about the limitations of their services.

Students of education have been conditioned by their courses to envision the ideal teaching situation as the harmonious pursuit of knowledge by a group of teachers and students who share the same culture, values, and information base. This joint pursuit of learning leads to the acquisition of those skills necessary to obtain rewarding jobs with equally enlightened employers. The fact is that this situation is not all that common; there are tremendous discrepancies among the demands of the learners, the school, and the marketplace.

The mismatch between the school society and the outside world is nowhere more evident than in poor communities. Middle class, mainstreamed American students usually find a school curriculum that is a continuation or even a replication of what they have been learning at home all along. They do well in school by "objective" standards such as norm referenced tests. However, they may not really be learning anything new. When they have to confront material outside of their experience, such as foreign languages or advanced math, they do not do quite so well. The vast majority opt out of these subjects altogether.

The economically, culturally, and linguistically different child, on the other hand, often faces a teacher who does not look, sound or act like anyone he or she has met before, and books that do not have familiar people or environments in them. In addition, this child must learn totally new information from the first day of his or her school career, and often he or she must learn this new information in a new language. (It is interesting that our nation, which has a worldwide reputation for total incompetence in the area of foreign languages, expects the linguistically different child to learn English the first week of school.) Is it any wonder that he or she is behind by objective standards? These standards do not reveal how much this child is really learning, how much new information he or she is assimilating, or how fast. The linguistically different child may in fact have learned much more than his or her mainstream counterpart.

It may be argued that the minority child is actually enjoying a much richer educational experience than the white middle class child. Studies by Wallace Lambert have revealed that bilingual/bicultural individuals have higher IQ's and cognitive and social flexibility indexes.[1] However, to the uninitiated, minority performance looks like school failure. It takes a while to master two languages; some say that bilinguals really come into their own in their twenties, well past the time for them to show their teachers their cognitive and social superiority.

Minority children must be prepared to enter mainstream society as economically viable participants. They must leave school with the same level of skill and competency as their mainstream counterparts. They must also have the social and cultural baggage that will enable them to be upwardly mobile. The exit criteria for all children must be the same, in spite of the fact that previous educational processes may differ. Certainly, childen should not have to give up one perfectly fine language and culture to learn another, that would be constricting their experience rather than enhancing it. Certainly, also, children of one culture should not be judged on the information and language of another until they have had sufficient time and exposure to learn them. The competent teacher knows how to suspend judgement about children's potential and demand the best from everyone. He or she knows that lacking specific information or the ability to speak English is not the same as being unintelligent, and he or she is loath to give any child a less than promising label.

On an average, more "different" children are sent to special education and fewer to classes for the gifted than their mainstream counterparts. This misplacement is due to ignorance and lack of imagination on the part of the professionals, not the students. (How does one react to an English-speaking psychologist labelling a Spanish-speaking child "non-verbal" simply because the psychologist or teacher cannot understand the child, who finally gives up trying to talk to this person?)

Being a compassionate professional does not mean lowering standards; it means teaching in such a way that most children can reach those standards. Sometimes, the steps must be made smaller and more numerous, and the motivation must be made stronger, but finding the way to do that is the essence of creative teaching.

There are many creative, sensitive and courageous teachers, and, in closing, I would like to praise the profession at large. Teachers, even more than parents, have the responsibility for training future generations. They impart the specific skills, information, and attitudes that will enable future geniuses to change the world and average Joes and Janes to lead successful and productive lives. The task is monumental, and the job is underrated in both pay and status. As to whether or not a career in education is worth the effort, I can only cite my continued excitement at being part of such an important and dynamic process, and the advice of Shirley Hufstedler, former Secretary of Education, to her successor:

> I am sure you will find, as I have, that a great many people are willing to fight over children, but precious few are willing to fight for them. Your job, shorn of the paper and the bureaucracy, is to fight forcefully and joyfully for those kids. It is not always an easy or a popular fight, but even the smallest victories can touch the lives and brighten the futures of hundreds and thousands of children. With each such victory you will feel, as I do today, happy to have passed this way.[2]

Notes

[1] Elizabeth Peal and Wallace Lambert, "Relation of Bilingualism to Intelligence," *Psychology Monographs* 76 (1962): 1-23.

[2] Shirley M. Hufstedler, "Open Letter to a Cabinet Member," *New York Times Magazine* (January 11, 1981) 384.

You've heard the expression, "Tell it like it is." Well, the following article by Leo Curran tells it like it is. However, since I believe that you should always examine different points of view, I suggest that you interview some teachers you know, and find out how they view "the teaching grind."

The Teaching Grind

Leo D. Curran
Council Rock High School, Pennsylvania

Most of us didn't go into teaching for the wealth and power. Teaching was a profession, a "calling," a hand on the rudder to the future, a celebration of reason and the democratic life, an adventure. But we recognize that many of our tribe can't adjust to the malevolent environments in which they find themselves. So we have our "burnouts" and "flame-outs" and "bail-outs." Are these people of weak constitution? No, for the most part. After all, they were selected for the classroom after extensive preparation and evaluation. They were ready. So was the environment.

It can be an atmosphere of morbidity; it certainly is an atmosphere of stress. In some schools, violence has become part of the daily routine. Stress leads to anxiety. Over time, anxiety is pathological.

Teaching today is more than stressful. Often it is also frustrating. Today's teachers face problems different from those that yesterday's teachers faced. Kids seem more challenging, and the job more demanding and complex. Accountability is greater and expectations are higher.

The public schools are the all-night diners of our society—they take everyone and serve them. Yet teachers, who don't control their students' backgrounds, are expected to produce a quality-controlled graduate from everyone who enters the door. The schools have been charged with making up for society's failings: bad housing and worse self-images, malnutrition, and neglect. Different teaching methods can help students at all levels achieve something, but the cry today is for equality of results. This is a demand for the impossible.

The classroom presents us with two major problems. The tactical problem is how to turn short-term memory into long-term memory. The strategic problem is motivation, which is more and more a struggle simply to lead the horses to water, let alone to get them to drink.

The clinker here is that the old incentives no longer work. The hope

Reprinted from the *NEA Reporter*, April/May 1981 by permission from the author.

of material rewards in the future has crashed with oil shortages, 20 percent interest rates, and the wreck of the greenback. Students in my suburban district have become used to a standard of living that it took their parents 20 years of hard work to achieve. The terror of graduation now is that a lifetime might not be enough to achieve a comparable situation. So why strive, sacrifice, study, or hope at all?

What we are asked to teach often lacks the crackle of relevancy, and we end up with a lot of people complaining, "These kids are so lazy! It's like pulling teeth to get them to do anything." Actually, lazy people probably don't exist. Students may not be motivated to do what you want them to do, but they can be observed moving heaven and earth if it's something *they* want to do. Relevancy is a great motivator.

Lacking tangible, if distant, rewards and relevancy, we can always fall back on punishment: low grades, detentions, scoldings. Kids don't scare as easily these days, though. There's always the strategy of getting the kids to like and respect you ("do it for me, guys"), but they don't "like and respect" as easily these days, either. So the satisfactions of the classroom, which used to go a long way toward making up for low wages and trying working conditions, aren't there in double handfuls anymore. In many instances teaching has become like sneaking medicine into cranky children.

The public's attitude toward teachers went down when we asked for decent wages and showed we'd hit the bricks if we didn't get a hearing. We are aware that our image suffered once we got "uppity," but there's more to it than that. As public employees, teachers have come to be seen as part of the government and so we take the heat for what the government does. This is why tax revolts zero in on us. We're within reach.

As teachers we have little control over our daily environment. We work in big, concrete egg crates and usually teach in isolation in crypt-like rooms for 35 years or more. It's a dead-end job. How many jobs are there that you can do for 35 years and still have the same job description? When people want a change, they're given a choice—between teaching ninth or tenth grades, if an opening occurs.

The main contact between the individual teacher and the overall school management is the principal—ideally, someone who can provide leadership without becoming autocratic, rigid, and bureaucratic. What teachers often get, however, are tyrannical or patronizing administrators who treat their staffs like children. They nitpick, "pull rank," and order people about until their staffs know to the day the principal's retirement date. Often teachers are allowed no voice in determining the professional and working conditions under which they teach—managerial prerogative, you know. School rules, constraints, and requirements create frustration and Catch-22 situations, often resulting in decline in creativity, initiative, and sense of humor.

Some day, after work, ask yourself, "What did I learn in school today? What did my environment teach me?" Now read a copy of your school's philosophy, inserting "teacher" everywhere it says "student." Interesting? Can teachers impart the high values of a community if they are denied the same?

Solutions, there are many. Once teachers achieve acceptable salary levels through the process of collective bargaining, we will undoubtedly turn our primary attention to the conditions which most affect our health and morale on the job. Until then, Mr. Chips, he's gettin' real tired.

———

Invite someone who is also interested in becoming a teacher for an ice cream cone and discuss with him or her the questions I have just mentioned. Without forgetting your idealism, try not to make that the focus of your talk. Take a good look at the teaching profession and, based on a realistic assessment of it, make sure that this is the profession you really want.

Every prospective teacher that I have met has wanted to become an effective teacher. Pause for a moment and recall your two best teachers. What similarities did they have, and how were they different? The following two articles suggest that good teachers are seen from two different vantage points: the first, "Good Teachers Make a Lasting Impact," is viewed from individuals who are professionally successful, and the second, "Characteristics of Superior and Average Special Education Teachers," from school administrators.

———

Good Teachers Make a Lasting Impact

Evelyn Reid
University of Wisconsin—Madison
Cheryl Utley
Governors State University, Illinois

Are teachers a cog in the wheel of success? A key to a good education? Although teachers have influenced each of us in positive ways, how important are they to preparing us for the professional paths that we choose to follow? When we ask successful people who in the past had contributed most to their present success, many times the response

Written expressly for *Preparing for Reflective Teaching*.

is a previous teacher. All of us have had teachers who have made a significant impact on us, and these impressions remain with us throughout our lives. In fact, their contributions have made us who we are today.

Collectively, however, the teaching profession is not always addressed favorably. If we were to sift through the literature of the fifties, when Rudolph Flesch astounded the American public with *Why Johnny Can't Read and What You Can Do About It*,[1] we would get a different picture of the teaching profession. Throughout this body of literature are comments like, "What is needed to upgrade the teaching profession is a massive overhauling of our educational system,"[2] and "Large numbers of teachers enter classrooms ill-prepared to meet the needs of students, therefore, they are unable to offer children those crucial elements necessary to success."[3] One newspaper article was even entitled, "Why Johnny's Teacher Can't Read, Either."[4]

However, rather than accept this dismal picture as the only view of the teaching profession, let us also remember that teachers have played a major role in the educational advances of American citizens in recent years. For example, according to statistics in the *Condition of Education*,[5] increases in educational attainment of both majority and minority students have been dramatic over recent years, and among the population 25 to 29 years old the proportion of those who have graduated from high school rose from 60 to 80 percent from 1960-1974.

The debate concerning the worth of our teachers is likely to continue for some time, and since bad news in general seems to receive more attention than goods news, it is necessary to try and present a balanced view. In order to illustrate some of the contributions of teachers to students, we interviewed a diverse group of successful professionals who were educated in various regions of the United States— East, West, Midwest, and South. Our sample included persons of both sexes and from many cultures—European-American, Afro-American, Native-American, Chinese-American, and Mexican-American. In addition, their professional occupations were varied: two circuit court judges, a senator, an attorney writer–historian, a public utilities commissioner, three school principals, a superintendent of public schools, a speech therapist, a school counselor, three higher education administrators, a literary author/university professor, a geologist, and five graduate students.

During the interview, we asked our respondents a series of questions about their past educational experiences with teachers. What we found was that they had acquired certain skills and developed attitudes in school which guided them to their present professions. They also felt that these skills and attitudes are clearly linked to previous classroom instruction and to particular teachers.

The following two examples are illustrative. The writer–historian lawyer recalled his tenth grade English teacher as "a stickler for precision." Every student was continually drilled in the rudiments of good writing. This teacher was viewed as an inspiration and a great motivator in his life because good writing skills are essential for a practicing lawyer. The literary author/university professor, in describing her early years of schooling during World War II, recalled that a sixth grade English teacher, the wife of a newspaper publisher, had made available to students each Monday a huge stack of newspapers. The writer chuckled when recalling the days she "was delegated the responsibility of keeping the bulletin board up-to-date with current events. It built my self-confidence because it required that I read the material." She had had to consider carefully which articles were worth reading because the teacher had told her to display "no crime stories and sensational news; things like that were of no value to young minds." It was such a formative experience that its impact has remained with her. Even today she states, "I love to read the newspaper and dare not miss it for one day." She also fondly recalled another inspirational and caring teacher that she met while at the university. "I admire him tremendously in every way. He was a fine teacher, a prolific writer, and a friend. He was always available to students and always projected a need for excellence. His standards became my own. I accept only the best from my students. I love him. He is fantastic. If it had not been for this experience, I would not be what I am today."

Two members of our sample felt that former teachers had contributed not only to their skill development but also to their overall progress. They noted that some former teachers had passed on to them traits such as sensitivity and fluidity, which helped them to be successful in later life. A speech therapist recalled a seventh/eighth grade teacher who had taught her respect for human diversity by the way she accepted and affirmed the individual differences of the students in her class, individualizing classroom instruction to meet the needs of different students. She said, ". . . there is a real need for sensitivity to differences among people and this teacher helped me to acknowledge these differences." The state superintendent recalled a first grade teacher as being "fluid." The teacher had been very smooth in handling her many responsibilities as librarian, guidance counselor, music instructor, physical education teacher, and hot lunch program coordinator for forty-five children. This trait of fluidity has been incorporated into the superintendent's repertoire of administrative strategies, and has been valuable to his profession because such a position involves coordinating many responsibilities in a manner similar to his first grade teacher. Our sample believes that many of the skills and attitudes important to their success today are a result of experiences with former teachers, and that teachers played an important role in their professional development.

As we mature, we are left with fond memories of a select group of friends. Such is the case with our memories of teachers. In order to discover why some teachers are so vividly remembered we asked our sample to tell us about their favorite teachers. Several of our respondents remembered these teachers as being well educated, dedicated to their jobs, challenging, caring, stimulating, and motivating in their efforts to offer children the best education possible. For example, one respondent recalled a favorite teacher as having had high moral and academic standards. "He was the kind of person who was interested in each student as an individual and dedicated his whole life to helping everyone within the classroom achieve his/her potential." He had set rigorous standards for academic achievement. Although one interviewee was often disappointed by his teachers, he did remember two teachers favorably. "My fifth grade English teacher was able to convey a strong sense of concern for me that suggested a keen sense of caring about my overall development. I also had a history teacher who projected a professional commitment to my personal well-being." Both of these teachers, in his opinion, had been "veterans to the profession."

Another respondent stated that a good teacher is "someone who is stimulating, who guides students and who is willing to model his/her own behavior in such a manner that students are able to respect and admire their personhood." Another stated that a good teacher has the "ability to deliver to students, is sympathetic, and has expertise and sensitivity." Still another felt that good teachers exhibit a strong sense of caring for children and are committed to doing the best job possible. Good teachers were also described as being those who "are able to challenge students; they are able to create an atmosphere where children are required to think critically and analytically."

Good teachers were further cited as having several other characteristics. One respondent viewed good teachers as being able to relate conceptual ideas and textbook knowledge to the real world. This is another admired professionalism in teachers. "I feel that good teachers are consistent in what they teach. For example, every voice teacher should give at least one recital a year. Faculty concerts are quite important to others so that they may share in one's expertise. The problem lies in the fact that piano teachers don't play enough and dance teachers don't dance enough. Good teachers are role models for their students." Finally, one commented that a good teacher can help children develop self-confidence and has the ability to teach children in such a manner that they become turned on to learning. A good teacher, as defined by our sample, can have a variety of skills and traits. However, there does seem to be one characteristic common to all the teachers that our respondents remembered: excellence in some area or areas of teaching.

We asked our sample if teachers' race, age, and sex influenced how they perceived their education. In discussing race, several respondents talked about how they perceived the race of a teacher as a child, indicating that, at the time, they did not see race as making a difference. For example, a respondent whose early years of schooling were spent in a desegregated school setting stated, "I once had an Oriental teacher. Her race meant nothing to me. She was only a teacher." Another interviewee, who reported having all white teachers said, "At that time, I didn't think about the teacher's race." Similarly, an interviewee who attended schools where the entire school population was black did not feel deprived in any way. He observed, "My early years of schooling were spent in segregated schools, and quite frankly, since I knew nothing else, I never considered or compared my educational experience to anyone else's. I knew that 'their' [white] schools looked nicer from the outside and now I am advised that they were better." Still another interviewee, who was educated in an integrated school during the 60s where the racial composition of the school staff was 90% white and 10% minority, felt that the teachers' race did not affect their abilities to do an effective job.

Others reflected on the impact of teachers' race, often observing that it did make a difference. For example, one who had attended private schools where all of the teachers were white feels that this kind of schooling was somewhat sheltered and artificial. Other views expressed were much stronger. Black teachers, said one, "were very positive, energetic, bright, articulate, and cared about all children. They were different from my tenth grade English teacher who was white. She did not really project an attitude of caring about us, neither did she attempt to tap our interest. Instead she drilled us in Shakespeare and other subjects of her own interest." One individual talked emphatically about those early years of schooling, which were spent in a poor rural area of North Carolina. "Teachers cared very little, if any, about our educational development. You see, to them, we were little black farm children who would never amount to anything anyway. I remember a situation during recess where the bell rang, yet we children asked, 'May we stay outside and play a little longer just to play another game or two?' These teachers were so accommodating that many times the children remained outside for as long as thirty to forty-five minutes more." In sum, many in our sample who did not believe that while they were students the teachers' race greatly influenced their education came to believe otherwise when they reflected upon their classroom days.

Their responses concerning whether or not the teacher's age was of importance were mixed. Some members of the sample preferred younger teachers. One commented, "If teachers were close to my age they seemed more in tune with what I was thinking and experiencing in life. The older ones were more out of touch with students." Similarly, "I experienced older teachers who did not keep up to date with what was happening in their fields and younger ones who kept abreast of changes, such as new strategies, techniques, research and so forth. I like the younger ones best." But one respondent thought older teachers were "more forceful . . . . One of the older teachers, whose course I took just before he retired at age 65 or 67, was a strong disciplinarian." In contrast, several respondents felt that the teacher's age did not make a difference, although they had had teachers of varying ages. One interpretation of these responses may be that being in tune with students, keeping up to date in one's field, and being a good classroom manager are things about teachers that students remember positively. However, it is important to remember that these items do not necessarily overlap with teacher's age.

Comments regarding the influence of teachers' gender were varied. The majority of people interviewed stated that they had had female teachers in elementary grades but, upon reaching high school, had male teachers in courses such as math, shop, and science. Most felt that teachers' gender did not make a difference. One remarked, "I think if I took some of the finest teachers that I knew, they would be fairly evenly divided between men and women." One respondent, who attended Jesuit schools, equally appreciated the nuns and priests in his schooling. He felt both male and female teachers represented positive figures and role models.

A female respondent, on the other hand, preferred male teachers as role models. Another individual felt that he could relate better to his male teachers because "they seemed to give one hundred percent." Still another respondent felt that male teachers were more competent in handling discipline problems. "I think I was more impressed with the male teachers in the way they would go about handling classroom situations, especially in high school where kids are kind of rowdy; it seemed like the females had a harder time controlling the class." Some of the most influential teachers in the educational experience of the female judge were female law professors. They had been good role models for those entering the law profession. Our respondents seemed to be telling us that there was no relationship between gender and quality of teaching. Gender of the teacher counted most when it came to the teacher's serving as a role model for students and being someone to whom students could relate.

Finally, many of the respondents spontaneously gave reasons why they believed that teachers today are not perceived positively. They pointed out that twenty years ago teachers may have been more dedicated to the profession for several reasons: the temper of the times may have determined how one functioned as a professional, and teachers may have been more content with their benefits and pay. As one respondent put it, "I am referring to a time when teachers were more in control of what went on in their classrooms. They were able to evaluate the content of materials used, the type of materials used, and the pace at which students achieved." Therefore, they may have been more positive about their work and their individual worth to the profession. Also, another respondent noted current problems such as "a lack of rewards, incentives, and encouragement for teachers to grow professionally, to realize their strengths and weaknesses, and have positive feedback to promote good leadership." He further stated, "One of our national goals should be to legitimize the teaching profession through improved salaries, prestige, and recognition from other professions so that the truly significant role of teachers may be appreciated."

Earlier we pointed out that there is a considerable amount of literature condemning teachers. This could leave you with the impression that you may have a difficult time being recognized as a good teacher. Yet, as our study shows, such an impression would clearly be in error. Each of our respondents remembered having had at least one good teacher, and most remembered having had several. These good teachers all had one thing in common: they excelled in some area of teaching. It is significant for you as prospective teachers to note that good teachers were not all described as being excellent in the same way. This might suggest that you develop your strengths with an eye to attaining excellence in those areas, while you continue to strive to improve in your weaker areas. You should do so without feeling a need to conform to any one particular mode of teaching excellence in order to be recognized as a good teacher. Finally, and perhaps more importantly, this study points out that good teachers make a lasting impact on their students.

Notes

[1] R. Flesch, *Why Johnny Can't Read and What You Can Do About It* (New York: Harper and Row, 1965).

[2] *Ibid.*

[3] M. C. Borrowman, *Teacher Education in America: A Documentary History*, No. 24 (New York: Teachers College Press, 1965).

[4] "Why Johnny's Teacher Can't Read, Either," *San Francisco Chronicle*, June 2, 1978.

[5] U.S. Department of Health, Education and Welfare, *The Condition of Education* (Washington, D.C.: Government Printing Office, 1975).

Characteristics of Superior and Average Special Education Teachers

David L. Westling and Mark A. Koorland
Florida State University
Terry L. Rose
University of Alabama

With the current trend in the field of special education to improve the quality of services for exceptional children, there has been a focus on the development of teacher competencies. Recent literature has included some discussion of competencies that should be demonstrated by teachers serving different severity levels and/or categories of exceptional children.

Review of Research

One problem regarding the development of such competencies is that they often lack empirical validity (Shores, Cegelka, & Nelson, 1973).[1] Relatively few studies have been conducted within special education to identify specific characteristics, strategies, tactics or other teaching variables that are more desirable than others.

Some of the studies conducted have investigated the relationship between the teacher's effectiveness and various personal variables not amenable to programmatic change. Meisgeier (1965),[2] for example, analyzed the relationship between the quality of teaching mentally or physically handicapped children and the teacher's scholastic aptitude, scholastic achievement, vocational interest, personality, and attitudes. As might be expected, the better teachers had favorable scores in each of these areas. Such information, however, is not very useful for identifying areas to be developed in order to improve the quality of special education through preservice or inservice training.

In a study similar to Meisgeier's, Scheuer (1971)[3] examined the relationship among certain personality variables of teachers of emotionally disturbed students, their competence as teachers, and student

Reprinted with permission from *Exceptional Children*, Vol. 47, No. 5, February 1981, pp. 357–363.

academic gains. The only substantial finding was that student gains correlated significantly with student evaluations of the teacher-pupil relationship. As with Meisgeier's results, Scheuer's study presented little information that could provide direction for improving the skills of special educators.

In another study, Blackwell (1972)[4] investigated the differences between good and poor teachers of trainable mentally retarded children. The teachers were ranked according to their supervisors' evaluations. Independent variables included personal data, personality traits, and attitudes toward children. Blackwell found that having more positive attitudes, being a woman, and teaching at the preschool level were related to better teachers.

The studies by Meisgeier, Scheuer, and Blackwell derived their dependent measures (i.e., teacher competence or effectiveness) from ratings by the teachers' supervisors. While this tactic is viable, a more empirical procedure was used by Fredericks, Anderson, and Baldwin (1977)[5] in differentiating the quality of teachers of severely handicapped students. They distinguished between good and poor teachers based on the gains made by their pupils during the previous year. Through questioning and observing the teachers, it was determined that four variables accounted for 90% of the variance in student gains: length of the instructional day, percentage of programs task analyzed, positive consequence delivery by volunteers, and the consequence delivery of teacher and aide. While such variables are not as specific as might be needed to translate them directly to teacher competencies, they do provide a significant departure from earlier studies in specifying the nature of tasks required to improve teaching performance.

Purpose of the Study

Like earlier studies, the present investigation used teacher responses to determine appropriate characteristics, strategies, and tactics that might serve as a basis for preservice and inservice training that would result in better qualified special educators. The study differed from earlier studies in two ways. First, instead of focusing on a specific categorical group of teachers, special educators teaching a variety of children with various exceptional learning conditions were included. The second difference was the nature of the independent variables studied. In attempting to determine predominant characteristics of superior teachers and differences between superior and average special educators, variables were analyzed that traditionally have been *directly* associated with special education teaching practices such as the classroom teaching arrangements used, reinforcement tactics, and testing procedures. High inference variables and variables that generally are not considered to be susceptible to change (for example, sex, personality) were not investigated. Basically, the research sought to answer two questions.

1. What characteristics, strategies, and tactics describing current classroom activities and related experiences would be identified by a majority of superior special educators in the sample?
2. What characteristics, strategies, tactics, and related experiences would be identified by superior special educators that would differ significantly ($p < .05$) from those identified by a contrast group of average special educators?

Method

Subjects

Initially, a letter was sent to all 67 district directors of special education in the state of Florida. The letter stated that the researchers were attempting to identify characteristics of superior special educators. Directors were asked to submit the names of three of their best special education teachers or at least three names of those considered to be among the best. In selecting the names, directors were asked to disregard degree level, certification status, number of years teaching experience, and area of exceptionality taught. Of the letters returned by the directors, 53 (80%) were usable. Each letter listed the name and school address of three special education teachers. Fifty of these lists were selected, and one teacher was randomly selected from each list. These 50 individuals were sent a letter explaining the purpose of the study, how they were selected to participate, a questionnaire, and a return envelope. Forty-five questionnaires (90%) were returned. These individuals were then designated as the group of "superior" special educators.

The three districts whose responses had been removed from the original 53 were used to provide the contrast data from an "average" group of special educators. In order to develop a contrast group of average special educators, it was thought that a heterogeneous sample would have to be questioned. The most feasible approach to achieve this was to select an intact group of educators from a given source. Therefore, directors from the three districts were asked to present the questionnaire to *all* of their teachers and return those completed. The total number of teachers in the contrast districts was 79. None of the superior special educators indicated in the original responses from the contrast district directors had been sent an individual letter and questionnaire. Instead, the directors were to ask all of their special education instructional personnel to fill out the forms. In doing so, the directors were requested to assure their teachers of anonymity and not to coerce them in any way to complete the forms. They were simply to inform them that the data were to be used as part of a study on characteristics and behaviors of special educators. A total of 60 responses (76%) were returned from the contrast districts. These individuals comprised the average group.

Questionnaire

The questionnaire used in the study was designed to reflect the status and behaviors of the teachers in several areas. A total of 100 questions were asked. The majority (88) were yes-no questions. The remaining questions were answered by selecting an answer from three or more choices. No question required the teacher to express an attitude, opinion, or idea; instead the teacher was asked to indicate the answer to the question according to his or her current or past experiences. The questionnaire was referred to as the Special Education Teacher Profile (Westling, Koorland, & Rose, 1978).[6]

The questions were divided into seven categories: personal/professional data; professional preparation; classroom teaching activities; classroom management; evaluation; professional interaction; and parental interaction. Personal/professional data included questions about the exceptionality being taught, the administrative arrangement, experience, and certification status. Professional preparation questions requested information about preservice and inservice training including practicum experiences and the number of journals currently received and read. The classroom teaching activities section allowed the teachers to respond in regard to the sources of their curricula and materials. In this section teachers were also asked about student-teacher ratios and the use of instructional media.

In the classroom management section, teachers were asked about the use of reinforcement, punishment, and various counseling techniques. They were also questioned about keeping systematic records of changes in students' behavior. Questions on evaluation focused on the manner and frequency of use of different kinds of pupil assessment techniques.

The final two sections presented questions regarding the teachers' interactions with other professionals and with parents. They were asked about types of interactions that occurred and the frequency of their occurrence.

Results

The data analyzed from the first section of the questionnaire (personal/professional) indicated only one significant difference ($p < .05$) between the two groups: 45% of the average teachers were in their first or second year of teaching their current exceptionality, whereas only 22% of the superior teachers indicated such limited experience. All other response frequencies within this section showed no significant differences when analyzed using the chi square test statistic.

The responses to questions in the remaining sections of the questionnaire were analyzed in two ways to answer the questions of the study. The first analysis found those items that were answered positively by a majority ($> 50\%$) of the superior group of special educators. Thirty items were found that met this criterion. They are indicated in Table 1 along with the percentage of superior teachers who answered "yes" to the question.

The second analysis compared differences in responses to individual items between the superior teachers and the contrast group of teachers. Each item was analyzed in a contingency table that was divided by groups and the number of yes and no or multiple choice responses. The chi square test statistic was used to determine significant ($p < .05$) differences in responses (Roscoe).[7] In this analysis the objective was to determine whether or not a significant difference existed between the two groups in terms of the frequency of types of responses. Significant

---

Table 1

Items Answered Positively by the Majority ($> 50\%$) of Superior Special Educators

Section	Item (percent answering yes)
Personal/professional	Certified in present area of teaching (96%)
Professional preparation	Holds BA/BS in area of exceptionality currently teaching (76%)
	Had voluntary experiences with exceptional children prior to entering training program (56%)
Classroom teaching activity	Develops own curriculum for at least 50% of instructional activities (83%)
	Uses commercial materials for at least 50% of learning activities (82%)
	Uses teacher-made materials for at least 50% of learning activities (82%)
	Uses instructional media at least once a week (91%)
	Uses a one-to-one instructional ratio for at least one-third of the day (82%)
	Uses small group (3–5 students) instructional arrangements for at least one-third of the day (88%)

Table 1   *(Continued)*

Classroom management	Commonly uses the following reinforcement tactics: smiles and gestures (91%), verbal praise (98%), physical contact (91%), verbal (71%), games and toys (62%), notes to parents (60%).
	Commonly uses the following punishment tactics: time-out (53%), verbal reprimand (83%), facial gestures (71%), loss of free time (51%), loss of special privileges (62%), ignores inappropriate behavior and reinforces appropriate behavior (51%)
	Uses value clarification activities (51%)
Evaluation	Uses standardized tests at the beginning of the year (84%)
	Tests are individually administered (84%)
	Uses the same tests at the end of the year (80%)
	Uses informal testing techniques with a majority of students (93%)
	Keeps records or graphs of individual students performance (69%)
Professional interaction	Consults with regular class teachers as part of regular teaching duty (58%)
	Assists guidance counselor in planning and/or conducting counseling sessions for exceptional students (58%)
	Keeps the principal informed of students' progress (73%)

differences ($p < .05$) in frequency of responses were found on 11 items. These items are indicated in Table 2 along with the percentage of both groups of teachers providing affirmative answers.

Discussion

As seen in Tables 1 and 2, a number of noteworthy items were found either to be indicated by the majority of the superior teachers or to differentiate the superior and average teachers. Before discussing the results and their implications, some consideration should be given to the limitations of the study.

Limitations of Study

In a study of this nature, certain limitations must be recognized. The first limitation of the present study was the manner of selecting the

---

Table 2

Items Having Significantly Different ($p < .05$) "Yes" Response
Frequencies Between Superior and Average Special Educators

Section	Item	Superior Teachers Answering "Yes"	Average Teachers Answering "Yes"
Professional preparation	Holds MA/MS in present area of teaching	31%	15%
	Number of courses taken that included practicum experience:		
	0	4%	23%
	1–2	22%	18%
	3–4	24%	8%
	5–6	11%	18%
	more than 6	38%	32%
	Had voluntary experiences with exceptional children prior to entering training program	56%	75%
Classroom teaching activity	Uses instructional media at least once a week	91%	73%
	Uses large group (more than 5) instructional arrangements for at least one-third of the day	29%	50%
Classroom management	Commonly uses facial gestures as a punishment tactic	71%	87%
Evaluation	Tests students at the end of the year (using same tests as at the beginning of the year)	80%	58%
	Uses informal testing techniques at least once a week	36%	55%
Professional interaction	Provides inservice training for non-special education personnel in the school or district	44%	12%
Parental interaction	Meets regularly with most students' parents	40%	18%
	Meets with most students' parents once a year	20%	38%

superior teachers. While it was assumed here that supervisors could accurately identify their best teachers, a more empirical approach (for example, one based on student gains) may be desirable. Even when such an approach is used, however, there will also be limitations, though perhaps of a different nature. For example, the variance in student gains may be due to sources other than teacher behaviors. In the present study, several selection procedures were considered. Given the variety of limitations that may affect any such process, it was felt that the most efficacious method was used.

A second limitation resulted from the manner in which the superior teachers were addressed. Their responses may have been influenced by their knowledge that they had been selected as superior teachers. Due to the nature of the questionnaire, however, this was considered by the authors to be a minimal threat. Because the teachers were asked to indicate facts, there was little leeway allowed to express what one *thought* should be the situation, which is often the case with attitudinal or other high inference scales.

A final limitation that must be considered is that even if the indicated responses correlate highly with actual classroom and related practices, this does not necessarily mean that the practices indicated by the superior teachers result in optimal student gains.

Factors Affecting Teacher Quality

Notwithstanding the recognized limitations of the study, there are various specific findings indicated in Tables 1 and 2 that could provide for extensive discussion. Also important is the lack of expected positive and/or differential responses to many of the items contained on the questionnaire. Due to space limitations, the present discussion can only highlight some of the more relevant results.

Years of Experience. As mentioned earlier, there were significantly fewer superior teachers in their first year or two of teaching than there were average teachers. In addition, as seen in Table 1, significantly more superior teachers held master's degrees. Despite the fact that district directors were asked not to select the superior teachers based on experience or degrees, they may have ignored this request. On the other hand, one could conclude that experience and graduate training is more typical of the superior teacher.

Practicum Experience. Perhaps a more important finding in the area of professional preparation is the extent of practicum experience differentiating the two groups. Since it is highly doubtful that the directors were aware of the particulars of their teachers' preservice training, it could be assumed that this finding is valid in its own right. Thus, it could be concluded that more extensive preservice practicum experiences are associated with a greater number of superior teachers.

Instructional Arrangements. One of the more interesting findings in the classroom teaching activity section regarded the use of instructional arrangements. A majority of the superior teachers provided individual and small group instruction, and significantly fewer of the superior teachers used large group instruction. Since one of the features of special education is to provide individualized instruction, it might have been expected that superior teachers would arrange for instruction to be delivered to smaller groups. The implication of this finding is not so much the obvious need to use small group instruction, but the need to train teachers in ways of managing instruction of children who, at a given time, are not receiving individual or small group instruction. It is possible that average teachers use so much large group instruction because they have difficulty managing the behavior of children not in the targeted instructional group. This may imply a need to provide teachers with better management techniques.

Use of Postyear Evaluations. Preyear and postyear evaluations of students using standardized tests (including achievement tests and adaptive behaviors tests) were reported by a majority of the superior teachers. When contrasted with the average group, significantly more of the superior teachers conducted postyear evaluations. This would indicate that an effort was being made by the superior teachers to document student gains during the year. This procedure, along with the common use of informal testing and record keeping, would indicate that the majority of superior special educators are attempting to comply with the spirit of legislative mandates. It is the responsibility of training programs to present this evaluation format to all preservice teachers, not only to encourage satisfying the requirements of law but also to enhance superior teaching performance.

Interaction with Parents and Other Professionals. The final point to be made is that the data depict most superior teachers as being extensively involved with other school personnel and with parents. Most superior teachers are working with regular educators. Additionally, more superior teachers are providing inservice training for non-special education personnel and are meeting regularly with parents. Since a majority of the superior teachers did not indicate consistently a significant frequency of meeting with parents, these data were not indicated in Table 1. However it was found, in combination, that a majority of the superior special educators met at least twice a year with their students' parents.

Conclusions

Two general impressions are relatively clear. First, as a group, special education teachers who are perceived by their district directors as being superior tend to have had more formal educational experience, particularly at the graduate level. The data also point out that as a group superior teachers have had more practicum experience in their preparatory course-work and more teaching experience with exceptional children. While the latter finding cannot be controlled at the preservice stage of training, the former certainly can.

The second general conclusion that may be inferred is that, by and large, the superior teachers are fulfilling the intent of current legislation affecting special education. This is clearly seen from the results in the sections on evaluation, professional interaction, and parental interaction. Other data that may also support this inference are in the section on classroom teaching activity, wherein a majority of the superior teachers reported developing their own curriculum. It may be reasoned that state and/or commercial curriculum guides simply do not allow for enough individualized planning. This hypothesis is somewhat supported by the extent of preyear and postyear evaluation conducted by superior teachers.

As in any profession, special education will always have members who range from superior to average to below average. It cannot be expected that this range, whatever may cause it, will ever be overcome entirely. It is felt, however, that by pointing out some of the characteristics and tactics that are common to superior teachers and differentiate them from average teachers, preservice and inservice training programs may be designed that will improve the overall quality of all special education teachers.

Notes

[1] R. Shores, P. Cegelka and C. Nelson, "Competency Based on Special Education Teacher Training," *Exceptional Children* 40 (1973) 92–197.

[2] C. Meisgeier, "The Identification of Successful Teachers of Mentally or Physically Handicapped Children," *Exceptional Children* 32 (1965) 229–235.

[3] A. Scheuer, "The Relationship Between Personal Attributes and Effectiveness in Teachers of the Emotionally Disturbed," *Exceptional Children* 37 (1971) 723–731.

[4] R. Blackwell, "Study of Effective and Ineffective Teachers of the Trainable Mentally Retarded," *Exceptional Children* 39 (1972) 139–143.

[5] H. Fredericks, R. Anderson and V. Baldwin, "The Identification of Competencies in Teachers of the Severely Handicapped," in *Research to Practice in Mental Retardation.* Vol. II ed. P. Mittler (Baltimore: University Park Press, 1977).

[6] D. Westling, M. Koorland and T. Rose, *Special Education Teacher Profile* (Talla-

hassee: Department of Childhood, Reading and Special Education, Florida State University, 1978).

[7] J. Roscoe, *Fundamental Research Statistics For the Behavioral Sciences* (New York: Holt, Rinehart, & Winston, 1975).

After reading "Characteristics of Superior and Average Special Education Teachers" and "Good Teachers Make a Lasting Impact," ask yourself how you can use your university experience to prepare to become the best teacher you can possibly be. What courses will you need to take? What kinds of projects will you need to be doing? What should you be reading? What kinds of things should you try to get out of your field experience?

Another thing you should begin to do in order to be a good teacher is to develop your own philosophy of teaching. Dan Pekarsky has offered a way to help you get started in the following article.

Back-to-the-Basics Reinterpreted:
Philosophy of Education and Educators

Daniel Pekarsky
University of Wisconsin

Is philosophy of education "relevant?" "Of course it is—but only to other philosophers of education, and even they don't seem able to agree about what philosophy of education is." This is a common view, and, unfortunately, it is shared not just by many who have never studied philosophy of education systematically but also by many who have been asked to do so on their way to professional life in schools and other education-related institutions. I say that this is "unfortunate," not because I believe that everything we study or do has to be "relevant" to some practical concern, but because, in actual fact, philosophy of education is of the utmost practical relevance to those entering the profession of education. If this has not seemed to be true, it is not because the concerns, methods, and questions of philosophy of education are irrelevant to practitioners of education but because this form of inquiry has too often been presented to students in a manner that makes its practical value something of a mystery. My purpose in this

Written expressly for *Preparing for Reflective Teaching.*

paper is to unravel this mystery, to explain what philosophical inquiry into education is in a way that will make its practical importance to educators obvious. In the course of doing so, I will be raising certain questions about the aims and process of education as a way of illustrating my general points, but I would be less than candid if I did not confess my hope that the reader will find these questions engaging enough to pursue further. And to explore such questions critically is already to be engaged in philosophizing about education.

Educational researchers ask many kinds of questions: What is the most effective way to teach reading, or to enhance creativity, or to encourage critical thinking, or to help students overcome their prejudices? What has been the actual impact of Head Start programs, of bilingual education programs, of mainstreaming programs? What is the most effective way of teaching teachers to be sensitive to the needs of students? What kind of teacher works best with what kind of child? And so on. These are all important questions, but though philosophy of education is interested in such matters, the questions it poses are of a different order. To engage in philosophical reflection on education is to step back and ask: What is it that we are really trying to do when, as parents or teachers, we participate in the educational process? What do we think the aims of education are, and what convictions about such matters as the nature and value of human life and knowledge, about the rights and duties of parents, teachers, and children, and about the circumstances in which human flourish which underlie our beliefs about the process and aims of education? Equally important, can we justify or defend our views on these questions or are they simply prejudices?

As the foregoing indicates, there are at least two stages to this kind of inquiry. The first stage is an attempt simply to get clearer about what we already believe—an attempt to bring to the surface and articulate those fundamental beliefs that guide both our understanding of education and our activities as educators. This may seem to be an easy thing to do, but in fact it is often quite difficult. For example, we may be inclined to say that one of the characteristics we think is important to cultivate in children is creativity, and perhaps it is. But what exactly *is* "creativity?" What are we really trying to say about a person when we describe him as "creative?" And what are we really endorsing when we say that "self-realization," "autonomy," or even "happiness" are desirable educational goals? Such terms are notoriously ambiguous, and it requires a lot of effort to spell out what we're really praising when we endorse them. Similarly, it is difficult to be clear about what we are condemning when we say that "indoctrination" or "authoritarianism" should have no part in the educational process. Suppose, for example, we are asked what we want to teach children about how to deal with authorities, and we answer, "We want to encourage them to adopt a questioning attitude, and to disobey when what is demanded of them is at odds with what they think right." But do we, on reflection, *really* believe this? Do we believe that we should disobey laws we think wrong, the court order we disagree with, or the decision of the captain of the football team if we happen to think him mistaken? Reflection may lead us to a much more complex but also much more accurate, account of our beliefs about authority and what we want to convey to children.

This kind of clarity can itself be of great value to the educator, be he or she a teacher, an administrator, a guidance counsellor, or a member of the school board. For the clearer we are about what we believe we should be doing, the more decisively and effectively can we set about our work with students and evaluate both our own performance and that of others. But though greater clarity about what we already believe is itself valuable, it represents only the first stage of philosophical reflection on education. In the second stage, we go on to assess our views, to see whether they can withstand our own critical scrutiny.

The fundamental issue at this second stage is whether, and how, we can justify our views: can we explain, to our own satisfaction and that of others, why they seem plausible to us? Supposing, for example, that we have gotten clearer about what we are pointing to when we endorse creativity, *why* do we think creativity worthy of nurturing? Is creativity necessary for happiness? Is society likely to benefit from the presence of many creative people? Or is there something else about creativity that makes it desirable to cultivate? Viewed from the other side, is it possible that creativity should not be a high educational priority? Is it conceivable, or likely, that a society of creative individuals might lack social stability, or that a creative individual living in the existing society is less likely to thrive than his or her uncreative counterpart? It is, of course, impossible to answer such questions until we have actually made explicit what we mean by "creativity," but this should not obscure the important point, which is that future educators as well as established educators can and should be addressing such questions.

The nature and value of creativity merit our attention because "creativity" figures prominently in the rhetoric of educational aims. Consider now a second kind of problem which, though it has to do with educational aims, more directly concerns the process of education itself. I am referring to the perennial debate concerning the place of freedom and authority in education. On the one side are lined up those who maintain that adults do not exercise enough control over the activities and the development of the young; on the other side are those who claim that adults already exercise too much control. How should we go about deciding our views on such a matter?

Our first step might be to stop and ask ourselves what our present views on this problem actually are, and let us *suppose* that our view is that children should have considerably more freedom than they ordinarily have in the educational process. Having announced our tentative commitment to this view, we might profitably proceed to articulate what we mean by "more freedom," for the meaning of this phrase is not self-evident. An alternative route, and one which I shall pursue, is to move directly to the question, *why* do we think children should have more freedom, on the assumption that in answering this question what we mean by "more freedom" will quickly become evident. If this assumption proves wrong, we can always return again and move directly to the problem of clarifying what "more freedom" means.

Let us therefore proceed to the question, Why do we think children should have more freedom than they now have? To this question one can imagine several possible responses. For example:

1. An appreciation for the needs, interests, understandings, and abilities of children is critical if the educator is to plan meaningful learning experiences for them. But existing educational arrangements are so confining and artificial that the children are generally unlikely to reveal to the educator who they are and what's on their mind. A more open educational environment that gives the child more room to express and act on his or her interests is therefore needed if educators are to understand enough about the children they are working with to develop an intelligent curriculum.

2. The use of threats and force to accomplish educational goals is counter-productive, in that children do not learn well, and probably will learn to hate, what they learn under duress.

3. The use of threats and force to accomplish educational goals is counter-productive in that this kind of treatment cripples the child humanly; in particular, it interferes with the child's development into an independent chooser and breeds instead an irrational, often unduly submissive, attitude towards authorities. To become effective choosers, children need many more opportunities for meaningful decision-making than they typically have.

4. Children are much better judges of their needs and interests —of "what is best for them"—than has been assumed traditionally. Too often they are interfered with in their supposed best interests when in fact they are the better judges of their best interests.

5. Many educational objectives that we try to attain through the use of force can be achieved without it. In fact, given a suitable environment, these objectives would be achieved through the child's own, uncoerced choices.

These are just a few of the possible rationales a person might have for urging that kids be granted more freedom than they currently have.

Which—if any of them—sound plausible? Notice that the answer we give, the rationale we choose, is very important because it will carry implications for the areas, the amount, and the kind of freedom we offer the child. Notice further, though, that the decision to adopt a particular rationale or a combination of different rationales is not the end but only the beginning of critical reflection; for of any rationale we propose it may, and should, be asked: can it be justified? what are our reasons for adopting this view, and, on reflection, are these reasons plausible?

Consider, for example, the third rationale proposed above, according to which children are emotionally scarred by the experience of being constrained and restrained by adult authorities. Anger, humiliation, and the erosion of the child's enthusiasm and spontaneity in the short-run, and the failure to develop meaningful independence as a chooser in the long run—these, so the story goes, are the consequences of the regime of authority. But is this really true? Or is it possible, and even likely, as some psychologists have argued, that sometimes children actually want (though they may not admit it) the adults in their lives to establish firm limits for them and to provide them with authoritative guidance, and that when adults fail to provide these things, the children are likely to feel insecure and unloved? Surely anyone considering adoption of this rationale should think long and hard about this question, drawing on his or her own experience of life and whatever knowledge may be available.

My own intention in this paper is not to try to answer such questions but only to raise them—and to urge on you the view that the attainment of clarity on such matters is both difficult and important. But I will express one view of my own concerning the rationales depicted above: the truth is that *each* of them probably applies in some situations but that none of them applies in all situations. The task of inquiry thus becomes to identify, without distorting, the element of truth in each of these rationales. It is, of course, true that, when all is said and done, the evidence on these kinds of matters may be inconclusive, as it is with many important problems. But this does not relieve us of the responsibility of trying to arrive at the most plausible view possible for us, with the proviso that the results of our investigation are themselves open to review in the light of further experience. (What are the results, for example, when we *act on* the views we have formed?)

Recent years have witnessed the rise of the "back to basics" movement in education, and it is important to note that the beliefs concerning the process and aims of education which this movement represents are themselves worthy of methodical scrutiny. But I mention the "back to basics" movement for another reason, and this is that philosophical reflection on education is itself a "back to basics" activity in an extremely important sense: for what could be more basic for educators than to reflect honestly and seriously about the beliefs that guide their participation in the educational process? True, such reflection, however productive, is not sufficient to make us good teachers or to create quality educational arrangements. For to be a good teacher or administrator involves a lot more than having beliefs that have passed the test of critical reflection; moreover, it may be very difficult to live by our beliefs, to act on them consistently and effectively, under existing educational arrangments. But surely coming to a critical understanding of what, as educators, we should be doing is a crucial stage in the effort to do our jobs well and to bring into being educational arrangements that we can genuinely endorse.

Finally, a warning is in order: to think seriously and critically about education (as about anything else) is to put our own beliefs in jeopardy and perhaps to suffer some moments of anxiety; for it is to risk the possibility that what we have thus far assumed to be obvious is only partially true, if not just plain wrong. But the compensating rewards of this kind of thinking are also substantial: at the end of the process we will be much clearer about what we believe and why we believe it; we will be better able to explain not just to other parties like parents and school boards but also to ourselves why we are committed to some educational practices and uneasy about others. And with this kind of understanding we will be better able both to guide and to evaluate educational practices intelligently. True, in the end of the process of critical reflection we will probably be left with unanswered questions in need of further examination, but for an educator this is as it should be—particularly if we genuinely believe that education is a life-long process.

In the first article, Zeichner and I suggested that you need to begin to articulate and clarify your beliefs about teaching in order to become a reflective teacher. Pekarsky has offered some suggestions to help you approach this task. Before going on to the other chapters in this book, stop and, after careful thought, write down your beliefs to complete each of the following statements:

The good life is . . .
The nature of society is . . .
Schooling should contribute to the good life by . . .
Schools should serve society by . . .
The things that are most worth learning include . . .
People approach learning in the following way: . . .
The teacher can best help children to learn by . . .

Now read the rest of the chapters in this book, keeping these topics in mind. Seriously discuss your beliefs with your peers as you go through this book. After you have finished the book, come back to these topics and see if your beliefs have changed or developed. This process will put you well on your way toward becoming a reflective teacher.

Chapter 2

Schools and Society

Do you think schools are designed to serve other purposes? If so, what are some of these other purposes?

By now you know that when you have answered one question that I have proposed, it will only lead to more questions. Read the article "Akwesasne Freedom School" and consider the following questions as you read.

How did the people of the Mohawk nation see the purposes of school?

Who did they think was benefitting most from those purposes in the public schools?

How did they restructure their own schools to make those purposes benefit them?

Akwesasne Freedom School
Sovereignty • Self–Sufficiency • Survival

Jose Barreiro and Carol Cornelius–Mohawk
Akwesasne Notes

Of the five processes that a people must control in order to call themselves sovereign, none is more vital and important than the education and socialization of their own children.

Children are a nation's most precious resource. The values, the skills, the very way of life we provide in their formative years determine the relative strengths and weaknesses of the nation through the lifespan of each successive generation.

Akwesasne Notes, Autumn 1980. Reprinted by permission from the authors.

61

Conscious of this fundamental principle of nationhood, the Mohawk People this fall established the Akwesasne Freedom School.

On September 8, 1980, the Akwesasne Freedom School opened with an enrollment of 63 students and an increasing waiting list of future students. Classes are held in the equivalent of pre-kindergarten to grade 12. At present they are held in two private homes plus the downstairs of a building which was constructed to house people in the Raquette Point Encampment. Construction is also presently under way on Mohawk Nation lands which will provide more usable space in the near future.

What happens within a community to compel it to move to regain control over the education of their young people? What are the deciding factors which bring people out of the talking phase into the action phase? Many, many native communities talk about educating their own children, but few communities are able to shake the feeling of helplessness with which the public schools control them and their children. The question that looms the heaviest is how does a nation of native people who have been able to successfully withstand attacks from the New York State Police, the New York courts, and vigilantes again and again for fifteen months, how does that community have the energy and motivation to tackle head-on the regaining of sovereignty in education?

The answers to these questions lie deep in the hearts of the People of the Mohawk Nation. Over the past year, they have seen some of their own people so sold out to the oppressor that they could take up arms to kill their own people. It was at this precarious point in history, June 13th, 1980, and the months of July and August that the People realized that these so-called vigilantes were totally uneducated about their own people's ways. Parents and Mohawk People with teacher certification began discussions. They realized that the public schools are syphoning off their young people to fit into the United States system to the detriment of the Mohawk Nation.

There seemed only one solution—we must educate our own children. We must stop the loss of children's minds to a foreign government which destroys their sense of being Mohawk. Ron LaFrance, coordinator for the school, says, "Their form of education (public schools) was not benefitting our community because we lost our young people. We are preparing our students to be good citizens of the Mohawk Nation just as the public school prepares their children to be good U.S. citizens. We have the right to do that. We have the right to prepare our students to be good citizens and community members of the Mohawk Nation. The whole concept of nationhood is strong in the school. If we're going to be a strong Nation we have to keep our young people and build educational, political, and economic sovereignty. That's our goal."

"We must all consciously challenge every model, every program, and every process that the West tries to force upon us. Paulo Friere wrote, in his book, *Pedagogy of the Oppressed*, that it is the nature of the oppressed to imitate the oppressor, and by such actions try to gain relief from the oppressive condition. We must learn to resist that response to oppression." (From *Basic Call to Consciousness*).

One of the most effective ways to pave a new path is to negate the system of hierarchy to which everyone is accustomed. In the Mohawk Nation's philosophy, everyone is equal. In the Freedom School everyone is equal and has a voice in developing the principles, the guidelines, the rules by which the school will function. The most effective way to make real changes in the educational process is to require parental involvement in all phases of the schooling process.

If you were to walk into the Akwesasne Freedom School any morning, you would find parents participating in the academics by conducting classes, tutoring, typing worksheets, cleaning up, and assisting the teachers with every aspect of the school day. Every Monday evening the parents have an open meeting where all problems, both short term and long term, are discussed. Long range planning for the acquisition of land and the development of self-sufficiency are discussed and decisions made. High school students have at least two representatives at these meetings.

Parental involvement in the school is not superficial, it is deliberately an in-depth process of total commitment of the parents to the students and for the community. The right to determine educational policy and to participate actively in the teaching of classes is essential if a Nation of Native peoples is to produce their own "citizens" who benefit themselves and the community.

Some parents have been timid about entering this process and it is easy to understand that after several hundred years of being kept out of their children's education, it is an entirely new idea to be welcomed into the education of their children. It's slow, at times, and painful, but it is worthwhile. The parents have organized and implemented the transportation system for the students. Money for gas comes out of their own pockets. In addition, each family is asked to donate $2 per week to the school to help with supplies.

One of the most important aspects of the school is that the parents are a resource. When asked what the Akwesasne Freedom School can offer students that they can't get in the public schools, the high school coordinator responded, "I think what we have here is an abundance of resource people that are invaluable to us. This week a lot of those resource people came into our classes—traditional people who have experience in a lot of different fields are coming in to teach our students. In the regular high school, you wouldn't get that, you'd get your regular subjects along the curriculum lines of New York State. We're developing our own curriculum line—something that pertains to our life and which balances things out more from our point of view. We're trying to get across the basic skills of reading, writing, math, and science, but we're doing that from the angle of native people. The books we're using are all oriented toward native viewpoints. We have the resource people coming in who can augment those books. I think that's valuable to the students. Mostly, we're trying to get them to get the idea to be responsible for education as much as possible."

When asked to define some of the values, she responded, "The two major items which I keep bringing up in class are respect and responsibility. These two concepts are the basis, I think, of how we should conduct ourselves. The first week most of the students were involved in what's going on here the whole year. We talked about what it is that we're all about here. What is the Mohawk Nation? Why does the Mohawk Nation seek recognition? What is it all about? Plus our recognition of the responsibility we have that goes along with that, the responsibility we have to act like a nation, and an individual within that nation.

"There are responsibilities and restrictions we have on ourselves too. Also the students felt that we have to be more disciplined if we're going to really strive to be a nation. Some of the students had heard that we're presenting papers in Geneva and they want to know more about that. Are we ready to take the responsibility to act like a nation? Are the students ready to take that kind of responsibility in five or ten years? They will be the ones who will be recognized as leaders, not that the older ones will be gone anywhere, but it will be their turn and a lot of the students seem like they really are responsible. That's amazing. They have a real 'want' to learn about things. They want more homework than they are getting, they want more reading. It's almost hard to keep up with them all the time."

One of the reasons the school was started is that the adults do see the students as future leaders. Are the students aware of that?

"I think a lot of them are aware of it," the high school coordinator replied, "but it seems that the school system outside teaches them to postpone that responsibility until they're out of college. Postpone that until you're thirty, don't take that responsibility now. According to the old ways we were carrying the responsibility of families when we were 14 or 15 years old, now we have that delayed by 15 years, and that's a long time. I think you go through the public system where it's always delayed and other people are always taking that responsibility for you. It gives you a whole different outlook and a lot of the problems that we see might even stem from that, or maybe that's the way it was planned.

"The students are beginning to realize that they have to take responsibility. For example, the remodeling that we are doing in the garage to make it into the high school—the idea was brought up and two of the students picked up the idea, and they are the ones who are making sure it gets done. They are not waiting for the adults. The students came to the parent committee the other day and asked for the money to get insulation and lumber. They want to get the project done, now. They took the responsibility of getting it done so it's their whole project right now. Students who build a building, who put their time and effort into it, are going to take care of it. That's something we don't see in the public school system."

The pre-kindergarten classes are entirely in Mohawk language. It is felt that it is necessary to establish the language first. Kindergarten is also in as much Mohawk language as possible.

The primary grades curriculum consists of Mohawk language, language arts, math, reading, social studies (home and community), and science. The afternoons are for culture-based learning with the focus on Mohawk oral language development integrated with their studies. Local community people, elders and leaders, work with the staff to develop the afternoon activities.

Traditional education of the Indian people is multi-disciplined, not simply mind development. Mini-home economics classes are being held to teach the students about foods and food preparation for the ceremonies throughout the year. One project the students will be working on is building a large earth oven to accommodate baking thirty loaves of bread at one time. The oven will be patterned after those used by the Southwest Indian people. This is one of the steps in building self-sufficiency. The most important goal is to facilitate learning so that the students will have a good self-image as Indians, promote self-reliance, and promote respect for and skills in living in harmony with others and the environment and mastering the academics and/or vocational skills necessary for self-sufficiency in a dualistic society.

The junior and senior high program has a core academic program with language arts, mathematics, science, and social studies. This program is also goal oriented, mixing academic studies with culture-based curriculum with emphasis on learning skills, completing tasks, research, and projects. Language acquisition as it relates to the cultural ceremonies and functions is stressed. For example, the various speeches that are given throughout the ceremonies contain a vast history and variety of concepts that are newly discovered phenomena in Western thought. Each elective has been thought through to determine how the skills learned will benefit both the student and the community. As the student learns, the community also learns, by doing; as participants, not as observers. It is planned that as the school grows, land is acquired and buildings built, that gardens will be planted which will support the school lunch program and will also contribute to the support of the school's families.

Self-sufficiency plans include alternative housing styles, bio-intensive gardening, solar green houses, processing/curing of foods, solar water heaters, waterless toilets, wind generators, earth ovens, and solar food dryers. These activities are being presented in theory now and will be hands-on projects when land is acquired. Woven into the curriculum are environmental and ecology issues which are presented from the viewpoint of Mohawk cultural beliefs.

"Our children should come out of our own schools knowing at least as much, and hopefully more, than they would coming out of the public school," says Brenda LaFrance, a biology teacher. "Science will help them realize and look at the world around them. They will know how the polluted air they breathe affects them, how the water with fluoride and mercury which they drink affects them and how pollution affects the food we grow in the earth."

The Mohawk Nation sits in one of the most heavily polluted areas of the United States. Alcoa and Reynolds aluminum plants are located nearby and a General Motors Chevrolet plant which dumps chemical pollutants on the land is within eyesight of the school. Across the St. Lawrence River, a Domtar Paper mill deposits mercury wastes into the waterways. We know these pollutants affect our health.

Land-based economics is self-sufficiency, another of the vital processes of sovereignty, a long-range goal of the school.

"The future of any Native Nation these days is directly linked to its ability right now to grow its sustenance on its own secure land-base," said one of the parents recently. "We know that. We have known that. The school community, the families, the parents, the teachers, the *Notes* staff—we all hope that this school process will be the process by which these perceptions will become a reality."

Now that you have finished reading "Akwesasne Freedom School," how do you think public schools could have modified the curriculum so that Mohawks could have been better served and not forced to create their own school? After all, are not schools supposed to serve all of the public?

Next time you are out in a school, if a student asks you what the purpose of schooling is, what would you say?

There are many different ways in which society influences schools. For example, society determines how much funding schools get, and what can and cannot be taught. In addition, social and political movements in society influence the perspectives of those who decide to enter schools as teachers. The following article provides an example of how the feminist movement influenced the views of three different generations of teachers regarding teaching. As you are reading the article you may want to consider the following questions: Why are many feminists

dissatisfied with teaching? Why don't they stay in school and make
schooling more feminist? Would the feminist view help to provide both
boys and girls with ideas about alternative lifestyles?

Women Elementary School Teachers and the Feminist Movement

Ruth Lebowitz
Public Schools, New York City

Much evidence exists that the teaching profession, especially at the elementary school level, continues to be sex-typed in a manner that is consistent with traditional sex-role concepts, even though, since the 1960's, the increasing vitality of the Feminist Movement has stimulated women everywhere to question the status quo.

The Feminist Movement, which has been responsible for the articulation of the dissatisfaction of women in general, has focused attention on the inequality of women in today's society and the discrimination against them in employment and education. In addition to pointing out salary inequities, the Feminist Movement has done much consciousness-raising among women teachers. It has made women more aware of their low, bottom-level status in the school hierarchy; it is the women who teach, and the men who administrate! Data on the distribution of men and women in the educational profession in the years from 1972 to 1974 indicated that although women made up 84 percent of the nation's elementary school teachers, only 19.6 percent of them were elementary school principals, 6.2 percent of them were associate superintendents, 5.3 percent were assistant superintendents, and 0.1 percent were superintendents![1]

The words "elementary school teacher" and "Feminist Movement" appear to suggest a dichotomy, or conflict, because our stereotyped notions of the kinds of women who are elementary school teachers and the kinds of women who are Feminists have placed them at opposite ends of a continuum.

Elementary school teaching has always been considered a "feminine" occupation, an extension of the female role that involves being sociable, passive, nurturant, cooperative, and helpful.[2] Recent research on women who support the Feminist Movement has found them to be less traditionally "feminine" in their personality characteristics, more achieve-

Reprinted with permission from: *The Elementary School Journal*, Volume 80, Number 5. © 1980 by The University of Chicago.

ment oriented, and liberal or radical in their religious and political ideology.[3] It would seem, therefore, that women who support the Feminist Movement would show a departure in their work as well.

The purpose of this research was to study the relationship of the views that women elementary school teachers in the New York City school system have of their work and their attitudes toward the Feminist Movement.[4] It was hypothesized that the women who are the most satisfied with their work as elementary school teachers would have the least favorable attitudes toward the Feminist Movement. Conversely, the women who have the most favorable attitudes toward the Feminist Movement would be least satisfied with their work as elementary school teachers, even though their dissatisfactions might stem as much from the conditions in the schools as from the women's awareness of the roles that they play in these schools.

The 327 women elementary school teachers who provided the samples for this study were all from a specific community school district in the New York City school system. Only classroom teachers were included, teachers who are scheduled to work all day with groups of children. Not included were such school personnel as guidance counselors, librarians, remedial reading teachers, or hearing and speech teachers. It was felt that this group has the opportunity to arrange flexible work schedules and is, therefore, not subject to the same kinds of pressures and problems that the daily routine of a classroom teacher presents.

The instrument used was a questionnaire containing 61 items and divided into three parts. The first part contained 27 questions designed to measure the attitudes, satisfactions, expectations, and perceptions of the teachers toward their work. These questions were drawn from previous studies and questionnaires developed by Wenoker, Simpson, and Mason, Dressel, and Baine.[5]

The second part of the questionnaire, the Feminist Scale, was a short form of the scale developed by Dempewolff at the University of Cincinnati in 1972.[6] It included statements about women's rights, women's competencies, and male-female relationships. High scores indicated favorable attitudes toward the Feminist Movement, and low scores indicated less favorable attitudes. Reliability of the Dempewolff Scale was estimated by using the Spearman-Brown formula, which yielded a reliability of .96. Split-half reliability using matched halves yielded a reliability estimate of .976. Dempewolff's test was validated by a two-way analysis of variance to see whether it effectively discriminated between two groups of students on campus who had opposing attitudes on the Feminist Movement. A significant difference was found between the two groups (p .001), thus demonstrating validation by discriminating between groups known to hold opposing views.

The third section consisted of questions on personal background, such as age, education, marital status, and number of years in teaching.

A scale total was computed for the items on the Feminist Scale (Part II of the questionnaire). The highest possible score was 4, and the lowest possible score was 1.

Because each question on attitudes, satisfactions, expectations, and aspirations dealt with a different aspect of these topics, it was necessary to treat each item statistically as a different entity. Therefore, one-way analysis of variance was used to test for significant differences between each of the variables in Part I of the questionnaire and the scores on the Feminist Scale.

One-way analysis of variance was also used to test for significant differences between background factors such as age, marital status, education, years in teaching, years in the present school, and scores on the Feminist Scale. In addition, relationships among pairs of variables in Part I and Part III were examined through the use of cross-tabulations.

Individual scores that respondents received on the Feminist Scale (Part II) ranged from 1.69 to 3.93. If a score of 1 to 2.5 can be considered as an indication of low or negative endorsement of the Feminist Movement and a score of 2.5 to 4 as an indication of positive endorsement, most of the subjects scored in the positive range rather than the negative range, as Table 1 shows. Only 5.6 percent of the respondents scored 2.5 or lower. The mean score was 3.19, and the median was 3.25, and the top quarter of the respondents scored 3.5 or higher. The standard deviation was .403.

The women elementary school teachers in this study were found to be decidedly pro-Feminist, and the majority of them also expressed satisfaction with teaching. However, findings from this study indicate that there are definite differences in attitudes toward teaching between women who are strongly in favor of the Feminist Movement and those whose feelings are less positive.

To summarize some of these differences, a composite picture was drawn of a teacher with a high score on the Feminist Scale and a teacher

Table 1

Distribution of Scores on the Feminist Scale

Range	Number of Teachers	Percent of Teachers
1. 1.69–2.50	18	5.6
2. 2.54–3.25	142	45.2
3. 3.26–3.48	78	24.1
4. 3.50–3.93	85	25.1
Total	323	100.0

with a low score. These portraits are generalizations drawn from the findings, not portraits that describe each teacher in the study. (See Table 2.)

High Scorers on the Feminist Scale

Using only those variables that showed a statistically significant relationship with attitudes toward the Feminist Movement, the researcher drew a profile of a woman elementary school teacher who is in strong agreement with the views of the Feminist Movement, as indicated by a score of 3.50 to 3.93 on the Feminist Scale.

1. The teacher is between 31 and 40 years of age.
2. She is probably married, but chances are strong that she is either divorced, separated, or widowed.
3. She has had from six to ten years of teaching experience.
4. She is not sure whether teaching in her school is a satisfying

---

Table 2.

Attitudes Toward Teaching Held by Women Elementary School Teachers Who Had the Highest and the Lowest Scores on the Feminist Scale

Variable	Highest Scores on the Feminist Scale		Lowest Scores on the Feminist Scale	
	Response	Mean Score	Response	Mean Score
1. Age	31-40	3.30	51-60+	3.11
2. Marital status*	Widowed, divorced, separated	3.24	Single	3.06
3. Teaching experience	6-10 years	3.27	21-42 years	2.90
4. Satisfaction with teaching in respondent's school	Not sure	3.28	Very satisfied	3.08
5. How satisfied do you think the other teachers in your school are?	Not satisfied	3.30	Very satisfied	2.90
6. Comparison of teaching with other careers.	Not sure	3.31	*The* most satisfying career	2.87
7. Would you advise your daughter to be a teacher?	Definitely no	3.32	Definitely yes	2.94

Table 2 *(Continued)*

8. How important is money a reason for your remaining a teacher?	*The* most important reason	3.23	Third most important reason	3.10
9. How important is professional status a reason for your remaining a teacher?	Not a reason for me	3.22	*The* most important	3.00
10. How would you rate the respect of people in your community for teachers?	Low	3.28	Very high	3.07
11. How do you feel now about your future as a teacher?	Would like to change to different work, outside education	3.36	Become a full-time housewife	2.95
12. Does teaching give you a chance to do the things you can do best?	Not sure	3.40	Very good chance	3.12
13. Has teaching lived up to your expectations?	Undecided	3.57	Yes, in all respects	3.06
14. If you had it to do over again, would you choose teaching?	Definitely no	3.34	Definitely yes	3.09

*Although the teachers who had the highest scores on the Feminist Scale were widowed, divorced, or separated, and those who had the lowest scores were single, the majority of the teachers in this sample (76 percent) were married.

experience for her, but she is sure that the other teachers in her school are dissatisfied.

5. She is not sure how teaching compares to other types of careers, but she would definitely not advise her daughter to become a teacher.

6. An important reason why she has stayed in teaching so far is that she needs the money, but she hopes to change some day to a different kind of work, outside of education.

7. She is not sure that teaching gives her a chance to do the things that she can do best, and she is undecided whether teaching has lived up to the expectations she had before she entered it, but, if she had it to do again, she would definitely not enter teaching.

Low Scorers on the Feminist Scale

Using those variables that showed a statistically significant relationship with attitudes toward the Feminist Movement, the researcher drew a profile of a woman elementary school teacher who has less favorable views of the Feminist Movement, as indicated by a Feminist Scale score of 1.69 to 3.10:

1. She is more than fifty years of age.
2. She is probably married, but chances are strong that she is single.
3. She has been teaching for more than twenty years.
4. She finds teaching in her school very satisfying and believes that other teachers in the school are very satisfied, too.
5. She believes that teaching is the most satisfying career one could follow and would definitely advise her daughter to become a teacher.
6. Her most important reason for staying in teaching so far is that she likes the professional status a teacher has. She believes that the respect for teachers in the community where she works is very high.
7. She believes that teaching gives her a very good chance to do the things she can do best and that teaching has in all respects lived up to the expectations she had before she entered it.
8. She would like to teach a while longer and then stop working to be a full-time housewife. If she had it to do again, she would definitely enter teaching.

Studies that date back to the late 1950's[7] have shown that teachers are generally not highly motivated toward achievement but are steady individuals who like stable, predictable lives, enjoy identifying with institutions and groups, and are socially oriented. Present findings generally agree, but only for older teachers. The 31- to 40-year-old group was found to be more in favor of the Feminist Movement than either the 21- to 30-year-old group or any of the older groups. The 31- to 40-year-olds went to college during the turbulent sixties and were exposed to the women's rights ideologies of that era. The absence of strong pro-Feminists among the youngest group would appear to suggest that they have already opted for careers other than elementary school teaching. This possibility is also confirmed by the finding that pro-Feminist teachers would not advise their daughters to become teachers, while teachers who had low Feminist scores would.

Findings from this study appear to suggest that women elementary school teachers who had the least favorable attitudes toward the Feminist Movement were the most satisfied with their jobs and anticipated lifelong careers as elementary school teachers or housewives. Women whose scores on the Feminist Scale indicated that they were the most pro-Feminist were found to be the most dissatisfied with, and the most ambivalent toward, their jobs as elementary school teachers. They planned to leave education for other lines of work, either immediately or in the future.

On aspirations for moving upward within the school hierarchy, no significant relationships were found between attitudes toward the Feminist Movement and the aspiration to become principal or assistant principal. Few teachers expressed aspirations for either of these two positions, as Table 3 shows.

Table 3

Frequency Distribution of Desire to Become Principal or Assistant Principal

	Principal		Assistant Principal	
Response	Number of Teachers	Percent of Teachers	Number of Teachers	Percent of Teachers
1. Would very much like to be	41	12.5	22	6.7
2. Have some desire to be	35	10.8	22	6.7
3. Not sure	21	6.4	17	5.2
4. Not especially anxious to be	62	19.0	50	15.3
5. Would not want to be	160	48.9	206	63.0
6. No response to question	8	2.4	10	3.1
Total	327	100.0	327	100.0

However, when levels of aspiration extended outside the school system, significant relationships were found. Teachers who had the highest scores on the Feminist Scale hoped some day to change to a different kind of work outside education and preferred to be in some other work now. These teachers were greater in number and had higher scores on the Feminist Scale than either the teachers who wanted to move to school administration or the teachers who wanted lifelong teaching careers, as Table 4 shows.

Education faces a crisis. At the same time that career opportunities in elementary school teaching are, for various reasons, declining, alternatives and options in other fields are widening. In an era of changing expectations for women, whether future elementary school teachers will be more feminine or more feminist will have important consequences for what happens in the classroom.

Table 4

Analysis of Variance of Scores on Feminist Scale and Responses·
to the Question: "Which One of the Following Statements Best
Describes How You Feel Now about Your Future as a Teacher?"

Response	Number of Teachers	Mean Scores on the Feminist Scale	Standard Deviation
1. I will reach retirement soon, so the question doesn't apply to me.	64	3.09	0.4202
2. I want a life-long career in teaching.	85	3.12	0.3570
3. I want a career in education but hope someday to move into school administration and leave classroom teaching.	42	3.24	0.4014
4. I want to teach a while longer but hope to stop working to be a full-time housewife.	22	2.95	0.4797
5. I want to teach a while longer but hope someday to change to a different kind of work, outside of education.	78	3.36	0.3716
6. I would really prefer to be in some different kind of work now.	25	3.33	0.3168
Total	316	3.19	0.4047

$F = 7.0842$ Significance $= 0.00000$

Notes

[1] Andrew Fishel and Janice Pottker, "Women in Educational Governance: A statistical Portrait," *Education Researcher 3* (July–August, 1974): 5-6.

[2] Cynthia Epstein, *Woman's Place* (Berkeley, California: University of California Press, 1970).

[3] Judith Ann Dempewolff, "Development and Validation of a Feminism Scale," *Psychological Reports 34* (April, 1974): 651-57; J. Goldschmidt, M. M. Gergen, K. Quigley, and K. Gergen, "The Women's Liberation Movement: Attitudes and Action," *Journal of Personality 42* (December, 1974): 601-17; Janet Schumacher-Finell, "The Relationship between Attitudes toward Feminism and the Sex, Age, and Background Factors of the Residents in a Small Town Setting" (Ed.D. dissertation, Columbia University, 1977).

[4] Ruth Lebowitz, "The Relationship of the Views Women Elementary Teachers Have of Their Work and Their Attitudes toward the Feminist Movement" (Ed.D. dissertation, Teachers College, Columbia University, 1979).

[5] Sidney Wenoker, "A Comparative Study of Teacher and Principal Role Expectations" (Ed.D. dissertation, Teachers College, Columbia University, 1976);

Richard Simpson, *The School Teacher: Social Values, Community Role, and Professional Self-Image.* (Chapel Hill, North Carolina: Institute for Research in Social Science, University of North Carolina, August, 1968); Ward Mason, R. Dressel, and R. Baine, "Sex Role and the Career Orientation of Beginning Teachers," *Harvard Educational Review 27* (August, 1959): 370-83.

[6] Judith Ann Dempewolff, "Feminism and Its Correlates" (Ph.D. dissertation, University of Cincinnati, 1972).

[7] R. G. Kuhlen and W. J. Dipboye, "Motivational and Personality Factors in the Selection of Elementary and Secondary School Teaching as a Career" (Washington, D.C.: Office of Education, 1959); Jack Mervin and Francis DiVesta, "A study of Need Theory and Career Choice," *Journal of Counseling Psychology 6* (Winter, 1959): 302-8; J. T. Gray, "Needs and Values in Three Occupations," *Personnel and Guidance Journal 42* (November, 1963): 238-44; Ward Mason, R. Dressel, and R. Baine, "Sex Role and the Career Orientation of Beginning Teachers," *Harvard Educational Review 27* (August, 1959): 370-83.

Perhaps you have met with a sharp retort or a steely glance when you have told people that you want to be a teacher. It was as if they were saying, "Why do you want to teach? Teachers do a lousy job. Just look at our schools."

In order that wisdom and knowledge rather than emotion guide your response, you need to know the facts surrounding many societal school-related problems. Read the following articles by Rowan and Royko and notice where they place the source of what are often described as school problems.

She Can't Spell, But at Least She's There

Mike Royko
Chicago Sun-Times News Service

In a Chicago schoolroom, a student raises his hand and asks a question about a math problem.

The teacher shakes her head and says: "I don't know the answer to that. I only know simple arithmetic. If you want to know the answer, you just look it up in your book."

A few days later, same school, same teacher, different classroom. A student asks about something she has read in her science book.

The teacher says: "I don't know anything about that stuff. Why'nt you just go on to the next part?"

And a few days later, same school, same teacher. This time the question is about punctuation.

The teacher says: "Sometimes you put that thing there, that punctuation, in front of the 's' and sometimes you put that thing in back of the 's,' but I'm not sure which is which. Just look in your book, and it'll tell you."

True story. But before you ask the obvious question—how did a person like that get to be a teacher—don't blame her.

She's not a teacher. Yes, she was teaching a class. She has taught many classes during the last semester.

But she's a high school dropout, hired under the federal Comprehensive Employment and Training Act (CETA) as a school security monitor. Her job is to break up fights in the schoolyard and watch the hallways.

But the Chicago schools are so financially desperate that the principal of that South Side school doesn't want to hire a substitute teacher when a regular is sick.

So instead of paying a substitute, the CETA employee more or less baby-sits the class.

I had a long talk with that CETA monitor about her experience.

"The first time it happened, I had finished monitoring the kids in the morning," she said. "I stay outside from 8 o'clock until 9, to break up fights and things like that.

"I came in, and the principal told me I should go in and take one of the classes because the teacher was home sick.

"I started to tell her I couldn't do that. But she's not the kind of person you argue with. She says to me: 'I'm your boss. You do as I say.' So after that, when she told me to do it—or the assistant principal or the clerk—I did it."

What did you teach them?

"Well, first of all I tell them that I don't know all that stuff so I'd ask them what word they are supposed to learn. Then they'd tell me, and I'd tell them all to write it five times or somethin' like that.

"I had this one class where the kids was supposed to be learnin' French. I don't know nothin' about French. So I ask them to teach me some of the French words, and they teach me words like "monjour" or somethin' like that.

"Sometimes kids would ask me about somethin', and I'd tell them I don't know things like that, and it would make them baffled. So I'd tell them that I hadn't gone to school for years, and when I went, I didn't go very long. So they should look up the answer in the book.

"I'd try to pacify 'em in some way. I'd tell 'em to skip the part they didn't know and go on to the next part. Or I'd tell 'em to remember the question and to ask the teacher when she came back.

"Sometimes I'd try to teach 'em things I knew, because I read a lot— the newspapers and some books and magazines.

"Like in 'word skills.' I guess that's English? I'd try to show them where to put that punctuation mark. Like in the word John when you have an 's' on the end of it. Sometimes you put the mark between John and the 's,' and sometime you put the mark after the 's.' But I wasn't really sure.'

How many times did you teach this semester?

"About 35 times. I have 'em all wrote down so I know how many times. It was about 35 times. We all did it. All the CETA workers.

"The teachers used to tell us not to. They said that we was being told to do this so they wouldn't have to hire a substitute. But we was afraid to argue with the principal. You argue with her, and she'll yell and won't even listen.

"But I can't teach anybody nothin'. All we was was baby-sitters. That's all. Just baby-sitters."

I talked to another CETA worker at the school, and she admitted that she, too, had been filling in as a teacher. But she wouldn't discuss details because she's afraid of getting into trouble.

Surprisingly, the school produces decent scores in the standard reading tests. They're not up to suburban scores but are not bad by Chicago inner-city schools standards.

That means somebody at the school is trying, which is why I haven't used the name of the CETA worker, the school or the principal. Any Chicago principal who can get even some results doesn't deserve a public rap.

But I think Chicagoans should know about the situation so they'll know what the future holds: As rough as things are now for the schools, they're going to get tougher.

If and when the RTA crisis is over, the next big crisis is going to be in the schools. They'll soon be scraping through the bottom of the barrel.

Then we'll have to ask the state legislature and Gov. James Thompson for help.

So far, they aren't willing or able to help white suburban commuters in the financial crisis of the Regional Transportation Authority. Imagine how much compassion those Down-state and boony-suburban politicians will feel for Chicago's black school kids.

And there won't even be half-educated CETA workers to baby-sit a class and try to learn what "monjour" means.

President Reagan wants to build more ships and bombers and tanks, even though we don't have enough military people to operate or maintain the ships and bombers and tanks.

To finance the arms race, he has to cut somewhere. And the CETA program is among the many social-help programs getting the ax.

The CETA worker added this thought:

"I've got an 11-year-old son of my own. Sometimes he comes home and asks me about something in his homework, and I tell him: 'I don't know how to do that. Tomorrow you ask your teacher.'

"But what if he gets a CETA worker like me, and she don't know either?"

Well, as bad as that sounds, what if he raises his hand, and there's nobody there?

Truancy Rate—A National Disgrace

Carl T. Rowan
Columnist

Remember when playing hooky from school could get you picked up by a truancy officer, plus a lashing at home with a razor strap or a black-gum switch?

When last did you see, or hear of, a truancy officer? Or hear anyone deplore the appalling rate of unexcused absences in our schools?

Educators, journalists and politicians wring their hands over the high number of teen-age dropouts, or the level of violence in public schools, but far too little attention is given to the fact that on any given day, some 4 million children who are supposed to be in school simply are not there.

Some educators have come to recognize that absenteeism is the first important indicator of a child being on the way to trouble—failing exams, losing interest, dropping out, joining the ranks of the unemployed, drifting into crime.

The Department of Education reports that on the average school day, one out of every 12 pupils across the country is not in class. Big city schools are harder hit. In New York and Boston, more than a fifth of public school students are likely to be absent on a given day. In

Chicago-Sun Times, June 26, 1981. © 1981 Field Enterprises, Inc. Courtesy of Field Newspaper Syndicate.

Cleveland, or here in the nation's capital, one out of six students is absent.

Some of these are "excused" absences granted because parents insist that a family trip is "more educational" than classroom studies, or because students are away with the band, the football team, the choir, or whatever.

But unexcused absences—truancy—have become a national disgrace and a woeful commentary on the social fabric of this nation. Those high-falutin' economic programs recently set forth by Jimmy Carter, Ronald Reagan, and John Anderson ought to be read in the context of what produces truancy, and why this society seems helpless to do anything about it.

Can you imagine that in New York City alone, on any school day, at least 100,000 pupils skip classes? Why so much absenteeism—especially when state aid money is given to schools on the basis of how many students show up for class?

The answer is that unexcused absenteeism and truancy reflect racial and economic injustices and the general malaise within this society.

We have today an appalling percentage of families headed by one parent, the poorest of families (19.3 percent) headed by women. Forty-six percent of black families (1,684,000 families!) are headed by women, against 18 percent when I was a high schooler. Kids from these mostly poor families skip school because:

Momma has to work, and she tells the eldest child to stay home and look after the younger ones. She can't afford day care.

Momma can't make ends meet when inflation is on the rampage, so the older children are told, or they sense, that they must go to work.

Welfare payments for a woman and three children, and no income, whether $476 a month in New York or $120 in Mississippi, don't allow youngsters from poor families to dress like their peers. A lot of children play hooky because they are ashamed of what they have to wear.

There are many other reasons why millions of American youngsters skip school—including the fact that a lot of parents have lost control of their teen-agers, or simply don't give a damn. Whatever the reason, every child playing hooky is courting personal tragedy—and is likely to become a burden on society.

———————

Schools do have an affect on society. And as a teacher you will often have a great affect upon what takes place in the home of your students.

As you read the next article, "A Teacher Too Outstanding," by Blattner, ask yourself what the teacher was doing to inspire such enthusiasm for learning in the student.

A Teacher Too Outstanding

Don Blattner
School District #172, Illinois

Dear Mr. Skinner:

This may be the first letter ever written by a parent to a teacher complaining that the teacher is doing his job too well. My wife and I have considered writing to you several times this year, but we felt that we were overreacting to a situation that would change. It wasn't until last Friday, when we received your monthly newsletter, that we decided that something had to be done.

Please do not misinterpret this letter as criticism of your ability. You are a good teacher—too good! Here's the problem. When I was a student, what I learned in school, stayed in school. It never occurred to me that this knowledge had any practical application in the real world. Your students, however, are motivated to use what they learn in their everyday life. Since Jeff, our son, has been making practical use of his schoolwork, the warm, harmonious relationship our family once enjoyed has been replaced by tension and discord. I have developed an ulcer and my wife is dangerously close to a nervous breakdown. Several incidents involving Jeff and his schoolwork have caused her nervousness to approach hysteria, then terror and finally despair.

Electronic Histrionics

When I came home from work one day last fall, I found my wife sitting at the kitchen table, obviously upset. Her eyes were wide, her face pale, her breathing shallow and labored.

"Go into *your* son's room," she said.

I've learned that whenever my wife disavows her maternal claims and Jeff becomes *my* son, there's a problem.

I went to Jeff's room and opened the door. A siren wailed, bells rang and red and white lights flashed.

Jeff sprang from his bed and flipped a switch which silenced the siren and the bells and also turned off the lights. "Electric eye, Dad." Jeff said. "In case of burglars. Mr. Skinner taught us how to make it in science class."

I looked around the room and could see why my wife was so upset. "Jeff, look at this room—clothes everywhere. On the floor, on the bed, on the chest, even on the lamp!"

"I didn't do it," Jeff protested. "Mom did. She was carryin' these clean clothes into the room when the alarm went off. Clothes flew everywhere." Jeff began to laugh. "You shoulda' seen it, Dad. It was really comical. Then she bent over to pick up the clothes right next to the closet and I flipped this switch." He flipped a switch on the wall and the closet door swung open. "I guess it kinda' hit her when she was bent over."

Jeff laughed again and then continued. "I helped her up and over to this chair so she could catch her breath and I turned on the radio for some relaxing music. Here," he said as he cross the room to the dresser. "You turn it on." He pointed to an old wooden, cathedral-shaped radio popular in the 1930's. "I found it at the dump," he said.

"Does it work?"

"Sure, I fixed it. Mr. Skinner helped me. Turn it on." I crossed to the dresser and removed a pair of socks draped over the top of the radio. Jeff's eyes were sparkling and he sported a wide grin.

"It doesn't shock, does it?" I asked skeptically.

"No, nothin' like that."

I turned the knob. The yellowish dial lit up and the radio began to hum. Suddenly a voice said, *"Who knows what evil lurks in the hearts of men? The Shadow knows."* There was a deep laugh. *"The Shadow who aids the forces of law and order is in reality Lamont Cranston, wealthy young man about town. Years ago in the Orient, Cranston learned a strange and mysterious secret—the hypnotic power to cloud men's minds. . . ."*

"Change stations," Jeff said. I was too surprised to move. Jeff reached out, grabbed the knob and twisted it until he got another program. For the next few minutes we listened to Bud Abbott and Lou Costello do their famous "Who's on First?" routine.

Jeff turned the dial again.

"Lux presents Hollywood," the announcer said. *"The Lux Radio Theatre brings you Rita Hayworth and Charles Korvin in* This Love of Ours. *Ladies and gentlemen, your producer, Mr. William Keighley."*

Again Jeff spun the dial. This time he found a station playing a Glenn Miller record. The song was abruptly interrupted by a voice which said, *"We interrupt this program to bring you a special news bulletin. The Japanese have attacked Pearl Harbor, Hawaii, by air,*

President Roosevelt has just announced. The attack was also made on all naval and military activities on the principal island of. . . ."

I stood in silence for some time before Jeff said. "What'd you expect, Dad? It *is* an old radio." He fell down on the bed, laughing.

"B . . . b . . . but that's impossible," I stammered.

"Hey, that's neat. You stuttered just like Mom did."

"That's impossible," I repeated.

"Look." He turned the radio around to reveal the workings of a tape recorder. "It's a stereo tape recorder. I bought it at a garage sale. All it needed was a new drive belt and some oil. I got the old radio programs at the library, recorded a different program on each track, and then hooked it up so that when you change stations, you are really changing tracks. Neat, huh?"

I stared at Jeff for several minutes. I was amazed. Amazed that he could conceive and design this machine, but still be unable to make his own bed. Amazed that he could spend endless hours building this apparatus, but still refuse to close a door because it takes too long. Amazed that he had the intense concentration necessary to complete such a project, but still could not remember to zip his pants.

Home Biology

While this episode was disconcerting, it was really not nearly as bad as what happened during one of your biology units.

One January evening as I entered the house, I saw my wife lying on the couch. Her hand was on her forehead, her eyes were half closed and her face was twitching noticeably. She didn't speak; she merely pointed to *my* son's room.

I knocked on the door. "Turn off the alarm," I called.

The door swung open. "Come on in, Dad. You wanna look at my specimens? We been studyin' biology in Mr. Skinner's class. Look." He gestured toward his bookcase. The books were gone. In their place were approximately 30 jars filled with various creatures.

"Aren't those our canning jars?" I asked.

"Yeah, I'm borrowing them for awhile until I can get something better. The top row is *Arachnida.*"

"What?" I asked.

"*Arachnida.* You know, arthropods like spiders, scorpions, mites. . . ." He picked up a pair of jars. "See, black widows. And here's a brown recluse—it's dangerous." He replaced the jars and pointed to the lower shelves. "The others are *Insecta, Crustacea,* and *Reptilia.*"

"Jeff," I began, "do you have any idea how much these bugs have upset your mother?"

"These aren't just bugs. These are classes, orders, and suborders of various organisms. Anyway, *these* didn't upset Mom. It was Rajah." He pointed to an aquarium on his desk.

I crossed to the desk and peered into the glass. The snake looked to be about four feet long, although its length was difficult to determine since it was coiled. It was shiny black with bands of yellow crisscrossing in a chainlike pattern.

"Rajah's a king snake." Jeff volunteered. "Mr. Skinner gave him to me." Rajah raised his head and flicked his tongue at me.

"You can't keep a snake in your room," I said. "What if he got out?"

"He wouldn't hurt anyone," Jeff protested. "He didn't hurt anyone today."

I asked the obvious question. "You had the snake out—what happened?"

"Well," Jeff began, "You know how snakes feed on mice. And you know how we've been bothered by mice in the basement. And you know how the washin' machine is in the basement. And you know. . . ."

"Never mind." I interrupted.

"He didn't bite her or anything. He just crawled over her foot." As I turned to go into the living room, I could hear Jeff continuing. "Anyway, she shoulda' been wearin' shoes."

The next problem occurred when I was out of town on business. About nine in the evening I received a call, but before I could even say hello, I heard a frightened voice say, "He has bones!"

"What?"

"He has bones," the voice repeated. It took a few seconds before I realized that the caller was my wife. "I went into Jeff's room to clean today," she continued, "and he has bones—piles of them. On the desk, in the drawers, under the bed. And skulls, too. He has skulls on his bed posts."

"Skulls?"

Her voice became more intense. "His class took a field trip to a museum and he saw skeletons of dinosaurs, elephants and whales. He's starting his own collection."

"But where did he get these bones?" I asked.

"At the dump. He dug them up." She began to sob. "He says they belong to cats and dogs and that he's going to put them together like a jigsaw puzzle—*in his room!*"

There was a long pause. Finally, I said, "I'll talk to him when I get home."

"You don't have to talk to him," she shouted. "Let him collect whatever he wants. But, I can tell you right now that I'm not going into his room again." Her voice sounded hysterical. "Bells, sirens, lights, snakes, spiders, animals and now bones and skulls! If you want that room cleaned, you clean it!" Then she hung up.

Beyond the Classroom

Things went fairly smoothly until the spring. I pulled my car into the driveway one evening, but a huge pile of material blocked the entrance to the garage. When I opened the door, the powerful smell told me immediately what was in the pile.

"Know what this is, Dad?" Before I had a chance to answer he said, "Manure." Did you know that animal manure is one of the oldest and most effective fertilizers known to man? On an average it contains 67.7 percent water, 0.465 percent nitrogen, 0.326 percent phosphoric acid and 0.485 percent potash. Mr. Skinner has some horses. He's gonna' bring me a load twice a week."

"Jeff, I didn't say anything when you started collecting insects, snakes and spiders. And I didn't say anything when you started collecting bones. But you're not going to start a collection of—"

"Not a collection," Jeff interrupted. "We're gonna have the best garden in town. We learned all about gardening in school. Planting, fertilizing, mulching—everything."

"Did your mother see this?" I asked.

"Yeah."

"What did she say?"

"Nothin'. Her face just started twitchin' and she started stuttering. You know, Dad, she's been doin' that a lot lately." He put the shovel down and pulled a wagon in the direction of the backyard. "I'm gonna' use nature's method for growing—natural fertilizer. I'm gonna' put ladybugs and praying mantises in the garden for natural pest control. And I'll use plenty of earthworms to enrich the soil."

"Earthworms?"

"Yeah, I got hundreds of 'em at the park today. They digest the soil and their castings are rich in nutrients. Did you know the average earthworm will produce its weight in castings every 24 hours?"

I had to admit that I didn't. Suddenly, from the house, I thought I heard a scream.

"Sounded like Mom," Jeff said. "Maybe she found the earthworms I stored in the refrigerator."

As I rushed toward the house, I could hear Jeff shouting, "Earthworms need cool air to thrive, so I put 'em in an empty milk carton between the ladybugs and the praying mantises."

This brings us up to the present. Last Friday when I came home, I found Jeff working in the garden.

"Where's your mother?" I asked.

"In her room. I think she's cryin'."

"What happened? What are you collecting now?"

"Nothin'," he protested. "I just came home and gave her Mr. Skinner's newsletter. She read it, started to cry, then went to her room."

Now as I stated before, Mr. Skinner, you are an excellent teacher. You have that rare and precious gift not only to motivate students, but also to inspire them. Jeff has been inspired to master the material presented in class. He has been inspired to work beyond classroom assignments on his own time in order to learn as much as possible. He has been inspired to throw himself into his schoolwork wholeheartedly to understand the theories and to apply what he has learned.

And that is the reason I am writing you now. I see in your newsletter that next week you plan to teach a unit on sex education. Jeff does *not* have my permission to participate.

Another way in which schools can influence society is discussed in the following article, an editorial that was published in the Boston Globe *as part of a program for racial peace. It suggested one way in which the school could foster peace efforts in Boston. Read the article and consider the relationship between schools and job opportunities. Do you think the program proposed here is appropriate? What is positive and what is negative about school's providing training for jobs?*

A Program For Racial Peace

Kirk Scharfenberg
Boston Globe

Almost all of Boston's racial incidents and much of its street crime (which often has a racial aspect) are perpetrated by young people.

The police can move the gangs from corner to corner and arrest the most troublesome. But that solves nothing. The irate citizenry can point

First appeared in the *Boston Globe*, April 8, 1980. Reprinted by permission of the *Boston Globe*.

to the page after page of "help wanted" advertisements in the Sunday paper and bemoan youth joblessness. But that solves nothing.

Social thinkers can ponder the implications of a rising generation of city kids that has no work experience and that may, in fact, have lost any ambition to acquire it. But that solves nothing.

What is needed is a visible, comprehensive, coordinated effort that links school and work for young Bostonians facing a narrowing job market. School and job-training programs must be designed to better meet the demands of the workplace. Employers in Boston should aid such efforts and then reward them by targeting hiring in Boston.

There is no master plan for an education-work policy in Boston and no fully applicable model elsewhere. But Boston might look to the state of Delaware for the outline of an approach applicable to its own needs.

Work-bound high school seniors there are the focus of a major initiative designed to find them jobs.

Every senior in the public school system is being interviewed three or more times to determine his plans, aspirations, abilities and needs.

Special counseling, remedial education and job-preparation programs are being offered to students. Job specialists are searching statewide for employment opportunities. Student organizations are being established in each high school to encourage participation in the effort, known as Jobs for Delaware Graduates.

Delaware Gov. Pierre S. DuPont has made a major commitment to the program. Many of the state's top elected officials and leading corporate executives sit on its board of directors and participate regularly.

The goal of the program, which is financed by the U.S. Labor Department and private foundations, is to find a job for every single graduate of Delaware's high schools.

Only an effort of comparable scope will reduce Boston's tragically high rates of unemployment and particularly youth unemployment, which is running 20 percent or more in white neighborhoods and 50 percent or more in minority neighborhoods.

There is no doubt that racial discrimination accounts in part for the incredibly high unemployment rate among black teenagers. Studies suggest that even when varying levels of education and training are taken into account, at most only half the difference in the unemployment rates of white and black youths can be explained away. Discrimination must be rooted out. But even the white youth-unemployment rate is unacceptable.

Only a concerted effort will prepare the graduates of Boston's schools and even dropouts, whatever their race, for a place in the city's increasingly sophisticated job market. Only when the frustrations born of idleness and poverty are reduced can this city hope to find the sustained racial peace that has so long eluded it.

What is required is a major attempt to introduce all young people in the city to the world of work, to help them develop the attitudes necessary to acquire a job, to aid them in obtaining the skills necessary to hold a job, and to provide the support they need as they enter the workplace.

Boston must develop a whole web of links between the schools and jobs, even links that appear to duplicate one another.

- Efforts to develop a strong career-education program in Boston should be focused on the new $30 million Occupation Resources Center (ORC) scheduled to open next to Madison Park High School next year. Policies for the center should be established by representatives from the School Department, the private sector and job-training programs. Curriculum content must win the approval of educational authorities, but private industry should help design the courses.
- The ORC's facilities should be available not only to students in the public school system but also to high-school-age dropouts. Federal job-training funds can be used to reimburse the School Department for the costs of training nonstudents.
- Where appropriate, personnel from the private sector should be welcomed as teachers at the ORC.
- In developing curricula, the Boston Private Industry Council (PIC) could help to gather data on projected job demands. PIC is an organization of business leaders, established at the urging of Washington to facilitate the use of CETA funds to train the unemployed for private-sector jobs.
- Community organizations, such as the Boston Jobs Coalition, which led the effort that prompted Mayor White to adopt a resident jobs policy on city-assisted construction projects, could provide outreach to locate those seeking training.
- An education-work policy should extend beyond the ORC. A consortium established there could serve at the same time as architect of work-related curricula for schools throughout Boston.
- To facilitate such programs, the pairing between schools and businesses established by U.S. District Judge W. Arthur Garrity must be strengthened. Businesses have worked primarily inside the schools. They should expand that effort, as Kaiser Aluminum has done in Oakland, California, to provide job-training sites and part-time job sites within their own facilities or at other private-sector locations for all high school students and former high school students from their "paired" schools.
- At each high school in the city, an office of school-community coordinator should be established to facilitate links between

the two, to oversee a variety of activities encompassing and building upon the Delaware model.

- The coordinator's duties should include a two-year follow-up of every student who leaves school, whether as a graduate or a dropout, and continuing job counseling where it is appropriate. That notion is embodied in a report issued last year by the Carnegie Council on Policy Studies in Higher Education.
- Finally, the office of school-community coordinator should assume the role of the school's career counselor, a function that would be distinct from that of the guidance counselor, who has come to serve more of a psychologist's role. Unlike the typical suburban student, many urban public school students lack the informal networks of family and friends to secure them jobs. A strong employment counseling service is essential to fill that void.

The recommendations above do not comprise a neat package. There is undoubtedly overlap in the proposed links between school and work. So be it. As the Boston economy becomes more service oriented and more dependent on relatively sophisticated communications skills, the gap between school and work becomes ever harder for many in Boston to bridge.

The more strands in the net between the two, the less likely that Boston youth, whites as well as minorities, will fall into the ever-wider gulf of unemployment. Much of the social unrest in this city, as elsewhere, is rooted in idleness and economic insecurity. An aggressive effort to provide jobs for Bostonians, coupled with innovative efforts to ensure that they are prepared for those jobs, will strike at the heart of Boston's racial problems.

For so long, teachers have received bad press. On your next trip to the library, see how many articles you can find that discuss teachers positively. If, after you have spent an hour searching, you have not found any, do not be surprised. An unflattering portrayal of teachers by the media has a number of historical reference points, as eloquently demonstrated in the following essay by Sabol.

Often society has a legitimate beef with the teaching profession. There are all too many hair-raising stories about what occurs in our classrooms. "Help! Teacher Can't Teach" is a cover story from an issue of Time *magazine. After you have read this article, ask yourself to what extent criticisms of the teaching profession are justified, and what you can do to become a teacher who deserves respect and who keeps from being one of the statistics in a future article criticizing teachers.*

Teachers Do Not Deserve Respect:
A Dickensian View in *Our Mutual Friend*

C. Ruth Sabol
University of Georgia

To put the case bluntly, teaching is not a profession because society as a whole does not view teachers with respect. This unhappy condition is not the fault of society, it is the fault of teachers themselves. But how has this condition come about? The answer is not to be found in sociological studies, nor in extensive statistics comparing the salaries of teachers with other professionals, nor in an analysis of the psychology of the American psyche, of the inadequacy of the home, the high rate of divorce, or the decline in learning. The answer is to be found in the literature of the culture—the words of the novelists, essayists, and (in some cases) the poets. In the literature of a culture are to be found the reflections, as in a million mirrors, of the myriad different aspects of the truths of the human condition.

If that sounds vague to you, I'll put it another way. When you look into a mirror, you see your reflection. But the mirror not only reflects the details of your features, it also casts light from its polished surface onto your features, illuminating every mark, line and blemish of those features. The truth of your actual appearance is exposed to you in a way that the casual observer never sees. This is what literature does: it mirrors and illuminates the truths of a culture or a society to which that culture or society would otherwise be blind. To know and understand the literature of a culture is to know and understand the conflicting truths of that culture.

We ourselves need look no farther than the writing of the great nineteenth century British novelist Charles Dickens to find one explanation of why society does not hold teachers as respected professionals.

In his great, last novel, *Our Mutual Friend* (1864-65), Dickens presents four different characters who are either teachers or behave like them: Miss Abbey Potterson, Charley Hexam, little Miss Peecher, and Bradley Headstone. Miss Abbey Potterson is hard and frigid, Charley Hexam is selfish and hollow, little Miss Peecher is foolish and inconsequential, and Bradley Headstone is intellectually fraudulent and murderous. In the images of these four typical teachers, the blemishes on the face of the teaching profession loom large.

Written expressly for *Preparing for Reflective Teaching*.

First, take Miss Abbey Potterson. Miss Abbey is the sole proprietor and manager of the riverside pub, the Six Jolly Fellowship Porters, where "they mulled your ale, or heated for you those delectable drinks, Purl, Flip and Dog's Nose." Miss Abbey is a hard woman who seldom softens to anyone. But when she did soften toward Lizzie Hexam, she became "like all hard people when they do soften"—she felt a great deal was owed her in compensation, and when that compensation was not paid in full by Lizzie, Miss Abbey "underwent reaction and became frigid." As Dickens judges, Miss Abbey "had more of the air of a school-mistress than mistress of the Six Jolly Fellowship Porters." On the surface Miss Abbey was respectable, but underneath she was as hard as a schoolmistress.

Can there possibly be a creature of more vicious, selfish ambition to be found in all of Dickens than Charley Hexam, the low-born son of a river rat. When Charley was young, he was a boy "of uncompleted savagery, and uncompleted civilization." Through the self-sacrifice of his sister Lizzie and the careful instruction of Bradley Headstone, Charley becomes a respectable schoolmaster. To retain his hard won respectability, he savagely rejects both his loving sister, whom he grows to consider beneath him in social status, and his former schoolmaster and friend, when he correctly suspects Headstone of attempted murder. That Headstone brutally and savagely attempted to bludgeon to death Eugene Wrayburn, the man Headstone views as his rival for Lizzie Hexam's affections, is of no consequence to Charley. His one concern is to keep his own hard earned respectability unsullied. Charley rejects Headstone with not a whit of gratitude or human concern because "there *was* none in his hollow empty heart." As the narrator laments: "What is there but self, for selfishness to see behind it?"

The third image of the teacher is presented in the trained, certified schoolmistress, little Miss Peecher. Secretly in love with Headstone, the object of her foolish affection, Miss Peecher "could write a little essay on any subject . . . strictly according to rule." (English teachers, beware!) Even Miss Peecher's favorite pupil, Mary Anne, converses with Miss Peecher in question and answer form and always raises her hand to answer Miss Peecher's catechism-like questions. Miss Peecher, unlike Charley Hexam or Bradley Headstone, is not vicious, secretive, spying, or plotting; she is just overly conscientious about useless, inconsequential rules and blinded by a "primitive and homely stock of love" for Headstone which "had never been examined or certificated out of her." Poor Miss Peecher. Her diligence and correctness were misdirected. It was not that she meant to do anything badly, rather that she never did anything of consequence well.

The master around whom these lesser educational lights shine is the villainous Bradley Headstone, a veritable model of the respectable schoolmaster Dickens describes him this way:

Bradley Headstone, in his decent black coat and waistcoat, and decent white shirt, and decent formal black tie, and decent pantaloons of pepper and salt, with his decent silver watch in his pocket and his decent hair-guard round his neck, looked a thoroughly decent young man of six-and-twenty. He was never seen in any other dress, and yet there was a certain stiffness in his manner of wearing this, as if there was a want of adaptation between him and it, recalling some mechanics in their holiday clothes. He had acquired mechanically a great store of teacher's knowledge. He could do mental arithmetic mechanically, sing at sight mechanically, blow various wind instruments mechanically, even play the great church organ mechanically. From his early childhood up, his mind had been a place of mechanical stowage. The arrangement of his wholesale warehouse, so that it might be always ready to meet the demands of retail dealers—history here, geography there, astronomy to the right, political economy to the left—natural history, the physical sciences, figures, music, the lower mathematics, and what not, all in their several places—this care had imparted to his countenance a look of care; while the habit of questioning and being questioned had given him a suspicious manner, or a manner that would be better described as one of lying wait. There was a kind of settled trouble in the face. It was the face belonging to a naturally slow and inattentive intellect that had toiled hard to get what it had won, and that had to hold it now that it was gotten. He always seemed to be uneasy lest anything should be missing from his mental warehouse, and taking stock to assure himself.[1]

Headstone has no deep knowledge of anything, although he appears to his students and the public to be very learned. Headstone is a trained, certificated schoolmaster who has earned the position of training other schoolmasters, but he is also a murderer. He murders the scoundrel Rogue Riderhood. On the surface Bradley Headstone has all the appearances of respectability and education. He trains other teachers, like Charley Hexam. But Headstone lacks genuine intelligence and depth of understanding. Education to Headstone is an acquired patina, rather than an indepth understanding of the social, psychological, philosophical, and aesthetic universe of thought. Yet, in his blind arrogance he has the temerity to announce: "Yes. I am the Master." Master of what, one might ask. Master of education, Dickens replies.

In *Our Mutual Friend*, Charles Dickens has given his answer to the question of why teachers do not deserve respect. Because the images of teachers which have persisted for well over a century—images taken from actual life—are the images of the hard, the selfish, the foolish, the inconsequential, the intellectually stupid murderers of children's minds. And these images reflect upon the teaching profession today.

Notes

[1] Charles Dickens, *Our Mutual Friend* (London: Penguin, 1971).

Help! Teacher Can't Teach!

On Free to Choose, *his popular public television series, economist Milton Friedman stands before Boston's Hyde Park High School as uniformed guards search entering students for weapons. In a voice-over Friedman says: "Parents know their kids are getting a bad education but . . . many of them can see no alternative."*

Speaking of educational reform, Richard H. Hersh, associate dean for teacher education at the University of Oregon, tells a meeting: "We've been rearranging deck chairs on the Titanic.*"*

Says Professor J. Myron Atkin, dean of Stanford University's School of Education: "For the first time, it is conceivable to envision the dismantling of universal, public, compulsory education as it has been pioneered in America."

Like some vast jury gradually and reluctantly arriving at a verdict, politicians, educators, and especially millions of parents have come to believe that the U.S. public schools are in parlous trouble. Violence keeps making headlines. Test scores keep dropping. Debate rages over whether or not one-fifth or more adult Americans are functionally illiterate. High school graduates go so far as to sue their school systems because they got respectable grades and a diploma but cannot fill in job application forms correctly. Experts confirm that students today get at least 25% more As and Bs than they did 15 years ago, but know less. A Government-funded nationwide survey group, the National Assessment of Educational Progress, reports that in science, writing, social studies, and mathematics the achievement of U.S. 17-year-olds has dropped regularly over the past decade.

Rounding up the usual suspects in the learning crisis is easy enough. The decline of the family that once instilled respect for authority and learning. The influence of television on student attention span. The disruption of schools created by busing, and the national policy of keeping more students in school longer, regardless of attitude or aptitude. The conflicting demands upon the public school system, which is now expected not only to teach but to make up for past and present racial and economic injustice.

But increasingly too, parents have begun to blame the shortcomings of the schools on the lone and very visible figure at the front of the classroom. Teachers for decades have been admired for selfless devotion.

More recently, as things went wrong, they were pitied as overworked martyrs to an overburdened school system. Now bewildered and beleaguered, teachers are being blamed—rightly or wrongly—for much of the trouble in the classroom.

One reason is simply that it is easier for society to find someone to blame than to hold up a mirror and see that U.S. culture itself is largely responsible. But the new complaints about teachering also arise from a dismaying discovery: quite a few teachers (estimates range up to 20%) simply have not mastered the basic skills in reading, writing, and arithmetic that they are supposed to teach.

Of course, among the 2.2 million teachers in the nation's public schools are hundreds of thousands of skilled and dedicated people who, despite immense problems, manage to produce the miraculous blend of care and discipline, energy, learning, and imagination that good teaching requires. Many newcomers to the field are still attracted by the dream of helping children rather than for reasons of security or salary. The estimated average salary of elementary school teachers is $15,661, and of high school teachers $16,387, for nine months' work. The average yearly pay of a plumber is about $19,700; for a government clerk it's approximately $15,500. The best-educated and most selfless teachers are highly critical and deeply concerned about the decline in teaching standards and educational procedures. Their frustration is perhaps the strongest warning signal of all.

Horror stories about teaching abound. In Oregon a kindergarten teacher who had been given As and Bs at Portland State University was recently found to be functionally illiterate. How could this be? Says Acting Dean of the School of Education Harold Jorgensen: "It was a whole series of people not looking closely at her."

In Chicago a third grade teacher wrote on the blackboard: "Put the following words in alfabetical order." During the weeklong teacher strike last winter, many Chicago parents were appalled by what they saw on television news of schools and teachers. Recalls one mother: "I froze when I heard a teacher tell a TV reporter, 'I teaches English.' "

In the Milwaukee suburb of Wales, Wisconsin, school board members were outraged when teachers sent them written curriculum proposals riddled with bad grammar and spelling. Teachers had written *dabate* for *debate*, *documant* for *document*. *Would* was *woud*, and *separate* was *seperate*. Angry parents waved samples of their children's work that contained uncorrected whoppers, marked with such teacher comments as "outstanding" and "excellent."

A Gallup poll has found that teacher laziness and lack of interest are the most frequent accusations of half the nation's parents, who complain that students get "less schoolwork" now than 20 years ago. Whether the parent perceptions are fair or not, there is no doubt that circumstances have certainly changed some teacher attitudes. At a Miami senior high school this spring, one social studies teacher asked his pupils whether their homework was completed. Half the students said no. The teacher recorded their answers in his gradebook but never bothered to collect the papers. Says the teacher, who has been in the profession for 15 years and has now become dispirited: "I'm not willing any more to take home 150 notebooks and grade them. I work from 7:30 a.m. to 2 p.m., and that's what I get paid for." A longtime teacher in a large suburban school outside Boston told TIME it is common knowledge that some of her colleagues, anxious to preserve their jobs as enrollments dwindle, fail children simply to ensure hefty class size the next year.

The new doubts about teachers have led to a state-by-state demand from legislators and citizen groups that teachers take special examinations to prove they are competent, much like the student competency exams that have become a requirement in 38 states. Asks Indiana State Senator Joan Gubbins: "Shouldn't we first see if the teachers are competent before we expect the kids to be competent?"

Some Burnt-Out Cases . . .

"Judy," 40, says: "What got to me was that I found I was not getting results." A Bryn Mawr graduate who always wanted to be a teacher in a big city, she successfully taught English for eleven years in a Manhattan high school. Her enthusiasm began to falter three years ago when each of her five high school classes crept above the union maximum of 34 students. Says she: "No English teacher should have five classes. If you're trying to teach kids how to read and write, you simply can't do it—that's 200 students a day." In effect, Judy gave up teaching because she wanted to teach. Says she: "Many of my colleagues were not making an effort. The administration failed to recognize excellence, failed to recognize mediocrity, and failed to recognize negligence—except if you punched your timecard a few minutes late."

"Diana," 38, has taught high school history for ten years in a mostly black Washington, D.C., school. Says she: "I'm not really burned out, but there are a lot of problems and not much hope."

Homework? "Mostly there's no homework because they can't read. Ten years ago it was different. But these kids today are the product of the time when people thought forcing blacks to learn English was unfair. Just let them speak black English and 'kinda let them do their thing' was the way it went. So they can't read. Parents are awfully upset. But when I call them to suggest they enroll their kids in remedial work, a lot of them are not interested. They just don't want to face the problem."

"Tracking," the grouping of students by ability, is no longer possible because it is discriminatory. "Too many whites are always in the upper track," Diana explains. But she finds that even in a virtually all-black school, just maintaining order among the nonlearners keeps her from working with the 5% of the class, again mostly black, who can read well and want to learn: "They just sit around and die of boredom while I try to keep the other kids from fighting."

"Harold," 50, is the son of a South Carolina millworker. With an M.A. in literature from Duke University, he headed north and took a job as a bank teller while working toward his New York teaching certificate. In 1963 he became an English teacher in a big New York City high school. Six years later, seeking a change, he spent a year at a suburban school, but was bored. "That's when I learned how much I identified with the deprived kids in Manhattan." Back in the city, Harold helped launch a special reading program. "We were all weary of failure in trying to teach academic subjects to high school kids who read on a fifth grade level," he says. "We saw reading as the key by which these kids could gain success." For six years, Harold's group faced constant opposition from the school's principal, who was embarrassed at all the attention to a remedial program for tenth-graders supposed to be taking high school courses. In 1974, during the city's big economic crisis, the program's teachers were let go or transferred.

"My plan now is to take early retirement in 1982 after completing 20 years in the classroom," says Harold. "I don't think many people believe any more in the validity of a democratic public education. That is, one where kids from various groups rub elbows and actually learn from each other. The question then is, what do we really want in education?" Harold still is an excellent teacher, and he likes the spirit of the children in his school. But, he says, "when I look out at a class of 35 sophomores and I know that the reading levels in it are everywhere from fourth to tenth grade, I know that society has presented me with an impossible teaching assignment."

"Dorothy," 36, a Chicago elementary school teacher, told school officials she had the flu for five days last month. In fact, she spent the time hiding at home reading *The Tale of Genji*, an 11th century Japanese novel of love and manners. Says she: "Some days I can't bear to go to school. My legs won't take me to the classroom." After 13 years of teaching, Dorothy is a classic case of teacher burnout, and she hopes to find a job in public relations. But she remembers proud moments from years ago: her rousing student production of *Tom Sawyer*, the months she worked with a nine-year-old Hispanic student until he finally learned long division. These days, though, she lets her student teacher run the class: "I told him I don't care what he does with the kids just as long as he returns them to me quiet."

Why has she given up? Paperwork, the yanking of her favorite subjects (science and geography) from the curriculum, she answers. But as she talks, what emerges is a general hopelessness and resentment of a faceless bureaucratic system. On pressure to bring up test scores, for example, she says: "It doesn't matter that the kid is Pakistani, and his home life is bad and he can't read English." Feeling she can neither help her students nor please the administration depresses her and makes her defensive and cynical—about the school and herself. Says she: "The good teachers have all quit to save their sanity. I hate to tell people I'm a teacher."

... And Some Who Carry On

Helen Lambert Scott is a legend at Detroit's inner city Angell Elementary School. "It is quite evident which children come up from Mrs. Scott's third grade," says Angell fourth grade teacher Dorothy Lindsey. "They are well behaved. They jump right in and attack their work. They listen. They participate."

Scott's classroom may be decorated with pictures of spaceships, but she is an old-fashioned, demanding teacher. Her classroom method is a blend of love, dignity, discipline, and self-confidence rooted in unshakable dedication to children. Says she: "I don't care what a child looks like, or what he smells like. He has a personal worth that God gave him, and that should be counted."

Scott has been teaching for 40 years, and much of the current talk about teacher burnout irritates her. She knows firsthand all the problems and questions that beset teachers. "There's a breakdown in family life. Everyone does his own thing," she admits. "The number of children actually doing the work and keeping up are in the minority." Excessive paperwork? "The only way I deal with it is to try to do it," she says, though she now often has to grade papers during lunch hour as well as at home. Kids who won't do homework? "I assign work to the child with a note of finality, and I keep after him until he realizes that I will pester until the work is done. He might as well do it in the first place." Demands that take teachers' time from teaching? "Sometimes you have to fight to teach the basic skills, but I'm going to have reading every day with every child so I know what he knows." Scott is in favor of teacher competency exams.

These days Scott's most rewarding moments occur "when children come back after high school and tell me, 'You were hard on us, but I found out what you were teaching was for our own good.'" One such is Linda Harris, now a high school teacher in Georgia, who was one of Scott's students in 1958: "She had a great deal to do with my wanting to become a teacher. She really wanted the kids to make something of themselves." Concedes Scott: "It's a labor of love to keep going. With that love, there's a mixture of frustration and agony." But, she adds, "there are minds to be trained. You must press forward."

Lillian Becker wanted to teach so much that she went back to college for her degree at age 42 and graduated from the City College of New York as a Phi Beta Kappa. Today, at Intermediate School 70 in Manhattan's Chelsea district, Becker scrubs the desks in her classroom herself and sweeps the floor three times each day. Says she: "Kids sense the order, and they like it. They behave differently in a clean classroom.

She has other practical suggestions "You have to keep calling parents. You have to keep trying to get homework done." She also believes in sentence diagraming and drill. "They can disregard it later on, but it only becomes part of you later on if you drill now." To discourage predictable student alibis like "I forgot my book" or "I lost my pencil," Becker spends her own money to keep an extra supply of paper and pencils on hand. She always has extra textbooks on her desk.

Recently she asked the class to draw such simple symbols as a flag or a dove of peace. Soon the lesson had blossomed into a study of the parts of speech. "I also had them drawing pictures of figures of speech, like 'you drive me up the wall.' They loved it. After that they seemed ready for similes and metaphors." Becker grades themes and tests at home at least three days each week, two to five hours at a stint.

She earns about $18,000 a year, but the payoff, of course, is that she knows her teaching works. Says she: "Most teachers don't teach for money. They teach for that recognition they see and feel when a student learns something. I think most teachers do a terrific job."

Carolyn Kelly, 33, whispers to a visitor: "I love this." Kelly has just led a spirited senior class debate on the best interpretation of H. G. Wells' *The Man Who Could Work Miracles.* "I feel rejuvenated when a kid expresses something in a manner that for him is totally new, totally his own."

The seniors are Kelly's star pupils. She also teaches a basic English class and acts as coordinator of teacher advisers at the Rindge and Latin School in Cambridge, Massachusetts. If need be she can reason with students from slum backgrounds in their own street-wise slang, and she spends a good deal of time trying to make students understand that public school is still a gateway to opportunity. Says she: "My goal is not just academic; it's teaching kids what it is to be a human being."

Like most teachers she decries the loss of public support for the profession. "It is vital that we all understand how things have changed:

the role of the teacher, the school, the church, the family. It does no good to isolate schools as the culprit when there are social changes that affect other institutions as well. Until we all realize that education is a reciprocal thing, we won't have understood much at all."

With 41 million pupils, public school education is one of the nation's largest single government activities. Current expenditures (federal, state, and local) run to $95 billion. So vast and costly an educational system does not cheerfully react to criticism or adapt to change.

The push toward testing teacher competency, however, depends less on Washington than on state and local governments. One of the most instructive battles fought over the issue occurred in Mobile, Alabama, and was led by conservative attorney Dan Alexander, president of the board of education. In 1978, after the board required competency testing of Mobile high school seniors, Alexander was besieged by angry parents, at least partly because 53% of the students who took the city's first competency exam flunked it. Recalls Alexander: "Parents came out of the woodwork saying, 'If you're going to crack down on my child, let me tell you about some of my children's teachers.' " One parent brought him a note sent home by a fifth-grade teacher with a master's degree, which read in part: "Scott is dropping in his studies he acts as if he don't Care. Scott want pass in his assignment at all, he a had a poem to learn and he fell to do it." Says Alexander: "I was shocked. I could not believe we had teachers who could not write a grammatically correct sentence. I took the complaints down to the superintendent, and what shocked me worse was that he wasn't shocked."

Alexander made the note public as the kickoff of a campaign for teacher testing. Says he: "Competency testing is probably a misnomer. You cannot test a teacher on whether he's competent, but you certainly can prove he's incompetent." The proposed exams for veteran teachers were blocked by Alexander's colleagues on the board. But they agreed that all new teachers should score at least 500 on the Educational Testing Service's 3¼-hour National Teacher Examination (N.T.E.), which measures general knowledge, reading, writing, and arithmetic. Only about half of the Mobile job applicants who took the N.T.E. in 1979 passed.

The American Federation of Teachers, which has 550,000 members, is opposed to testing experienced teachers, though it approves of competency exams for new candidates. The much larger National Education Association is against any kind of competency testing for teachers, claiming teacher competency cannot be measured by written tests. Even so, some form of teacher testing has been approved in twelve states (Alabama, Arizona, Arkansas, Florida, Georgia, Louisiana, Mississippi, North Carolina, South Carolina, Tennessee, Virginia, West Virginia). Proposals for teacher testing have been introduced in Colo-

Scott is dropping in his studies he acts as if the don't Care. Scott wont pass in his assignment at all, he a had a poem to learn and he fell to do it.

Portion of a note sent home in Mobile, Alabama, by a teacher with a master's degree.

rado, Illinois, Iowa, Kansas, Missouri, New York, Vermont, and Wisconsin, and a bill in Oklahoma is scheduled to be signed into law this week. Polls say the teacher-testing movement is supported by 85% of U.S. adults.

Thus far actual test scores of teacher applicants seem depressing. In Louisiana, for instance, only 53% passed in 1978, 63% last year. What about the ones who fail? Says Louisiana Certification Director Jacqueline Lewis: "Obviously they're moving out of state to teach in states where the tests are not required." The results of basic achievement tests taken by job applicants at Florida's Pinellas County school board (St. Petersburg, Clearwater) are not encouraging. Since 1976, the board has required teacher candidates to read at an advanced tenth-grade level and solve math problems at an eighth-grade level. Though all had their B.A. in hand, about one-third of the applicants (25% of the whites, 79% of the blacks) flunked Pinellas' test the first time they took it in 1979.

In 1900, when only 6% of U.S. children graduated from high school, secondary school teachers were looked up to as scholars of considerable learning. Public school teachers were essential to what was regarded as the proud advance of U.S. education. By 1930, 30% of American 17-year-olds were graduating from high school, and by the mid-1960s, graduates totaled 70%. The American public school was hailed for teaching citizenship and common sense to rich and poor, immigrant and native-born children, and for giving them a common democratic experience. "The public school was the true melting pot," William O. Douglas once wrote, "and the public school teacher was the leading architect of the new America that was being fashioned."

The academic effectiveness of the system was challenged in 1957, when the Soviet Union launched its Sputnik satellite. Almost overnight, it was perceived that American training was not competitive with that of the U.S.S.R. Public criticism and government funds began to converge on U.S. schools. By 1964, achievement scores in math and reading had risen to an alltime high. But in the '60s the number of students (and teachers too) was expanding tremendously as a result of the maturing crop of post-World War II babies. In the decade before 1969, the number of high school teachers almost doubled, from 575,000 to nearly 1 million. Reading expert Paul Copperman writes in *The Literacy Hoax:* "The stage was set for an academic tragedy of historic proportions as the nation's high school faculty, about half of whom were young and immature, prepared to meet the largest generation of high school students in American history." To compound the problem, many teachers had been radicalized by the 1960s. They suspected that competition was immoral, grades undemocratic, and promotion based on merit and measurable accomplishment a likely way to discriminate against minorities and the poor. Ever since the mid-1960s, the average achievement of high school graduates has gone steadily downhill.

Ironically, the slide occurred at a time when teachers were getting far more training than ever before. In the early 1900s, few elementary school teachers went to college; most were trained at two-year normal schools. Now a bachelor's degree from college is a general requirement for teaching. Today's teaching incompetence reflects the lax standards in many of the education programs at the 1,150 colleges around the country that train teachers. It also reflects on colleges generally, since teachers take more than half their courses in traditional departments like English, history, and mathematics.

Research by W. Timothy Weaver, an associate professor of education at Boston University, seems to confirm a long-standing charge that one of the easiest U.S. college majors is education. Weaver found the high school seniors who planned to major in education well below the average for all college-bound seniors—34 points below average in verbal scores on the 1976 Scholastic Aptitude Test, 43 points below average in math. Teaching majors score lower in English than majors in almost every other field.

Evidence that many graduates of teacher-training programs cannot read, write, or do sums adequately has led educators like Robert L. Egbert, president of the American Association of Colleges for Teacher Education, to urge higher standards on his colleagues. The National Council for Accreditation of Teacher Education has become warier about issuing its seal of approval, which is largely honorific, since state boards of education issue their own, often easygoing approval for teacher-training programs. Nevertheless, with an awakened interest in "consumer protection" for parents and pupils, the council denied accreditation to teacher-training programs at 31% of colleges reviewed in 1979, compared with 10% in 1973. Says Salem, Oregon, School Superintendent William Kendrick: "For too long, we've believed that if you hold a teaching certificate you can do the job."

Many teachers favor rigorous teaching standards, including the use of compulsory minimum-competency tests—at least for candidates starting out in their careers. They are dismayed by the public's disapproval. Says Linda Kovaric, 32, a teacher at Olympic Continuation High School in Santa Monica, California: "The administration tells you you're doing a crummy job, parents tell you you're doing a crummy job, kids even tell you you're doing a crummy job. A lot of teachers these days feel and look like soldiers who returned from Viet Nam. You see the same glazed look in their eyes."

Many teachers have come to see themselves as casualties in a losing battle for learning and order in an indulgent age. Society does not support them, though it expects them to compensate in the classroom for racial prejudice, economic inequality, and parental indifference. Says *American School Board Journal* managing editor Jerome Cramer: "Schools are now asked to do what people used to ask God to do." The steady increase in the number of working mothers (35% work full time now) has sharply reduced family supervision of children and thrown many personal problems into the teacher's lap, while weakening support for the teacher's efforts. Says Thomas Anderson, 31, who plans to quit this month after teaching social studies for seven years in Clearwater, Florida: "I know more about some of my kids than their mothers or fathers do."

A teacher's view, in short, of why teachers cannot teach is that teachers are not allowed to teach. "The teacher today is expected to be mother, father, priest or rabbi, peacekeeper, police officer, playground monitor, and lunchroom patrol," says David Imig, executive director of the American Association of Colleges for Teacher Education. "Over and above that, he's supposed to teach Johnny and Mary how to read." Adds Edith Shain, a veteran kindergarten teacher at the Hancock Park School in Los Angeles: "The teacher doesn't know who she has to please. She's not as autonomous as she once was."

In the past 15 years the number of teachers with 20 years or more experience has dropped by nearly half. Four out of ten claim they plan to quit before retirement. In 1965 more than half of America's teachers told polltakers they were happy in their work. Now barely a third say they would become teachers if they had to make the choice again.

For many teachers, whether to leave their profession is not seen as a question of choice, or economics, but as a matter of emotional necessity. The latest pedagogic phenomenon is something called "teacher burnout." It is a psychological condition, produced by stress, that can result in anything from acute loss of will to suicidal tendencies, ulcers, migraine, colitis, dizziness, even the inability to throw off chronic, and perhaps psychosomatic, colds.

This spring the first national conference on teacher burnout was held in New York City. Surprisingly, the syndrome seems nearly as common in small towns and well-off suburbs as in big cities. The National Education Association has already held more than 100 local workshops round the country to help teachers cope with the problem, which University of California Social Psychologist Ayala Pines defines as "physical, emotional, and attitudinal exhaustion." Last March, Stress Consultant Marian Leibowitz held a burnout seminar in Edwardsville, Illinois (pop. 11,982). It drew a paying audience of 250 to a hall big enough for only 100.

According to Dr. Herbert Pardes, director of the National Institute of Mental Health, what emerges from the familiar litany of teacher complaints is that administrative headaches and even physical assaults on teachers can be psychologically less wounding than the frustrating fact that teachers feel unable to do enough that is constructive and rewarding in their classrooms. Whether it is blackboard jungle, red-tape jumble, a place of learning or a collective holding pen for the hapless young, the modern classroom, teachers claim, is out of teachers' control. Some reasons:

Discipline and Violence. Last year 110,000 teachers, 5% of the U.S. total, reported they were attacked by students, an increase of 57% over 1977–78. Teachers believe administrators tend to duck the subject of violence in the schools to avoid adverse publicity. More than half the teachers assaulted feel that afterward authorities did not take adequate action. Today one in eight high school teachers says he "hesitates to confront students out of fear." One in every four reports that he has had personal property stolen at school.

Since the *Wood* vs. *Strickland* Supreme Court decision of 1975, which upheld the right to due process of students accused of trouble-making, the number of students expelled from school has dropped by about 30%. As always in a democracy, the problem of expulsion turns in part on the question of concern for the rights of the disruptive individual *versus* the rights of classmates and of society. School officials argue that it is wiser and more humane to keep a violent or disruptive student in school than to turn him loose on the streets. But, says John Kotsakis of the Chicago Teachers Union, "schools are now being asked to be more tolerant of disruptive or criminal behavior than society." In a Washington, D.C., high school, a jealous boy tried to shoot his girlfriend in class. The boy was briefly suspended from school. No other action was taken. Says a teacher from that school: "These days if you order a student to the principal's office, he won't go. Hall monitors have to be called to drag him away."

Student Attitudes Toward Learning. In a current hit song called *Another Brick in the Wall*, the rock group Pink Floyd brays: "We don't need no education." There is near unanimity among teachers that many students are defiantly uninterested in schoolwork. Says one West Coast teacher: "Tell me kids haven't changed since we were in high school, and I'll tell you you're living in a fantasy world." A New York panel investigated declining test scores and found that homework assignments had been cut nearly in half during the years from 1968 to 1977. Why? Often simply because students refuse to do them. Blame for the shift in student attitude has been assigned to such things as Watergate, the Viet Nam War, the "Me" culture, also to television, which reduces attention span. There are now 76 million TV homes in the U.S., *versus* only 10 million in 1950. By age 18, the average American has spent an estimated 15,000 hours in front of the set, far more time than in school. Whatever the figures, teachers agree, television is a hard act to follow.

Shifting Tides of Theory. Because it is American, American education dreams of panaceas—universal modern cures for the ancient pain of learning, easy ways to raise test scores and at the same time prepare the "whole child" for his role in society. Education has become a tormented field where armies of theorists clash, frequently using language that is unintelligible to the layman. Faddish theories sweep through the profession, changing standards, techniques, procedures. Often these changes dislocate students and teachers to little purpose. The New Math is an instructive example. Introduced in the early '60s without adequate try-out, and poorly understood by teachers and parents, the New Math eventually was used in more than half the nation's schools. The result: lowered basic skills and test scores in elementary math. Exotic features, like binary arithmetic, have since been dropped. Another trend is the "open classroom," with its many competing "learning centers," which can turn a class into a bullpen of babble. There was the look-say approach to reading (learning to read by recognizing a whole word), which for years displaced the more effective "phonics" (learning to read by sounding out syllables).

Pedagogues seeking a "science of education" are sometimes mere comic pinpricks in a teacher's side. For example, Ph.D. theses have been written on such topics as *Service in the High School Cafeteria, Student Posture,* and *Public School Plumbing.* But many studies are hard on teacher morale. Sociologist James S. Coleman's celebrated 1966 survey of pupil achievement seemed glum news for teachers. That study argued that family background made almost all the difference, and that qualities of schools and teachers, good and bad, accounted "for only a small fraction of differences in pupil achievement." Later researchers, examining Coleman's work, found that pupils do seem to learn more when they receive more hours of instruction.

The sensible thing for any effective teacher would be to fend off such theories as best he can and go on teaching. As teachers are fond of saying, "Teaching occurs behind closed doors." But theory, some of it foolish and damaging, inexorably seeps under the doors and into the classrooms. For example, the sound idea that teachers should concentrate on whetting the interests of students and stirring creativity has been unsoundly used as an excuse to duck detailed schoolwork. Says Columbia's Teachers College Professor Diane Ravitch: "It is really putting things backward to say that if children feel good about themselves, then they will achieve. Instead, if children are learning and achieving, *then* they feel good about themselves." Ravitch believes U.S. education has suffered much from such pedagogic theories, and especially from the notion, which emerged from the social climate of the 1960s, that the pursuit of competency is "elitist and undemocratic."

Textbooks and Paperwork.   Teachers are consulted about textbooks but rarely decide what books are finally bought. The textbook business is a $1.3 billion a year industry. Books are ordered by editorial committees and updated at the pleasure of the publisher to sell in as many school systems as possible. Since the late 1960s, according to Reading Expert Copperman, publishers have found that if a textbook is to sell really well, it must be written at a level "two years below the grade for which it is intended."

Paperwork done by teachers and administrators for district, state, and national agencies proliferates geometrically. Though it all may be necessary to some distant bureaucrat—a most unlikely circumstance—when teachers comply they tend to feel like spindling, folding, and mutilating all the forms. Paperwork wastes an enormous amount of teaching time. In Atlanta, for example, fourth- and fifth-grade teachers must evaluate their students on 60 separate skills. The children must be rated on everything from whether they can express "written ideas clearly" to whether they can apply "scarcity, opportunity cost, and resource allocation to local, national, and global situations."

Administrative Hassles.   School procedures, the size and quality of classes, the textbooks and time allotted to study are all affected by government demands, including desegregation of classes, integration of faculty, even federal food programs. One way or another, teachers are bureaucratically hammered at by public health officials (about vaccinations, ringworm, cavities, malnutrition), by social workers and insurance (about driver education and broken windows), by juvenile police, civil liberties lawyers, Justice Department lawyers, even divorce lawyers (about child custody).

Mainstreaming as Nightmare.   Since the passage of Public Law 94-142 in 1975, it has been federal policy that all handicapped children, insofar as possible, be "mainstreamed," that is, educated in the same class with everyone else. The law is theoretically useful and just, as a means of avoiding unwarranted discrimination. But in practice it often puts an overwhelming strain on the teacher. "Mainstreaming is ludicrous," says Detroit Counselor Jeanne Latcham. "We have children whose needs are complicated: a child in the third grade who has already been in 16 schools, children who need love and attention and disrupt the classroom to get it. Ten percent of the students in Detroit's classrooms can't conform and can't learn. These children need a disproportionate amount of the teacher's time. It's a teacher's nightmare—she can't help them, but she never forgets them."

The tangle of teaching troubles is too complex to be easily unraveled. But one problem whose solution seems fairly straightforward is the matter of illiterate and uninformed teachers. Competency tests can—and should—be administered to screen out teachers, old as well as novice, who lack basic skills. Such screening would benefit pupils, but it would also put pressure on marginal colleges to flunk substandard students bound for a career in teaching. Indiana University Education Professor David Clark asks rhetorically: "Is it more important to make it easy for kids to reach professional level, or to have good teachers?" Pressure is also needed to ensure adequate funding for teacher training. As a typical example, at the University of Alabama last year total instructional cost for a student in a teacher–education program was $648, in contrast to $2,304 for an engineering student.

In a classic 1960s study titled *The Miseducation of American Teachers*, James D. Koerner, now program officer at the Alfred P. Sloan Foundation, called for the opening of new paths to careers in teaching. At present a state certificate is required for public school teachers, who earn it by completing practice teaching and specialized education courses (such as philosophy of education and educational psychology). According to Koerner there is little evidence that this program of study improves teacher performance. Koerner calls for more intellectually demanding but more flexible requirements to make the field more attractive to talented people who lack specialized teaching credentials. A small step in this direction is a three-year-old pilot program run by the school board in Hanover, New Hampshire. There, college graduates who want to teach are carefully screened for such qualities as imagination and love of children, as well as academic competency. After a year of probationary teaching, chosen candidates become certified teachers.

It has been argued that teaching needs to be more professional. But in some ways it is too professional now—too encrusted with useless requirements and too tangled in its own obscure professional jargon. The impenetrable language of educators has evolved into what Koerner calls "an artificial drive to create a profession." But it is more damaging to the country than the jargon of law, say, or even government, because it sabotages the use of clear writing and clear thinking by tens of thousands of teachers, and through them, hundreds of thousands of students.

Violence in schools has got to be dealt with effectively. A muscular and unprecedented step in the right direction may have just been taken in California. Over a six-year period, Los Angeles County schools lost an estimated $100 million as a result of school muggings, lawsuits, theft, and vandalism while city and school officials ineffectually wrung their hands over jurisdictional problems. Last month the attorney general for the state of California sued, among others, the mayor of Los Angeles, the entire city council, the chief of police and the board of trustees of the Los Angeles Unified School District, demanding that authorities put together some coordinated program to punish the criminals and cut down on violence and theft.

A promising proposal was made by legislators in Pennsylvania last year. They introduced bills requiring that schools report all attacks on teachers to state authorities and that criminal penalties be stiffened for school offenses. Under one of the measures, carrying a gun or knife in school would be treated as a serious crime, and a student who assaulted a teacher would face up to seven years in jail.

Principals need to be more willing to manage their schools. When necessary, the resignation of bad teachers must be sought, even though union grievance procedures can be costly and time consuming. "Too many principals are afraid of grievances," says William Grimshaw, professor of political science at the Illinois Institute of Technology. More important, it should be easier to reward good teachers—if only with public recognition, which is rare at present. As Sylvia Schneirov, a third-grade teacher in Chicago, puts it: "The only praise you get is if your class is quiet and if your bulletin boards are ready when the superintendent comes—you better not have snowflakes on the board when you should have flowers."

Public praise for a job well done matters a great deal. Last year Raj Chopra, the Indian-born superintendent of schools in Council Bluffs, Iowa, raised Council Bluffs' S.A.T. scores, which had slumped below national norms, by starting a systematic campaign to encourage "positive thinking" by—and about—Council Bluffs teachers. Says he: "We make them feel proud of their profession by emphasizing that what they do will have an impact on the country for years to come." On May 6, the city celebrated Teachers Day. Retailers, who had earlier been visited by a "teacher recognition task force," gave discounts to teachers that day.

Teaching children to read and write and do sums correctly is not so complicated a business as it is often made to seem. As Koerner puts it: "Almost any school can significantly improve its performance by the simple act of deciding to do so." Indeed, much of the trouble boils down to a failure of will, of old-fashioned teacherly "gumption" in the schools and outside them. As Marcia Fensin, a former teacher and mother of two daughters enrolled in Chicago's Joyce Kilmer Elementary School, says: "The teachers just don't care. They give busy work straight from the textbooks, and meanwhile our kids are not being motivated."

Ironically though, lack of care about education is also a favorite complaint of educators today. Echoing the view of many in the schools, President Lawrence Cremin of Columbia's Teachers College observes: "By and large, society gets what it deserves out of its school system. It gets what it expects. If you don't value things, you don't get them."

The evidence suggests that something so simple as caring can improve the schools. One of James Coleman's undisputed findings: all other things being equal, students achieve better in schools that have active Parent-Teacher Associations. PTAs can provide pressure to improve a teaching staff or school programs and facilities. More important, a widely supported PTA is the tangible sign of parental responsibility for education. Caring shows in other ways as well. Observes Cremin: "A number of studies indicate that certain kinds of schools are unusually effective. Whether the students are rich kids, poor kids, blacks, Hispanics or whites, these schools look very much alike on some criteria. The *principal* leads his teachers. The teachers become committed to teaching the basic skills. *Expectations* become high. Time is spent on classroom tasks, and a happy order pervades the school. Rules are widely known and quickly enforced. Parents are brought into the act and are supportive. In such schools, black kids learn, white kids learn, green kids learn."

Yet such is the dilemma of education today that even so clear-cut a matter as agreeing to establish very low minimum competency tests for teachers becomes a hot political issue, arousing fear that the tests will only serve as racial discrimination. Significantly, one of the most eloquent advocates of tough standards, and the man who speaks most probingly and practically about American education, its problems and possible salvation, is not an educator but a black leader, the Rev. Jesse Jackson. "Nobody can save us for us but us" is a Jackson slogan. He insists that parents sign a contract stating that they will get personally involved with school and require their children to do two hours of work a night, without benefit of television. "Many of us allow our children to eat junk," Jackson accuses, "watch junk, listen to junk, talk junk, play with junk, and then we're suprised when they come out to be social junkies." And again, "Tears will get you sympathy, but sweat will get you change." Ostensibly, he is exhorting black ghetto kids and their parents. But he could just as well be setting up a program for everyone, blacks and whites, middle-class parents and burnt-out teachers.

The salvation of the public schools lies, most of all, in just such individual dedication to learning, spread societywide. The schools are simply too big, too close to families and neighborhoods, and too diverse for the improvement of teaching to be ordered by a legislature. Governor, university, or school superintendent. They do not need a social program as complex as, say, the Apollo space program, as the continued existence of good public schools throughout the nation shows. They need agreement by the many groups that shape them—parents, teachers, taxpayers, government—that teaching and good teachers are in trouble and need society's support. As to the historic issue, Thomas Jefferson put it well: "If a nation expects to be ignorant and free, in a state of civilization, it expects what never was and never will be."

An important step you can take to help improve society's image of teachers is to learn how to establish parent-teacher rapport. The following article by Bloch offers important insights about parent-teacher relationships.

Parent-Teacher Relationships: Complementary, Supplementary, or Conflicting?

Marianne Bloch
University of Wisconsin

Parents and teachers are both considered to be responsible for the socialization and education of young children in the United States. Yet, in an increasingly complex American society and in the world in general, it is more and more difficult for parents and teachers to identify the roles and responsibilities for which children should be trained. The task of both parents and teachers now, in contrast to the past, is to identify strategies that prepare children for an uncertain future, one in which flexibility and adaptation to new circumstances and people may be crucial. For such a future, it is necessary to identify those skills which are most likely to be adaptive in various contexts and to identify the ways in which parents and teachers can best help them to attain them. In this essay, the particular ways in which parents and teachers might collaborate in this task are explored. The essay begins with a brief

Written expressly for *Preparing for Reflective Teaching*.

description of some similarities and differences in parent-teacher roles and relationships followed by an historical review of the way roles, responsibilities, and interaction have changed in America. The last section of the essay focuses on current practice and perspectives on the way in which parents and teachers might function together more meaningfully in the future.

Conceptual Similarities and Differences Between Parents and Teachers

Parents most often interact with their children in the home, a physical and social context quite different from the school. Parent-child interaction also takes place within a different emotional setting than that of teacher-child interaction. Parents and children interact with an affective bond that is formed in early childhood and which endures over many years; teachers and children interact usually without the advantage (or disadvantage, in some cases) of such an affective bond, and their relationship does not last as long.[1] Parent roles and responsibilities toward children differ from those of teachers also. Parents' roles and responsibilities are considered to be "functionally diffuse" in the sense that they are all encompassing yet informally prescribed. Teacher roles and responsibilities, on the other hand, are "functionally specific," and usually concern the role of instructor with explicit responsibility for the transmission of basic information (the "3 R's") to children.

Increasingly, the ways in which parents and teachers influence each other and children are being examined. Books and chapters with titles such as *The Family and Community as Educators*[2] or *Worlds Apart: Relationships between Families and Schools*[3] reflect our knowledge that families and schools have domains of interest and influence in common. Head Start and Follow Through programs, federally financed programs to increase low-income children's opportunities for success in schools, have mandated parent involvement components in these programs because the interaction between school and home was found to be such an important factor in the success of the programs.[4] Other programs in school districts across the nation are emphasizing increased contact between homes and schools and are studying ways to make such interaction effective.

While some have suggested that the family has the most important influence on children,[5] it seems obvious that parents and teachers both influence children's lives and opportunities for success in important ways. The following example illustrates more concretely only one of the ways in which parent-child interaction might overlap with a teacher's work in the school setting.

In one family, the child played with her cousin as the mother looked on. The two children played a game, played with dolls and stuffed toys, and played "store" with a cash register and play money. The mother watched them making suggestions and comments, helping when necessary, and laughing at the children's humorous remarks. The child suggested they play "teacher." The child and the cousin pretended to be teacher and student. The cousin began to read a book, then the child read. The mother looked on as the child read, correcting when necessary.[6]

Although there are ways in which parents and teachers interact with children that are complementary, there are also differences in the content and type of interaction parents and teachers have with children. Parents' roles and responsibilities at home include a broad range of activities which include interaction with many children, and the transmission of information, as well as cultural values and attitudes. Teachers, on the other hand, may use strategies with children or portray values or attitudes that reinforce or conflict with those of the parents. While diversity in a pluralistic society is often healthy for children and society, the extent and effect of differences or similarities in parents' and teachers' behavior and attitudes needs to be more closely examined. In the following paragraphs some of the ways in which parents and teachers have complemented, supplemented, or conflicted with each other are explored.

Parent-Teacher Roles and Responsibilities: A Brief History

Parents and teachers *complement* one another in their common need to train children to be flexible, competitive, and cooperative for the future. They complement each other's tasks, in addition, in the extent to which they model and reinforce each other's values and styles of moral, cognitive, and social behavior with children. Parents and teachers, finally, complement one another in the joint roles they play in children's lives as critical adult socialization agents; both are advocates for children's development, although within different contexts of learning (community, home, and school).

Parents and teachers appear to supplement each other to the extent that one group seems to have, be assigned, or take more responsibility for support, maintenance, or training in one area than the other. A brief historical review will be used to illustrate the changing ways in which parents and teachers have appeared to supplement or complement each others' tasks.[7]

During the seventeenth and eighteenth centuries, families were primarily responsible for children's social and physical well-being and for their moral character training (including literacy training to be able to read the Bible).[8] By age seven, however, children were also "schooled" in the skills needed for future work through apprenticeships outside their home. In the eighteenth century, primary schools in villages and early cities began. Teachers were considered part of the community and were in close contact with parents and their children as they saw families in the community or in their homes. While parents, church, and communities continued to share responsibility for the moral and social behavior training of children, teachers and schools were perceived to have major responsibility for academic skill training. The vast majority of children, however, still learned out of school through on-the-job training in apprenticeships.

During the latter decades of the nineteenth century and into the twentieth century's "progressive era," the number of schools grew enormously as America expanded and schooling became mandatory for the masses. Around the turn of the century, schools took on an explicit social reform as well as an educational role as they took on more explicit responsibility for training the moral and social behavior of the large urban immigrant group of children coming to America; Americanization and universal education for "citizenry" were responsibilities increasingly thought (by empowered groups, at least) to be the province of schools and teachers. As the twentieth century progressed, scientific knowledge of children, education, and technology advanced and began to dominate school and parent group discussions and relationships. Teachers' and parents' roles and responsibilities appeared to diverge more than they had in the past. Teachers learned an increasingly complex body of knowledge at universities and teacher training institutions; parents were increasingly guided in the "best" child-rearing techniques for children's physical, social, and emotional well-being. Increasingly, it seemed that parents were perceived responsible for children's development during the pre-primary school years but only with the advice of doctors, and other child-rearing "experts."[10] Teachers were perceived to prepare children for a wider more complex society through academic and social training while parents were perceived responsible for emotional and intellectual *support* of children as they entered into schools. In the 1960's changes in our knowledge of child development signaled the important role of the home in cognitive and language development.[11] As a result, cognitive and language stimulation were added to parents' "list" of responsibilities particularly during the preprimary years. In fact, children were perceived to be "deprived" cognitively or emotionally if their homes were not considered to be adequately stimulating school-like language or cognitive competencies, or were not stable or supportive emotionally.[12]

An Historical Review of Parent-Teacher Interaction

At the turn of the century, advice was distributed by well-meaning reformers (kindergarteners, psychologists such as G. Stanley Hall, philanthropic groups, social welfare workers) to working class immigrant parents. Kindergarten teachers often went to children's homes during the afternoons after morning programs to visit with parents, or sent children home with new ideas or modes of behavior (to train the parents). Others, such as the participants of the newly formed (1897) National Mothers' Congress (which became the National Congress of Mothers and Parent-Teacher Associations in 1908, and subsequently the PTA),[13] sent literature to parents, visited families, or held meetings to communicate new (or old) knowledge about scientific ways to rear children. Middle- and upper-class parents were involved in the National Mothers' Congress and other social reform or philanthropic movements aimed at helping immigrant urban families rear children better. They were also, however, part of the growing group of parents seeking "expert" advice on the newest ideas in child-rearing and education for their own children. As teachers became more "professional" through training and schools became more centralized and bureaucratic (and often farther from the homes), teachers and administrators increasingly distanced themselves from all groups of parents. Teacher-parent inter-action became formal, occurring in specifically defined settings and times (parent-teacher association meetings) or in formal conferences or day-to-day meetings between parents and teachers centering on superficial reports of children's behavior or performance. Parent-teacher association meetings after World War I were more and more oriented toward communicating administrative facts, details of school curricula, and child-rearing advice to "less knowledgeable" parents of all classes; educational issues that might have been of common concern to parents and teachers of particular children were not explored. Control of school hiring, firing, and curriculum decision-making had also been an area in which parents and teachers collaborated during the 18th and part of the 19th century. But as schools grew during the early years of the 20th century such decision-making became the province of physically distant, relatively elite centralized school bureaucracies. In the 1960s community control and/or advice on these issues became a demand of many groups again; while demands for such collaboration or control have decreased since the 1960s, efforts to develop successful models of community-school collaboration have continued.[14]

Current Conceptions of the Past and Present

By describing the historical shifts in the roles and responsibilities of parents and teachers (church and society), and in their interaction during the past several centuries, some of the areas where parents and teachers complement or supplement one another's tasks have been described; in addition, some of the areas in which one might perceive them to be in conflict have also been mentioned. Although parents and teachers have collaborated in the task of educating children in the past, it should be apparent that the pattern of collaboration has depended upon changing conceptions of the nature of children and their development in a changing American society. It might also be apparent that changes in conceptions of parent and teacher responsibilities were a function of changes in scientific knowledge, reliance on such knowledge, and of various group and class perceptions of what intellectual, moral, and social education should be.

In the last two decades (since the early 1960s at least), scientific knowledge has changed our conception of the importance of the early environment in the cognitive development of children. We have also increasingly recognized the difficulty of the task of equalizing educational opportunities through the schools alone. For both of these reasons, parents have been recognized by teachers and society as "educators" of children in all areas of development. Similarly, over the last two decades, the implicit or "hidden" curriculum of the school in the areas of moral and social behavior training has also been recognized.[15] While schools have had explicit mandates to teach academic skills, their implicitly defined but important educational role in other areas of development is now being described. Thus it now seems clear that parents, communities, and schools need to coordinate their ideas and efforts for children's development.

Cooperation and Competition Between Parents and Teachers in the 1980s

As we begin the last two decades of the twentieth century, schools and families face the difficult task of defining a joint course, a less competitive and more collaborative one, for the education and socialization of children. The goals for children's education seem still to be to equalize the educational and occupational opportunities of all children, and to prepare children for the somewhat unknown roles and responsibilities they will have as adults. There are various ways in which this collaboration might be achieved, while minimizing unhealthy conflict. Several important ways to accomplish this task with examples to illustrate the points are outlined below.

First, *parents and teachers must recognize that the people they must be most concerned about are children.* A community involvement program in New Haven, Connecticut[16] was able to develop much more individualized, culturally "relevant" teaching-learning techniques for children once parents and teachers began to talk with one another and work together with children's benefit foremost in their minds.

Second, *parents and teachers must recognize each other's competencies and appreciate each other's values*. Much of the historical and present-day conflict in the failure of various parent-school relationships (regardless of parental class or ethnic background) stems from a lack of knowledge of both parent and teacher about each other. This lack of knowledge results in stereotyped perceptions of parent, community, teacher, and administrative groups. An extreme example of this point stems from an unsuccessful community involvement program begun in the Midwest. In this program, native American parents and community members were to be included in a massive school reform program. Due to stereotypes about the native American group held by school officials, teachers, and by representatives of the funding agency in Washington, control of funds and decision-making was held at the government and school level and not given to a joint native American-School group. This original decision, based on inaccurate ideas about the competencies of the native American group, eventually undermined the reform program.[17]

Third, *parents and teachers need to interact in situations where both groups perceive themselves as having status and competence*. This point stems from research on the effects of prejudice and its reduction. The results suggest contact alone between disparate groups fails to significantly reduce stereotypes; however, contact under *equal status* conditions helps.[18]

An example of this principle is reflected in the research of the effectiveness of various parent education programs. In those programs in which parents were involved as low-status, inexpert "teachers" of children, few of the program objectives were achieved. In contrast, those programs[19] in which parents maintained their status as primary teachers of their children and were included in decision-making in the parent education program affected children's achievement, parental self-esteem and participation.

Fourth, *parents and teachers need to accept the diversity of skills and attitudes that allow children to function successfully in various settings*. Various cultural groups have patterns of interactions relating to values and belief systems which are inherent to their culture. These may be distinct or different from those valued by teachers and schools within the "culture" of the school. Parents and teachers might work more toward recognizing the strengths of the behavior children and parents use in their home/community settings, and accept and encourage these differences more readily in school settings. For example, Heath[20] describes a program that used knowledge about school and home patterns of communication to fashion a more successful school setting for children.

In Heath's study, the style and function of questions addressed to both preschool and elementary children in their homes and at school were observed and analyzed. Heath noted the differences in questions used in various settings by adults addressing children. In the community of "Trackton" parents, other adults, and siblings of children addressed questions to children that required "analogies" ("What's that like?"), "story-starters" ("Did you hear what happened to Maggie's dog?"), were "accusatory" ("What's that all over your face?"), or required information that was unknown by the questioner. In schools, by contrast, the following types of questions were most frequently asked by teachers, questions in which the information required was already known to both the teacher and child ("What's your name?" "What color is that?"); questions to clarify, confirm, or repeat previous utterances ("What do you want again?"); "I wonder" questions that no one was expected to answer ("I wonder why the sky is dark?"); or indirect directives ("Would you go to the closet and get my coat?").

The children from Trackton, according to Heath, were not prepared for the type of questions used in classrooms. Because of this, the children failed to respond to the frequent questions of the well-intentioned teachers or responded incorrectly. Heath helped to institute a successful intervention program that allowed teachers to ask questions in a way that was more familiar to children or to establish informal situations in which children could more comfortably respond to unfamiliar types of questions. She also worked closely with parents of the children in efforts to prepare a program that would be compatible with the children's skills and their success in school.

Finally, *parents and teachers need to communicate effectively with one another on a frequent basis about the children so that they can both work more effectively with them.* Several examples will illustrate this point better than discussion.

In one family, a child was doing very poorly in school and was in the lowest group in each subject area. Nevertheless, the teacher encouraged the child throughout the year and put "smiling faces" and "good work" on many of his papers that went home. At the end of the year, when the child was kept back a grade, the child's mother complained that she never knew he was doing poorly.[21]

Another example I have encountered in my own work in school:

A child was in an advanced math group. After about three weeks in the group, he began to complain to his mother that he was having trouble and that he needed to be helped by both the teacher and the other children to complete his assignments. The mother received a brief note from the math teacher suggesting one type of problem the child could use help with at home. On the basis of this note and queries to the child about the type of problems he was doing in school, the mother helped the child. She thought he was doing much better. A week later, the child mentioned he had been moved into a less difficult math group. The mother felt defeated in both her attempt to discern the areas in which the child needed help and by her lack of knowledge about the day-to-day activities and problems (or successes) of her child in school.

Both examples show not only well-intentioned behavior on both teachers' and parents' parts but clearly and unfortunately a lack of communication concerning children's progress. The parents perceived themselves as passive or powerless recipients of knowledge about their children from school. In these cases both teachers and parents might have taken more initiative in remedying the "communication gap," which in retrospect is so obvious.

Conclusion

The problems described above reflect some of the conflicts in the roles, responsibilities, and relationships of parents and teachers. Parents, of all classes, feel "inexpert" and of unequal status with teachers in areas concerning "school knowledge." The distance that parents feel toward teachers and schools, fostered throughout the twentieth century, influences parent-teacher relationships to the schools', parents', teachers', and children's disadvantage. Teachers, too, often try to guard their domain against other types of knowledge or status parents, communities, or larger school bureaucracies may have. If we expect day-to-day conflicts between parents and teachers to diminish and equal status collaboration to increase, more ways of informal, equal status contact between parents and teachers need to be developed.

What can teachers do specifically to remove the barriers that have been up for so long between parents and teachers? Unfortunately, there are no easy answers to this question. The importance of parent-teacher collaboration must first become apparent to teachers and parents before successful strategies for collaboration can be identified. Through an historical review of some of the changes in parent-teacher responsibilities and relationships and a presentation of some successful and unsuccessful parent-teacher collaborative/communicative efforts, the importance of this relationship has hopefully been established. Parents and teachers from various communities and diverse backgrounds must determine that they are in the "education act" together and that the relationship between them is important to them. If so, both groups will, it is hoped, developed ways to share information and goals and to work together to support one another for the children's benefit.

Notes

[1] This difference is changing in certain schools where mixed-age grouping or "attachment" groupings of children increase the time children have with the same children or teacher.

[2] H. Leichter, *Families and Communities as Educators* (New York: Teachers College Press, 1979); K. Marjoribanks, "Family Environments," in *Educational Environments and Effects*, ed. H. J. Walberg (Berkeley: McCutchan, 1979).

[3] S. L. Lightfoot, *Worlds Apart: Relationships between Families and School* (New York: Basic Books, 1978).

[4] U. Bronfenbrenner, *Is Early Intervention Effective?* Report on longitudinal evaluation of preschool programs. Vol. 2: Office of Child Development (Washington, D.C.: Department of Health, Education and Welfare, 1974).

[5] J. S. Colemen, *Equality of Educational Opportunity* (Washington, D.C.: Department of Health, Education and Welfare, 1966); C. Jencks, *et. al., Inequality: A Reassessment of the Effect of Family and Schooling in America* (New York: Basic Books, 1972).

[6] D. Scott-Jones, "Relationships Between Family Variables and School Achievement in Low-Income Black First Graders." Paper presented at the Conference on Home Influences on School Achievement. University of Wisconsin-Madison, 1981.

[7] Any "brief" historical review is problematic both for the author and for the readers because of the generalizations that must be made. In the following, many statements suggest simple transitions from one period or situation to another. In fact, in many areas of the United States, and for many groups, the history could be expressed differently. There were also many important political, social, and economic changes that affected the course of the history that are only quickly presented here. For more elaboration of these points see S. M. Clarke, "Changing Meanings of Equal Educational Opportunity," *Theory into Practice* (1976), or S. L. Schlossman, "Before Home Start: Notes toward a History of Parent Education in America, 1897-1929," *Harvard Education Review*, 1976.

[8] J. Demos, *A Little Commonwealth: Family Life in Plymouth Colony* (New York: Oxford University Press, 1970).

[9] S. L. Schlossman, "Before Home Start: Notes Toward a History of Parent Education in America, 1897-1929," *Harvard Education Review*, 1976.

[10] *Ibid.*; M. Apple, *Ideology and Curriculum* (Boston: Routledge and Kegan Paul, 1979).

[11] J. McV. Hunt, *Intelligence and Experience* (New York: Ronald, 1961); B. S. Bloom, *Stability and Change in Human Characteristics* (New York: Wiley, 1964).

[12] Again, primarily by "empowered groups."

[13] Schlossman, "Before Home Start: Notes toward a History of Parent Education in America, 1897-1929."

[14] B. R. Hatton, "Community Control in Retrospect: A Review of strategies for

Community Participation in Education," in *Community Participation in Education*, ed. C. A. Grant (Boston: Allyn and Bacon, 1979); D. B. Tyack, *The One Best System* (Cambridge: Harvard University Press, 1974).

[15] M. Apple, *Ideology and Curriculum* (Boston: Routledge and Kegan Paul, 1979).

[16] J. P. Comer, "Relationships between School and Family-Policy Implications of an Inner-City School Program," in *Care and Education of Young Children in America*, ed. R. Haskins and J. J. Gallagher (n.p.: Ablex Publishing Co., 1980).

[17] T. S. Popkewitz, "Reform as Political Discourse: A Case Study," *School Review*, November 1975.

[18] M. Sherif, O. J. Harvey, B. J. White, W. R. Hood, and C. W. Sherif, *Intergroup Conflict and Cooperation: The Robber's Cave Experiment* (Norman, Oklahoma: University Book Exchange, 1961); E. Aronson, "Social Psychology," in *Psychology*, ed. P. Mussen and M. R. Rosentweig (Boston: Heath, 1977).

[19] P. Levenstein, "The Mother-Child Home Program," in *The Preschool in Action*, ed. M. C. Day and R. K. Parker (Boston: Allyn and Bacon, 1977). B. D. Goodson and R. D. Hess, "Parents as Teachers: A Summary of Some Program Results" (Unpublished manuscript, Stanford University: School of Education, 1975).

[20] S. B. Heath, "Questioning at Home and at School: A Comparative Study" in *Doing the Enthnography of Schooling*, ed. G. Spindler (New York: Holt, Rinehart, and Winston, 1982).

[21] Scott-Jones, personal communication.

After reading the previous papers you may be feeling overwhelmed and concerned about the role of school in society. That's OK—such an important relationship demands continual examination and constant reflection.

As you sort out what you think the relationship between school and society should be, read the statement by Kleinmann. He has done an excellent job of putting his beliefs into words.

Schools Should Stand For Something

Jack H. Kleinmann
National Foundation for the
Improvement of Education

The problems of the schools reflect the problems of society. We need to acknowledge this in order to determine the role that schools should play in society. In recent years, schools have accepted responsibilities in helping to cure familiar social problems too numerous to mention.

Originally published in *Counterpoint*, November 1981. Used by permission from the author.

Although these attempts have not yet been altogether successful, the totality of this change process itself will stretch across a generation. Unfortunately, there is too often a rush to judge education and other institutions for failing to produce instant results in endeavors whose gains, if they are to be substantial, must of necessity be gradual, layered, and deliberate.

In examining appropriate roles for schools to play in society, it is also relevant to ask whether education should lead or follow in matters of general social concern, such as issues of war and peace, social systems, and other types of advocacy. Popular thought holds that education should not take stands on issues of this sort.

On the other hand, it is also relevant to ask whether education should be vulnerable to ever-changing social and political trends and bandwagons, reversing entire philosophies and curricula in reaction to the variability of public temperament. It is one thing to alter education's policies and procedures to incorporate technological advances and objective discoveries and developments in the realm of teaching and learning. It is quite another thing to reverse the content and function of the schools several times during each generation of school children. Among all of the other reasons suggested for the perceived decline in achievement test scores, these fluctuations and interruptions may represent a central problem.

Schools should stand for something that students, teachers, parents, and the public can depend upon. And we as educators need to believe in something beyond ourselves. It is not to say that education should lead society. And it certainly does not mean that education should blindly follow every transient social trend. There is, rather, a middle ground. Education should be concerned with improving the organization of human thought and activity here and now.

The schools can teach children to be narrow-minded, or selfish, or biased, or unconcerned. The schools can teach children to lead unexamined lives. Or the schools can teach children how to be rational and productive members of a free society. These decisions are apart from the content of education; they are decisions involving the processes of education and the processes of helping children develop into reasonable, concerned, and thinking citizens.

Schools will do best if they teach students to think, to listen, to evaluate, to develop their critical faculties, to assess information, to interpret their experiences, and to come to reasonable conclusions about events and information. From a very early age, it is possible for children to develop the integrity that comes from reasoning and thinking.

Schools will do best if they teach students how to work with others cooperatively in groups, how to solve problems together, how to engage in both leadership and collaboration. And schools will do best if they involve students in the outside world at the earliest opportunity. The more meaningfully students can interact with the community, the more they will respect and participate in the work of the community, and the more they will experience society as an aggregate of individuals and endeavors, not as a set of compartments and schisms.

The achievement of these or any other educational goals depends, of course on teachers. Teachers form the critical mass, that is education. Possibly the most important thing that any of us can do is to keep teachers alive, stimulated, interested, and hopeful in a society that seems no longer to fully support or respect their work. At the same time, we should be helping society (our critics and advocates alike) to understand what education is really doing and to learn first-hand what teachers are accomplishing.

Finally, we as educators need to come together in agreement on stable directions for education, a set of values that can endure fleeting changes and that can preserve the purposes of educational honesty and opportunity in a free society. In this regard, I cannot think of a more important event in the history of education than America's support of the education of all handicapped children. This has been a momentous step in manifesting education's belief in equality of education for all.

Our mutual willingness to collaborate for and about education is more important now than ever. New funding and leadership patterns are sure to bring about disequilibrium. Because viewpoints differ among states, block grants will spawn varying levels and standards of service across the nation, both in the varieties of specialized programs and in education overall. Moreover, our central sense of direction may disintegrate unless we work together to continue and enhance the special and general qualities of education that we have worked so hard to achieve.

The schools should stand for something. Education cannot abrogate this responsibility—least of all now.

Chapter 3

Curriculum and Materials

Have you ever thought that what you choose to teach could have important political implications or may suggest to your students a way of viewing the world? When you choose to teach something, at the same time you choose not to teach other things. Does this sound confusing? Let me give you an example. You may be expected to teach certain specific units in social studies and materials to use and topics to include may be suggested in your school district's curriculum guide. But you, as the teacher, will have an important and often the final say on which concepts are actually taught, and which materials are actually used. In deciding which concepts are important to teach, say, about the Industrial Revolution, you are also deciding that other concepts are not as important. You may feel that the political events of the Industrial Revolution are more important to study than the lives of farmers who lived at that time. You may decide to use a chapter in one particular book instead of another book. You may decide to discuss how women viewed the Industrial Revolution, or you may present only the men's perspectives.

The article by Apple and Taxel discusses how these decisions about your curriculum are political decisions, and why you need to pay attention to the decisions you make in curriculum planning and in selecting instructional materials. Besides this apparent and well thoughtout curriculum, there is also a hidden curriculum in every classroom. It influences students too. Take some time to try to figure out what the hidden curriculum might be and compare your definition with the one given in the following article.

Power and Curriculum Content

Michael W. Apple
University of Wisconsin
Joel Taxel
University of Georgia

In a recent study about the nature of power in our society, two economists concluded that the distribution of wealth and income in the United States had changed very little since before World War II. Another investigation showed something even more graphic. In our attempts to make our society more equal, to eliminate the awful disparities of wealth and power that still remain, most programs that have been attempted have had a rather interesting effect. Eighty percent of the benefits have gone to the top 20 percent of the population.[1] Schools have not been immune to these unequal benefits, unfortunately. While doing well in school is helpful, it seems again to be more helpful to some groups than to others. As Christopher Jencks and his colleagues have just found out, the benefits that white students get from school are still twice as great as blacks. Furthermore, finishing high school pays off primarily for students who are already relatively economically advantaged. Getting a high school diploma actually has very few economic benefits for people who were not advantaged to begin with.[2]

We bring these facts to your attention not just to shock you, though the facts are not at all pleasant. Rather, we want to remind you that even though we may think that the economic and educational system of the United States presents great opportunities to its population, many of our institutions may have effects that are less helpful than most thoughtful and concerned people would like. Because of the possibility that schools may be connected to the creation and maintenance of these inequalities, it is very important for those of us in education to be critical of our own actions, of our methods, and of the curriculum that we teach. In the following, we examine this by raising some critical issues about the methods and content that tend to be accepted too easily in our schools.

The Question of Ethics

The traditional model of curriculum planning and evaluation stresses method over content. This may seem abstract but what we mean here is

Written expressly for *Preparing for Reflective Teaching*.

that the model itself tends to focus on *how* you select your teaching techniques and content, not on *what* you should do or teach. Let us give an example here. Curriculum planning and evaluation usually employs what is called the "Tyler Rationale," so named because it was proposed in the late 1940's by Ralph Tyler, a professor at the University of Chicago. The model has changed little in the thirty or more years since it was first proposed, even though the pressures on schools and teachers have gotten quite a bit more complicated. It has four or five basic steps.

1. Define your objectives in behavioral terms—for example, in precise language, tell what a student will actually do when he or she completes the task. Usually these objectives look something like test questions.
2. Determine the experiences, activities, and tasks that will meet these objectives.
3. Organize these experiences according to scope and sequence— for example, how much knowledge should be covered and what knowledge should be taught first.
4. Teach.
5. Evaluate. Usually this has meant simply giving a test. And then start the whole process all over again.

In more current variants of this model, a prior step is added. We often now give a pre-test to find out what our students know already before we do anything else.

Notice that the emphasis in this model is on how to plan technically and efficiently. It tells us very little about what should go on. This is very important and needs to be stressed. This kind of strategy—let us call it process/product thinking—defines a curriculum as working well if one's behavioral objectives are met. However, the appropriateness of the goals and of the teaching techniques you employ are made less consequential. That is, if we are primarily interested in getting from point A to point B relatively cheaply and efficiently, we tend not to ask whether B is where we should be going in the first place, nor do we tend to ask whether the process we use to get there is morally or educationally sound.[3]

However, questions about what we should do, what our goals should be, what content we should teach, and so on are not technical ones. They are not easily answered by merely plugging into a process/product model which says first do this, then do this, and so on. Instead, they are ethical and political problems. They involve some difficult and personal questioning about how we should work with children, who after all depend on us for their future in many ways. Take this example. Remember in the process/product model success is defined as meeting the objectives set down. Suppose I decide that I shall use behavior modification in teaching reading. I give concrete rewards—like tokens or candy—to my students when they give the prespecified answer or "behave correctly." I judge my plan a success.

However, suppose I find that behavior modification—with its emphasis on discipline, on doing exactly what an authority figure tells you, on following specific directions, and on engaging in specific bite-sized tasks, and so on—is usually seen in schools that serve a poor population or have large numbers of black or brown students. It is employed much less frequently in schools in economically advantaged areas. The methods found in these more advantaged schools stress something significantly different. Here one finds an emphasis not on obeying authority and doing something just to get a small immediate reward but on intellectual open-mindedness, curiosity, teaching based on discovery techniques, less stress on discipline, and much more flexible rules.

What does this comparison tell me? Yes, behavior modification was "successful," but successful according to what? Is it ethically correct for me to teach, say, black and brown students in a way that stresses obedience, doing things for small rewards, and so forth, while teaching their more advantaged counterparts something totally different? I got from A to B, but what kinds of unequal social roles am I preparing each group for? We do not mean to imply here that behavior modification has no use in education—though it certainly can be and sometimes is being overused. What we do want to do is demonstrate that decisions about curriculum and teaching are not merely "how to" or technical matters. They require us to think fairly carefully not only about how we should do something, but about whether it is *right* for someone to treat another person this way. In the case of children, this needs special attention. Given the unequal outcomes of the economic and educational institutions of our society, our goals, and methods need careful scrutiny if we are to act correctly.

While our focus here has been mainly on the ethics of the procedures we use, we shall next look more closely at the content of the curriculum itself. As we shall see, in order to do this we shall have to examine not only the ethical but the political nature of education.

The Question of Power

As we saw in the prior section, curriculum planning and evaluation is not a simple act of just putting together knowledge in some sort of efficient arrangement, teaching it, and then testing to see if our plan worked or not. If it were that simple, the work of teachers and others would be made much easier (though probably less interesting). Instead, thinking about curriculum is a much more complicated undertaking, one which is as concerned with engaging in ethically correct and socially responsible activities and outcomes as it is with getting knowledge across to students. Yet something else needs to be accented. At its very heart, curriculum deals with *power*.

The issue of power is important in three distinct ways. First, curriculum concerns power in that not everyone's knowledge is taught in school. Unfortunately, just as our society is relatively unequal by race, class, and sex, so too is the knowledge that gets into texts and curricular materials often a reflection of these same inequalities. Some groups' knowledge—often those who have been discriminated against because of their race, sex, or class—is simply not represented, or misrepresented, in schools.

Second, curriculum is concerned with power because schools themselves are fundamentally important sorting and selecting devices for the larger society.[4] How well do you do on mastering the formal curriculum (for example, mathematics, science, social studies, reading, and so forth) is related to where you come from and where you will wind up later on in life. The knowledge that is chosen, hence, helps sort students and can either help or hinder them.

We need to remember, by the way, that there are actually two curricula in schools. Besides the formal curriculum, there is something called the "hidden curriculum." This includes the norms and values that children learn from the routines and rituals that go on everyday in most classrooms, like lining up, the ringing of bells, using a pass to go to the bathroom, not sharing answers, and many, many more. Norms and values of punctuality, neatness, obeying authority, waiting in line, accepting institutional and bureaucratic rules instead of personal needs and beliefs are part of this more hidden teaching that goes on in many classrooms.[5] Our previous discussion of behavior modification offers an example of this. Clearly, the two distinct styles of teaching tacitly communicate very different norms and values to their students.

A third, and just as significant, sense of power is a more interpersonal one. At a time of fiscal crisis when budgets are being cut and programs and positions slashed, internal and external power conflicts arise. These conflicts over building new and better curricular programs, withstanding or supporting special interest groups, or simply maintaining the quality of one's teaching now, are apt to be rather intense. This is exactly what we are seeing today as different groups both within and outside the school jockey for position to have more power over the school curriculum. Some of these groups—it is hoped the teachers, for instance— have the interests of students in mind. Some groups may wish the schools to serve the needs of business and large corporations at the expense of the large proportion of the population. And other groups are even more reactionary, seeking to transform the classroom into a platform for their own social and religious beliefs.[6]

All of this indicates how very important it is for educators to both be aware of how power functions in and out of the school and be armed with a background of knowledge about how to argue about and deal with it. We need to understand, for instance, the economics of curriculum, who supports what, and what benefits it will give to different groups. Above all, we need to be critical of what we take for granted about the educational process and the knowledge we are told to teach. Rather than talking abstractly about the issue of whose content is often taught in schools, however, it would be wise to get more specific at this point. Then we can return with a bit more background to the questions of the economics of curriculum and who has power.

Content and Power

A good deal of research has shown that the content and organization of school curricula has reflected the culture, history, and values of dominant groups, while tending to exclude that of the poor and ethnically diverse. As a result, a number of individuals have argued that because of the knowledge that is taught, schools actually function to "legitimate" (give support to) the social positions of dominant social groups in our society and thus contribute to the reproduction and perpetuation of social inequality. We shall use history, race, class, and sex as our primary examples of how this goes on.

The writing of curricular materials is necessarily a complicated and, above all, a selective process. In writing a history textbook, for example, an author must take into account the ever increasing fund of knowledge about the past. Some knowledge is chosen. A large portion is omitted. In addition, as we shall see later, an array of political and economic decisions reflecting the realities of modern textbook publication, marketing, and adoption procedures exert important, and too rarely considered, pressures that influence the final content and format of a textbook. Despite these often conflicting pressures, authors are compelled to choose from among the myriad events, personalities, and points of view in reconstructing a vision of the past. The textbooks that are the result of this process of selection and omission are, however, rarely perceived as such by students who generally read their textbooks as bodies of established facts. Consequently, a student's vision of the past is shaped by what may actually be a subtly biased selection by a group of authors or editors.

The real importance of the perspective used to select or omit content in history textbooks becomes readily apparent when we examine the manner in which native Americans, blacks, and women have been treated in curricular materials. Research has consistently shown that stereotypes, derogatory, racist, and sexist language, and a white perspective on events have characterized the presentation of these groups in instructional materials. The popular image of Native Americans, for example, as "tribes" of "blood thirsty savages" who callously "massacre" peace-loving settlers has been imprinted on the minds of generations of American school children through textbooks as well as countless novels, television programs, and motion pictures. While this stereotype may accurately reflect the sentiments and perspective of several generations of those who "settled" the frontier, it completely ignores the native American point of view. An Indian perspective on America's westward expansion might justifiably see the native American response to the white "invasions" as the determined actions of a brave people determined to resist the actions of an "alien" people bent on their destruction. This perspective is evident in the following remarks made by Frank James, a descendent of the Wampanoag Indians, a nation whose kindness to the Pilgrims is celebrated every Thanksgiving.

> Even before the Pilgrims landed, explorers captured Indians, took them to Europe and sold them as slaves for 20 shillings apiece. The Pilgrims had hardly explored the shores of Cape Cod four days before they had robbed the graves of my ancestors, and stolen their corn, wheat, and beans. . . .
> Massasoit, the great leader of the Wampanoag, knew these facts; yet he and his People welcomed and befriended the settlers. This action by Massasoit was probably our greatest mistake. We, the Wampanoags, welcomed you, the white people, with open arms, little knowing that it was the beginning of the end; that before 50 years were to pass, the Wampanoags would no longer be a Tribe; that we and other Indians living near the settlers would be killed by their guns or dead from diseases that we caught from them. . . .
> Down through the years there is record after record of Indian lands taken, and reservations set up for them upon which to live. The Indian, no longer having any power, could only stand by and watch—while the white people took Indian lands. This the Indian couldn't stand, for to him, land was survival, to farm, to hunt, to be enjoyed. It wasn't to be bought and sold to make money. . . .
> History wants us to believe that the Indian was a savage, illiterate, uncivilized animal. Let us remember, the Indian is and was just as human as white people. The Indian feels pain, gets hurt, has dreams, bears tragedy and failure, suffers from loneliness, needs to cry as well as laugh.[7]

James's remarks are a poignant reminder of the extent to which accounts of white-native American relations have excluded the Indian perspective. The persistently stereotyped depiction of native peoples as ruthless, uncivilized, if at times noble savages, is indicative of the difficulty that oppressed, powerless groups have in making known their point of view. Such negative portrayals have also provided an important source of justification and legitimation for policies toward native Americans that can, in fact, be considered genocidal. In addition, distorted accounts of the native American experience in curricular materials, and in the culture at large, may serve to frustrate attempts by native Americans themselves to gain an accurate perspective on their own history and culture, thus contributing to their continued oppressed, second class status.

Similar cases have been made for the way that blacks, women, and labor unions have been treated in a variety of curricular materials. This selection and omission has had a very long history. Elson's analysis of over a thousand widely used nineteenth century schoolbooks demonstrates this quite clearly. Elson characterizes as "consistently conservative" the stance taken by the books on a variety of social issues. On race, for example, the books suggest that the progress of America was possible only with "the conquest and subordination of inferior races."[8] Women were seen existing solely to serve their husbands and children, with fulfillment coming in helping males fulfill their ambition.[9] Many of the books also expressed a strong belief in class distinctions and attempted to portray poverty in attractive colors, asserting that in a society stratified by classes, "contentment with one's lot" is a major duty to society and God. Finally, there is virtual unanimity among the early schoolbooks about the evils of unions, charging them with irresponsible violence and doctrines "subversive" to American institutions. Importantly, the books never suggest that an alternative perspective on these issues was possible. While it is difficult to determine the precise effects which these, and similar books, have on their youthful reader, it does not seem unreasonable to suggest that the racism, sexism, and anti-union sentiment in such books both reflected and contributed to the development of a consciousness and mind set in and among children that made possible the perpetuation of the powerlessness of racial minorities, women, and many labor groups.

More recent research has indicated that most contemporary materials are more free of the chauvanism and *overt* racism and sexism of those examined by Elson. Nevertheless, studies do indicate that the history, culture, and perspectives of racial and ethnic minorities, women, and workers continue to be minimized, distorted, and, in some instances, ignored altogether.[10] Male characters continue to dominate fiction written for children, and one prominant black author recently suggested that children's book publishers have become *less* favorably disposed in the past several years to publish books about the black experience.[11] Furthermore, several commentators have increasingly decried the more subtle, though still insidious racism that they insist characterizes more contemporary children's fiction including such award winning books as Armstrong's *Sounder*, Taylor's *The Cay*, and Fox's *The Slave Dancer*.[12] Finally, an interesting recent study by Harty has documented the alarming extent of teachers' utilization of "free" materials distributed by wealthy corporate interests for instructional purposes. Labeling these materials "propaganda," Harty shows how product advertising is passed off as nutrition education, nuclear power advocacy is presented as energy education, and industry public relations "taught" as environmental education in materials "contributed" free of charge "in the public interest."[13] The question of unequal benefits, of whose interests are actually served by such materials is, of course, not addressed within them.

Finally, those taking a more critical approach to curriculum have examined not just the omissions but the nature of the curricula made available to *different* groups of children. For instance, Frances Fitzgerald, in her widely read study of conflict and change in social studies textbook publishing, points out the differences in the content of textbooks geared toward students of different backgrounds. Thus, while the more sophisticated "inquiry" books, geared to largely white, upper-middle-class children, discuss cultural diversity and social conflict, those designed for a "less literate" audience (for example, inner city blacks, working class whites) emphasize that America is growing stronger, gaining respect, and fighting communism. As Fitzgerald noted, up until quite recently, the textbook formula seemed to "educate the children of different age groups and different social classes differently."[14]

Much more could be said about these issues, of course, especially about the treatment of women in curriculum, for example. However, even though there have been changes in content because of the continuing attempts by minority people, women, workers, and thoughtful teachers to get better material in classrooms, so much more needs to be done. Thus, a more critical look at the curricula in use in our schools would have us remember the facts about inequality with which we began this discussion. We would have to ask questions like: Whose knowledge is it? Why is it taught to this particular group, in this particular way? Who may tend to benefit from its teaching? Does it reflect and legitimate the interests and points of view of the powerful?[15] As committed educators, we need to be quite careful not to let this happen.

The Issue of Economics

In order to understand why this kind of content has been found in schools, we need to know something about some of the economics of curriculum.

Most texts and commercially produced curricular materials in the United States are written with state adoption policies in mind. Though this differs from state to state, what it basically means is this. A number of states, such as Mississippi, have lists of officially approved curricula and texts. A local school district is usually free to choose any text that is published by a reputable publisher, but if you choose one from the approved list you are reimbursed for a significant portion of the purchase price. This has two effects. In a time of financial difficulty especially, districts will be under considerable budgetary pressure to select texts that have been screened and passed for inclusion on the statewide list. More importantly, publishers aim their sales *and* the content of their material at those states with such adoption policies. Thus, it is much more difficult for honest and/or provocative material to be presented. Since part of the business of text production is exactly that—a business— it is very important for publishers that no powerful lobbying group be offended.

Texts, hence, are carefully "homogenized" and made relatively bland so that they are "acceptable." After all, the difference between getting on such a list and not getting on it may be thousands upon thousands of books sold. It may also be that since some of the areas of the United States that have state adoption policies have historically been the most conservative and the most resistant to social, racial, and sexual equality, the content of the curricular materials that are selected (and, therefore, the content of the bulk of the texts written and produced for American public schools) will reflect these unfortunate beliefs.

Even though we can now begin to see how and why all this happens, it is still very important to act on it. Unfortunately, a number of conditions that are currently emerging in education may make it more difficult for teachers and others to band together to design or select ethically and politically just curricula.

Teachers themselves are caught in a contradictory situation. On the one hand, more and more of them are on curriculum selection committees and over the years have gradually won the right to have an extensive say in what it is they will teach in their classrooms. This is a significant difference over practices years ago when curricula were often mandated by central authorities.

On the other hand, teachers are losing control of curricula in other ways, ways that need to be understood since they are very subtle and powerful. Two movements are worthy of note here. The first concerns the pressure for accountability. More and more state legislatures and education departments are attempting to specify the "competencies" that students are to have at each successive grade level.[16] While the attempt to take all of the knowledge, skills, and values that are important to teach and reduce them down to a list of competencies is in our view not very sound educational practice, notice that individual teachers are *losing the power* to decide what should go on in their classrooms.

The second tendency is that of the rapid growth of prepackaged curricular materials in use in classrooms. These materials have all of the objectives of one's teaching built into them. They specify nearly everything a teacher needs to know, say, and do.

They often list acceptable student responses as well. Furthermore, in a good deal of some of the more widely sold material, all of the diagnostic and achievement tests and all of the teaching materials you will "need" are included, as well. Little of any consequence is left to the individual teacher. This seems to be having an effect similar to what sociologists have called *deskilling*. That is, when skills are not used they atrophy. The people who developed and needed these skills tend to lose them. This is quite possibly the case here. Since so much of what the teacher does is already preorganized and given to you by someone outside the situation, skills such as curriculum planning for individual student needs, making ethically responsive material, creating new and better evaluation techniques that really get at what your students know, and so forth are slowly lost. Teachers lose the power to create their own curricula because they no longer have the knowledge and skill to do it.[17]

In both of these ways—the pressure for accountability and for mass-produced and standardized material that is test-based—power becomes increasingly centralized and teachers lose their hard won gains. In the process it may be harder for them to act on what are important social goals—making the knowledge we teach, the techniques we use, and the outcomes of the institutions equally responsive by race, class, and sex.

Conclusion

Even though we have discussed some of the relationships between what schools teach and unequal power, we should not be pessimistic about the situation we have described in this chapter. The fact that changes *have* been made shows how important it is to keep trying. A recent case in Mississippi, for instance, where a "non-racist" textbook was finally approved for statewide use after years of litigation, illustrates the fact that concerted efforts by groups of concerned parents, community groups, and educators can be successful.[18] The fact, as well, that many teachers today are raising questions about the content they teach, about the methods of curriculum selection, teaching, and evaluation that have been handed down to them, about the necessity of some of the bureaucratic rules of their schools, all of these provide positive signs of what can and is being done.

We do not need technicians in classrooms, teachers who only use process/product models and do not really care about the ethics or politics of their actions, methods, or curricula. What we do need are individuals who really care about the present and future of their students and who are willing to question continually what curriculum and teaching are about. Would you want someone teaching your children who did not care or question?

Notes

[1] These findings are summarized in Martin Carnoy and Derek Shearer, *Economic Democracy* (White Plains, New York: M. E. Sharpe, 1980), and Vincente Navarro, *Medicine Under Capitalism* (New York: Neale Watson Academic Publishing, 1976).

[2] Christopher Jencks, *et al. Who Gets Ahead?* (New York: Basic Books, 1979), pp. 174-175.

[3] For a discussion of the Tyler Rationale and its history and problems, see Herbert Kliebard, "Bureaucracy and Curriculum Theory," *Freedom, Bureaucracy and Schooling*, ed. Vernon Haubrick, (Washington: Association for Supervision and Curriculum Development, 1971).

[4] A thorough review of most of the literature on this subject can be found in Caroline H. Percell, *Education and Inequality* (New York: Free Press, 1977).

[5] Philip Jackson, *Life in Classrooms* (New York: Holt, Rinehart and Winston, 1968).

[6] See, for example, Michael W. Apple, "Curricular Form and the Logic of Technical Control," *Cultural and Economic Reproduction in Education: Essays on Class, Ideology and the State*, ed. Michael W. Apple, (Boston: Routledge and Kegan Paul, 1981), and Sheila Harty, *Hucksters in the Classroom: A Review of Industry Propaganda in Schools* (Washington, D.C.: Center for the Study of Responsive Law, 1979).

[7] Frank James, quoted in Council on Interracial Books for Children, "A Thanksgiving Lesson Plan: Celebration or Mourning? It's All a Point of View," *Interracial Books for Children Bulletin* 10:6 (1979): 13.

[8] Ruth Elson, *Guardians of Tradition: American Schoolbooks in the Nineteenth Century* (Lincoln: University of Nebraska Press, 1964), p. 70.

[9] *Ibid.*, p. 301.

[10] See, for example, Dorothy Broderick, *Image of the Black in Children's Literature* (New York: Bowker, 1973); Council on Interracial Books for Children, *Human —and Anti-Human—Values in Children's Books* (New York: The Racism and Sexism Resource Center for Educators, 1976); Council on Interracial Books for Children, *Stereotypes, Distortions and Omissions in U.S. History Textbooks* (New York: The Racism and Sexism Resource Center for Education, 1977); C. Swanson, "The Treatment of the American Indians in High School History Texts," *The Indian Historian* 10 (1977): 28-37; John Stewig and M. L. Knipfel, "Sexism in Picture Books: What Progress?" *The Elementary School Journal* 76 (1975): 151-155; and Jean Anyon, "Ideology and U.S. History Textbooks," *Harvard Educational Review* 49 (1979): 361-386.

[11]   Walter Meyers, "The Black Experience in Children's Books: One Step Forward, Two Steps Back," *Interracial Books for Children Bulletin* 10:6 (1979): 14-15.

[12]   Council on Interracial Books for Children, *Human—and Anti-Human—Values in Children's Books* (1976).

[13]   Harty, *Hucksters in the Classroom.*

[14]   Frances Fitzgerald, *America Revised: History Schoolbooks in the Twentieth Century* (Boston: Little, Brown, 1979), pp. 142-143.

[15]   This is discussed in much more detail in Michael W. Apple, *Ideology and Curriculum* (Boston: Routledge and Kegan Paul, 1979), and Joel Taxel, "Justice and Cultural Conflict: Racism, Sexism and Instructional Materials," *Interchange* 9:1 (1978/1979): 56-84.

[16]   Arthur Wise, *Legislated Learning* (Berkeley: University of California Press, 1979).

[17]   Apple, "Curricular Form and the Logic of Technical Control."

[18]   Council on Interracial Books for Children, "Non-Racist Text Wins Mississippi Court Battle," *Interracial Books for Children Bulletin* 11:5 (1980): 11-13.

What do publishers say about the publishing of instructional materials? Are publishers mere servants of educators, doing their bidding? Or is the relationship between publisher and educator complex and in need of strong direction from the educational community? Tom Hutchinson provides some important insights into publishing and education that require your attention.

Publishing and Education:
The Ambiguous Union

Tom Hutchinson
Charles E. Merrill Publishing

The rise of special education in America over the last three decades has been accompanied by a corresponding rise in the publication of learning materials specifically intended for handicapped students. How much these materials have contributed to the improvement of education for the handicapped is far less clear than the dramatic increase in their

Originally published in COUNTERPOINT, November, 1980. Reprinted by permission of author and publisher.

number and variety in classrooms. In criticizing the less than systematic progress of improving education in recent years, Dr. Thomas Lovitt[1] has faulted, along with schools of education and bureaucratic agencies of government, the publishers of educational materials. In his words, publishers "have done nothing to stem the tide of confusion. They have profited from the fact that educational practice, particularly in the form of materials, has changed so rapidly. . . . In order to keep their merchandise flowing, the publishers have also taken a cue from the life insurance people; they try to program guilt. By constantly harping at teachers to buy the best, the latest, publishers are often successful in making them feel guilty. . . . Like the life insurance industry, the publishers promote the idea that if you care, you buy; therefore, if you do not buy, you do not care."

Dr. Lovitt's distress with publishers impressed me when, as a publisher myself, I was considering his manuscript in which these comments appeared. And I suppose the fact that I elected to publish his book suggests that I did not find his criticisms wholly unfair. Perhaps like him, though, I felt the contributions of publishers to be only part of a much larger spectre of confusion in education. Moreover, his comments gave substance to my growing conviction that educational publishers have a role and responsibility in education that seems curiously disproportionate.

One example of that disproportion surfaced when, to celebrate the fiftieth anniversary of *Saturday Review* in 1974, its editors asked a wide variety of prominent educators for their opinions on the most influential figure in American education during the fifty years since *SR* had begun publishing. Most of those polled chose the educational philosopher John Dewey. One notable exception among the nominations, however, was that offered by John I. Goodlad, Dean of the Graduate School of Education at UCLA. Goodlad not only named Dewey but also added the name of behavioral psychologist E. L. Thorndike. "I put them together," Goodlad said, "because they so well represent the productive dimension between humanism and behaviorism that has influenced American education so much throughout the twentieth century." Goodlad elaborated by reflecting on a question a friend had once asked: What might have happened in American education if Thorndike had won over Dewey in influence? "I wonder if it is not just the opposite," had been Goodlad's reply. "Thorndike got into the textbooks used by millions of American children."

Goodlad's response intrigued me then and has stuck with me since. "Getting into the textbooks," it seemed, could be more important in shaping educational change than other, more philosophical explorations of teaching and learning. When I read that issue of *Saturday Review*[2] in 1974, I was early into a career in educational publishing. In the years since, I have come to suspect that Goodlad may be right, though for reasons that bring up more questions than answers.

The Educational/Commercial Enterprise

The American textbook, for all its apparent powers, is itself a curious child of free enterprise, born of both pedagogical and commercial parentage. For that matter, the notion of a "textbook" has evolved in recent years to include the larger vision of "educational materials." The traditional book bound between covers has given way to a myriad of print, audiovisual, and manipulative aids for teachers and learners. Now, the larger revolution of the computer is knocking, quietly for the moment, at the schoolroom door, and visionaries both commercial and educational are prophesying an explosion of learning software in the not very distant future. Regardless of what may be coming, though, the present for educational materials is very much filled with this mingling of commercial and educational interests.

This union of commerce and pedagogy is nowhere more evident than in the marketing and selling of these materials. Many companies have their own forces of salespeople and so-called "consultants," often composed of former teachers, who travel thoughout well-demarcated territories in search of "adoptions." Other companies establish channels through hundreds of local dealers, who sell both audiovisual hardware and educational software. Nearly all of the companies have colorful brochures and catalogs which they mail regularly to thousands of teachers, curriculum supervisors, and school administrators. Many advertise their wares in the dozens of educational journals and teachers' magazines, helping to support those publications. Many spend from a few hundred to many thousand dollars to exhibit at conferences and conventions attended by educators. Thus, on the one hand, the promotion of educational materials is solidly rooted in the commercial experience of American free enterprise.

On the other hand, the schools have responded to these armies of sales and promotion people with their own armies of materials evaluation experts. At the local level, for instance, school districts usually maintain staffs of curriculum consultants or materials evaluators who decide, or help to decide, which materials are worthy of use. In more than twenty states, state-level committees review the offerings of publishers to decide which shall be allowed on the state adoption lists. Once on such a list, the publisher then has a hunting license to seek adoptions within the state. At the national level in special education, the notion of regional instructional Materials Centers was implemented several years ago, evolving into a network of large Regional Resource

Centers and Area Learning Resource Centers. Now, virtually every state has some kind of center for collecting educational materials, evaluating them, and informing teachers about them.

Commerce and education are more subtly joined in the development of materials for education. While the popular myth may be that professional educators—subject experts and master teachers—create most materials, the reality is that the commercial companies are more heavily involved. Most have their own editorial staffs who assess market needs and trends, who identify educators who will write or act as consultants in the writing of materials, and who oversee the development of the new product from its beginnings to its final form. Often these editorial staffs are composed of former teachers who have given up the classroom for greater challenges, more money, or, in many cases, because teaching children proved more demanding than rewarding for them. Quite frequently, it is these editors who actually write the textbooks, workbooks, filmstrips, and other materials which the company manufactures and sells. Often they are hired not so much for their expertise in teaching or in the subject matter but because they can produce edited American English, that is, prose which is grammatical and appropriate for the intended audiences. More often than not, no one editor writes a textbook. Rather, a team of editors and artists collaborate to create a patchwork of component books, chapters, units, or sections which come together under the supervision of a managing editor. Quite often, editors leave in the middle of such projects only to be replaced by new editors who take up where their predecessors left off. Of course, nearly all of these editors remain nameless. The title pages of the books generally list a few, select educators as the authors, often balanced between at least one big-name subject matter specialist from a university and one or more school curriculum specialists or classroom teachers. But like the contemporary movie, the contemporary textbook is most often the product of a collective effort, and the list of editors involved in a basal text series could rival in length the credits which crawl up the theater screen, ignored by the audience as it gathers up hats, coats, and kids on its way out.

These somewhat ambiguous ties between commercial and educational interests do not fully explain the force which the textbook exerts on American education. Nor does the size of the educational materials industry explain it. In fact, the total dollar expenditure for educational materials of all kinds amounts each year to only a tiny fraction (about one percent) of the total spent to educate children. This represents about one twenty-fifth of the amount spent each year on teacher salaries and less than half of the amount paid in interest on the schools' debts each year. To use another measure of comparison, the combined sales of all educational materials each year makes the entire industry—

hundreds of companies—smaller than many of the nation's individual corporations. Just one division of General Motors, for example, accounts for sales far in excess of the entire educational materials industry. The pond is a very small one indeed.

Publishers' Responsibilities

Nevertheless, the power of the textbook is both philosophical and practical. For example, if the society determines that is has slighted women or ethnic minorities in the past, then the textbooks are in time rewritten to stress more heavily the presence of women or minorities, both in history and in the present. As a result, schoolchildren learn that some women and some members of minority ethnic groups played significant roles in the shaping of America. Likewise, they learn that women can be pilots or doctors or scientists or whatever else they choose to be. They see blacks and Chicanos and Orientals and members of other ethnic minorities side by side with whites in all kinds of settings and all walks of life. The textbook thus serves as a subtle but influential agent of social change, because in all this children are supposedly learning to view their culture in ways markedly different from the ways their parents learned to view it.

No wonder, then, that Dean Goodlad saw Thorndike as influential for getting into the textbooks used by millions of schoolchildren. No wonder, either, that Dr. Lovitt is unhappy with publishers who have taken advantage of the "cry" in special education to "match the materials to the needs of the child." According to Lovitt (1977),[3] "Special education has been beseiged by a plethora of materials. Many publishers have responded, even capitalized, on these deviations of our young people. Materials have been designed for every need. In fact, materials have been designed for needs that have yet to be pointed out." Implied in the comments of these two educators is the notion that those who produce and select textbooks bear, or ought to bear, some heavy responsibility for the education of children in general and of "special needs" children in particular.

One of the difficulties in exercising this responsibility derives, as Lovitt suggests, from the publisher's need to grind out new products every year. That is perhaps the bogey which being commercial carries with it. Stockholders and venture capitalists do not seem particularly tolerant of a company's failure to increase both sales and profits each year, and they become even less tolerant when a company's sales and profits decline. But they could conceivably turn downright hostile if a company were to explain declining sales with the excuse that "we didn't publish anything new this year because last year's products were really top-notch and we felt the market didn't need any more until it learned to use to its best advantage what we had already sold it." No doubt the new management which would be brought in under such circumstances would be charged with the task of finding something the market did need or, at the very least, finding something it wanted. No doubt, either, that the new management would find a way to produce something the market wanted, whether it needed it or not.

This little scenario should not be interpreted to mean that a commercial publisher's only motives are higher sales and greater profits. Most of the people in educational publishing are in fact well-meaning, literate, responsible people who believe that they are producing useful products for teachers and children. Moreover, most of them earn far less in salaries than their counterparts in bigger, more profitable businesses but stay in publishing at least partly out of a sense of commitment. Further, many of the people who produce and sell educational materials are, as I pointed out earlier, former educators themselves. And while they may see themselves as better off in publishing than in teaching, they almost never see themselves as taking advantage of hapless, incompetent educators who blindly buy whatever is put before them. Yet, to come full circle, most people in educational publishing see that they must continue to produce and market new products if they are to maintain sales, increase profits, and move up the management ladders in their own companies.

Perhaps a second obstacle to publishers' exercising a kind of wholly altruistic responsibility to education is their essential conservatism. This conservatism, which I define as the tendency to continue to do things as one has always done them, is again partly a result of the financial conservatism that comes from reading profit-and-loss statements. In any case, this conservatism manifests itself in the tendency to give the market what it wants, or is willing to use, rather than what it or someone else thinks it needs, but might not use. For example, a few years ago educational technologists predicted a future aglow with the light and enlightenment of teaching machines. A few companies responded with truly sophisticated teaching hardware; many more jumped in with arrays of nonprint media for use in all kinds of wonderfully individualized, self-paced, self-instructional ways. But sales of such media have lagged in the latter half of the 1970's, and the number of teaching machines available today is barely countable. In contrast, basal and supplementary textbook series continue to sell well, despite their increasingly "homogenized" appearance. Thus, publishers find themselves spending more and more on market research, not so much to find what the market needs but to learn what it will buy.

There is perhaps no better example of the problem which educational publishers face than in the publication of standardized tests. Nearly every educational test published in the last twenty-five years has come under criticism from some educators, and each year the educational journals and professional books criticize tests for being culturally or racially discriminatory, for lacking adequate norming samples, for poor validity and reliability studies, for fostering a climate in which teachers must teach to the test rather than to some set of higher purposes, for a host of other weaknesses. The disheartening truth is that some of the worst tests, by these criteria, continue to sell the best. The reasons are partly that educators tend to use what they have always used (publishers call this phenomenon "product loyalty") and partly that the probable sales of a test which met all these criteria (if they could be met at all) would scarcely ever justify the costs to create it. Perhaps even more disheartening is that the best constructed and most carefully standardized of all tests, at least by prevailing standards, are also those most heavily threatened by legislation such as New York's recent "truth in testing" law. (I am not defending here the continuation of standardized tests, by the way, so much as pointing out the disparity between what educators claim to want and what they proceed to buy.) Despite what one industry source calls "an uncertain political climate" for educational tests over the next decade, the future of tests is in far less jeopardy than the future of such new marvels as the microcomputer and the videodisc in education.

Education's Responsibilities

If much of this has sounded like a publisher's stock defense of its right to sell whatever the educational marketplace is willing or well-enough conditioned to buy, I have made my point badly. Publishers are not merely a group of well-meaning folk who always sell only the best which education and commerce can pool their respective talents to produce. I doubt that it was an educator who first voiced the somewhat insidious notion that "a good book is a book that sells good." No, indeed, publishers are by and large a collection of aggressive, profit-oriented business people. But they are not, on the other hand, an unprincipled lot of hucksters for whom the only rule is "Let the buyer beware." What they are, more often than not, is a collection of people with widely diverse backgrounds, some commercial and some educational, who want to make money to the benefit rather than the detriment of learners.

The real point, however, is this. In none of these good intentions and marriages of educational and commercial values should one expect commercial publishers to produce and market only the highest quality materials. What one should expect, what many if not most publishers would welcome, is precisely what Lovitt wants: a little less confusion and a little more data. Quite simply, it is the teacher (or curriculum supervisor or adoption committee) who determines what sells or does not sell and, therefore, what will be produced in the future and what will not be produced. The point to be made is equally simple: American education must first look to itself to shape, change, and improve educational practice, not to those who publish the materials which partly effect that change. When educators begin to agree on what children need, on what makes them learning disabled, or simply on what works in helping them overcome special learning problems, they will find publishers rushing to respond with materials that fit the bill. In the meantime, however, Lovitt's words will continue to haunt education: "The divorce rate between pupils and materials has been scandalously high."[4] In the meantime, for better or worse, educators can expect to find in the diverse quality of educational materials a mirror of the diversity in theories and practices which have characterized American education throughout this century and special education over the last few decades.

Notes

[1] T. C. Lovitt, *In spite of my resentment, I've learned from my children* (Columbus, Ohio: Charles E. Merrill Publishing Co., 1977).
[2] *Saturday Review/World*, (August 10, 1974,) 86–87.
[3] T. C. Lovitt, *In spite of my resentment, I've learned from my children* (1977).
[4] *Ibid.*

You are probably aware that what should be taught in school (for example, sex education) and which materials can be used in school (for example, Catcher in the Rye) *are being hotly debated by citizens groups. Read the following* Newsweek *and* New York Times *articles and discuss this question with a friend and/or someone who has children in school.*

The Right to Ban Books

Aric Press with Emily Newhall
Newsweek

Few images are more abhorrent than that of the censor picking his way down a library shelf, consigning volumes to a dustbin or a bonfire. Few ideas of government are better accepted than the right of local communities to run their own schools. What happens when these fixed ideas of American democracy collide? Increasingly the answer has been to turn to Federal judges, who have tried to pick their way through the troubling issue of book banning in the schools. In three recent decisions, however, the judges have left school boards and students with conflicting views of how well the First Amendment protects young readers from older bowdlerizers.

The latest cases came from places as diverse as a New York City suburb and an Indiana town best known as the orthodontic-appliances capital of the nation. In those disputes, the courts ruled that board members can ban vulgar and distasteful books from school shelves as long as the officials are not imposing a "rigid orthodoxy" or suppressing an entire body of ideas. Other judges, however, have declared that school boards cannot remove books they find objectionable once they are part of a library's collection, even if they contain vivid expletives. "There's no bright, clean line when you try to apply the First Amendment in these cases," says Bruce Ennis, legal director of the American Civil Liberties Union. "It's an extremely fuzzy one and that drives judges up the wall."

Armbands: The fundamental question is, what does the First Amendment protect—and prevent? Twelve years ago the U.S. Supreme Court declared that "it can hardly be argued that either students or teachers shed their constitutional rights to freedom of . . . expression at the schoolhouse gate." Action and speech by students and teachers are clearly protected. They may wear black armbands to protest an unpopular war, or criticize the school in their newspapers. But those guarantees have little application to book banning cases. What's involved instead is an opposite notion: do students have a constitutional right to be exposed to controversial ideas—a passive right to hear as well as to speak? Several lower courts have created such a privilege. The U.S. Supreme Court has never addressed the issue, although it has protected the rights of prisoners, consumers, and citizens to receive mail and other information.

The First Amendment does not confer rights; rather, it serves as a flat prohibition on governmental interference with free speech. Ordinarily the courts view very strictly any official limits on expression. But judges have always treated schools differently. They usually have accepted the statutory right of local authorities to "inculcate" their pupils with their community's values—unless school boards range too far. Where that line is drawn, however, depends on which judge wields the pen.

The three cases decided since August [1981] have not clarified the issue. The first involved a challenge to the Warsaw, Indiana, school board's controversial attempt to eliminate courses and books it found objectionable. One of the board's first targets was a course called "values clarification"—a class where students discussed divorce, marijuana, and premarital sex. After eliminating the elective class, the board gave the 40 "values" textbooks to a local senior citizens group. In order to show support for the board, the group promptly burned the books in a local parking lot. Then, embarking on a wider purge, the board banned four other books, fired three teachers, and dropped nine literature courses.

Two students went to court, charging a denial of their academic freedom. In August a Federal appeals panel dismissed the suit. ". . . Nothing in the Constitution permits the courts to interfere with local educational discretion until local authorities begin to substitute rigid and exclusive indoctrination for the mere exercise of their prerogative to make pedagogic choices," wrote Judge Walter J. Cummings. The majority refused to side with Federal courts in Ohio, Massachusetts, and New Hampshire, which held earlier that officials may not remove library books or magazines just because they object to their content.

A fuzzier ruling was handed down last month in New York. The Island Trees, New York, school board removed nine books from high school libraries, including Bernard Malamud's *The Fixer*, Kurt Vonnegut's *Slaughterhouse Five* and Eldridge Cleaver's *Soul on Ice*. The board seized the books after three members attended a conference of parents worried about the tone of public education; at the meeting a list of "problem" books was circulated. A district judge upheld the board, but an appeals court reversed in a 2-to-1 vote. One judge in the majority suggested that the ban reflected improper political motives; the other wanted a trial to see if the board was condemning ideas and not just books. Wrote U.S. Judge Jon O. Newman, "Teachers and students alike have a right to freedom from 'a pall of orthodoxy'."

Potpourri: The Island Trees board has asked for a rehearing. It argues that the ban rested solely on the books' offensive language. If the board can prove that point, it may ultimately prevail. On the same day that the judges in New York ruled against Island Trees, they also upheld a Vermont district's ban on *Dog Day Afternoon* and *The Wanderers*, two books that local officials found vulgar.

This potpourri of opinions confuses school officials who feel the urge to protect their children by limiting what they read. Eventually, if enough courts disagree among themselves, the U.S. Supreme Court might try to resolve some of the issues. But parents and school boards cannot eliminate all offensive material available to children, no matter what the courts decide. They may have the right to control libraries' card catalogs, but private book stores, movie houses, and television networks are beyond their legal reach.

Parents' Groups Purging Schools of 'Humanist' Books and Classes

Dena Kleiman
The New York Times

In Onida, South Dakota, birth control information has been removed from the high school guidance office, and the word "evolution" is no longer uttered in advanced biology. *Brave New World* and *Catcher in the Rye* have been dropped from classes in literature. The award winning children's book *Run, Shelley, Run* has been banned from the library.

In Plano, Texas, teachers no longer ask students their opinions because to do so, they have been told, is to deny absolute right and wrong. In Des Moines, Iowa, a high school student production of "Grease," the hit Broadway musical, was banned. In Mount Diablo, California, *Ms. Magazine* is off the school library shelves; it is available only with permission from both a parent and a teacher.

Lobbying Methods Sophisticated

Emboldened by what they see as a conservative mood in the country, parents' groups across the nation are demanding that teachers and administrators cleanse their local schools of materials and teaching methods they consider anti-family, anti-American, and anti-God.

Armed with sophisticated lobbying techniques, and backed by such national organizations as Moral Majority, the Eagle Forum and the Christian Broadcasting Network, these parents are banding together to remove books from libraries, replace textbooks, eliminate sex education courses and balance lessons of evolution with those of Biblical creation, at least. They also seek to revise such things as the open classroom, new math, and creative writing, asserting that these relatively unstructured academic approaches break down standards of right and wrong and thus promote rebellion, sexual promiscuity, and crime.

There have always been disgruntled parents of one political persuasion or another. But visits to several cities and interviews with educators and leaders of the movement in cities around the nation show that today's groups are far more numerous, well organized and vocal. Their focus is no longer a specific book or course of study but rather the very nature of public education itself. The philosophy of "secular humanism," they say, permeates every facet of school life, from learning the alphabet to high school lessons in American history.

"Secular humanism is the underlying philosophy of all schools," said Terry Todd, national chairman of Stop Textbook Censorship, a group based in South St. Paul, Minnesota, which argues that "decent" books such as *The House of Seven Gables, A Midsummer Night's Dream, Huckleberry Finn* and *Robinson Crusoe* have been censored in favor of "humanist" literature. "Those of us who understand know how it is infiltrated, know how it is inculcated in the children."

Lottie Beth Hobbs, president of the Pro-Family Forum in Fort Worth, Texas, which distributes a leaflet entitled "Is Humanism Molesting Your Child?" said, "Humanism is everywhere. It is destructive to our nation, destructive to the family, destructive to the individual."

According to these groups, "humanism" has become the unofficial state religion. Its omnipresence, they contend, particularly within the nation's schools, is responsible for crime, drug abuse, sexual promiscuity, and the decline of American power.

The Philosophy Called Humanism

There is a philosophy called humanism, which places man at the center of the universe, encourages free thought and scientific inquiry without deference to a supreme being and offers no absolute standard of ethics.

But critics of the antihumanist movement, including teachers, parents, and administrators, charge that the campaign is based more on hysteria than fact. They see "secular humanism" as a meaningless catch-all term used by these groups to describe all the nation's ills. While they acknowledge that humanism is the underlying philosophy of modern society, they dispute the belief that its acceptance is a result of conspiracy. Nor do they believe that it has been destructive to mankind.

"I think secular humanism is a straw man," said Paul Kurtz, a professor of philosophy at the State University at Buffalo, a leading humanist. "They are looking for someone to blame."

"Substitute the word humanist for Communist of the fifties or Bolshevik of the twenties," said Dorothy Massie of the Nation Education Association. "This time the target is public school education."

Based primarily in predominantly white suburbs and small towns, the protesting parents' groups, which number in the hundreds, have names such as Young Parents Alert, People Concerned With Education,

Parents of Minnesota and Guardians of Education. They include many parents who have never been involved in organized activity before but have decided to join with others now because they fear that the problems of urban school systems are slowly encroaching on those of their own home towns. Direct mail, toll-free telephone numbers, and cable television provide easy access to others who share their concerns.

Through brochures, films, and pamphlets distributed at parents meetings, these parents are being told that humanism "brainwashes" students to accept suicide, abortion, and euthanasia and that it encourages them to lie, alienates them from their parents, fosters such "socialistic" anticompetitive practices as the open classroom and conditions them to think that there is no such thing as right or wrong.

"Some of you may have elementary or secondary children who experience stomach aches, headaches, nightmares, or other similar complaints and/or disorders that cannot be accounted for," warns a pamphlet entitled "Parental Guide to Combat the Religion of Humanism in Schools," distributed by Parents of Minnesota. "Look in your schools! Modern educational materials and the techniques used may be what is causing those problems."

"I worry about my sons," said Lore Finley, whose two sons attend grade school in Blunt, South Dakota, and who only recently has become aware of the movement against secular humanism. "We do not have any rules in school; no right, no wrong. I don't like secular humanism. It teaches anything goes: if you feel it's O.K., do it."

What these parent groups are asking for, they say, is a return to many of the teaching practices and textbooks of 30 years ago, as well as the Christian values and principles upon which, they argue, the country was founded. They are asking specifically for history texts that emphasize the positive side of America's past, economics courses that stress the strengths of capitalism and literature that avoids divorce, suicide, drug addiction, and other harsh realities of life.

On another level, they advocate a return to academic "basics," contending that the abandonment of such disciplines as penmanship has led to slackening of standards and declining achievement. They want reading programs that focus on phonics rather than whole word recognition, writing programs that stress good spelling over creativity. They also want, they say, a curriculum and an approach to teaching that clearly delineates between right and wrong.

Rating Textbooks for Parents

"There is just too much negativism," said Mel Gabler, who with his wife, Norma, operates the largest "textbook clearinghouse" in the country, advising parents' groups on the moral acceptability of textbooks from their home in Longview, Texas. The Gablers say inquiries have increased 50 percent since President Reagan was elected in November.

"There is an uneasy feeling that maybe we've bent over backwards with being broadminded," said Dr. Scott Thompson, president of the National Association of Secondary School Principals.

According to Judith Krug of the American Library Association, since last November there have been attempts to remove, restrict or deny access to 148 different books in 34 states.

In Buhler, Kansas, for example, *The Kinsman,* a science fiction novel by Ben Bova, was removed from the library of the Prairie Hills Middle School because parents complained that it was sexually suggestive. In Gretna, Virginia, a parent-teacher committee at the high school voted to cut out or ink over "Howl" by Allen Ginsberg and "Getting Down to Get Over" by June Gordon, which involves the trauma of a woman who was raped, both of which are in "The Treasury of American Poetry."

Because of successful challenges by such groups as the Gablers, numerous health, social studies, English, and science textbooks have already been removed or revised to comply with parental complaints. Most recently, the Alabama Board of Education voted to remove *Justice in America* and *Unfinished Journey,* both published by Houghton Mifflin and widely used in social studies classes across the country, from the state's approved textbook list in response to parental complaints that they were filled with secular humanism.

"We feel we brought the best of scholarship and accumulated as accurate and objective a book as we can possibly publish," Gary Smith, corporate counsel for Houghton Mifflin, said of *Unfinished Journey.* "We found it difficult to find substance to support the charges made."

Many attempts to ban books have met failure. Others are still tied up in litigation, such as Pico v. Island Trees, a case involving a ban on Long Island in 1976 of nine books, including *Slaughterhouse Five* by Kurt Vonnegut, Jr., *The Fixer* by Bernard Malmud, and *Down These Mean Streets* by Piri Thomas. The Long Island case is currently on appeal to the Supreme Court and could become an important test case of a school board's right to decide the contents of a school library.

Even in areas where censorship efforts have failed, teachers and others say that the battles themselves have had a chilling impact in certain cases on what goes on in the classroom.

"I think about what I'm doing twice," said Betty Duke, who teaches ninth grade history at Vines High School in Plano, a suburb of Dallas, where no specific book has been eliminated. "Is there anything controversial in this lesson plan? If there is, I won't use it. I won't use things where a kid has to make a judgment."

In South St. Paul, a suburb of St. Paul, Minnesota, all books that could possibly be considered controversial must be so labeled. They must then be reviewed by committee and either rejected or accepted by the school board. Rather than be subjected to that procedure, teachers in the school system simply have not changed the curriculum in more than six years and continue to use books that may in fact no longer be relevant.

"We want and need to update contemporary literature," said Joyce Johnson, who teaches language arts at South St. Paul Senior High School. "But we won't make suggestions because they would only be labeled out of context."

Peter Carparelli, the principal of Helena Senior High School in Montana, said that many of his teachers had become anxious since a meeting last month when a discussion of the sex education curriculum turned into a forum on the ills of secular humanism. "There is this feeling that you're being questioned," he said.

"Anything that I think possibly controversial I tape," said George H. Tanner, one of several teachers at Montello High School in Wisconsin who began taking cassette tape recorders to class after parents accused them of "anti-God" statements they deny making.

Parents become aware of "secular humanism" and the campaign to cleanse the schools in different ways. Some first heard about it by means of religious television, newspapers, or at religious services. Many others have been invited to community meetings and have been shown films and given pamphlets from such national organizations as the Gablers, the Pro-Family Forum, the Eagle Forum, Moral Majority, the Heritage Foundation and America's Future.

Some of the pamphlets currently in circulation include "Weep for Your Children," "The Hate Factory" and "Anti-God Humanists are 'Conditioning' Our Children."

A 29-minute film produced by the Christian Broadcasting Network and entitled "Let Their Eyes Be Opened" has already sold over 1,800 copies at $125 each to individuals and groups across the nation. The film shows, among other things, aborted fetuses and teen-agers who have taken an overdose of drugs. It attempts to show that teen-age prostitution, pornography, and murder are all a result of secular humanism in the schools.

"We have to get rid of secular humanism," said Donald J. Rykhus, superintendent of schools in Onida and Blunt, South Dakota. The only way that can be done, he said, was by getting rid of "liberal, real liberal, personnel."

"I worry for my son," said Vicky Brooks, who teaches English at Sully Buttes high school and opposed the ban. "I don't want him to be in a community where if you disagree you are wrong. I want him to be able to evaluate opinions and be able to think. People who can't think are ripe for dictatorship."

Having read these two articles, how would you answer the question: Who should decide what should be taught in school?

Review the philosophy that Pekarsky challenged you to begin to develop. Does your response to this question agree with other beliefs that constitute your philosophy? On what basis do you justify your response to this question? Did you use the procedure suggested by Pekarsky to help you think it through?

Often K–8 teachers have a fear of teaching science and math, feeling that they lack a solid background in these areas. In order to make certain that you do not become a member of this group, try approaching these subjects with a little more vim and vigor during your preservice days. Also read the following two articles that provide beginning frameworks for thinking through your math and science curriculum. As you read the science and math articles, consider the importance of your role in selecting curriculum in all subject areas.

Science in the Elementary School: Some Basic Considerations

James Stewart
University of Wisconsin—Madison
Fred Finley
University of Maryland

"I have to teach science to 4th graders during my student teaching!" This realization might cause prospective teachers to feel like the rope in a tug-of-war. On one hand, they begin to question the adequacy of their science preparation. It may seem to have been minimal or so abstract that it could not possibly be meaningfully relayed to elementary school students. Counterbalancing this apprehension is the recognition that science lessons are often the most exciting, active, and enjoyable part of the school day. Conscientious teachers cannot help but be influenced by such experiences.

We hope that we can, in these few pages, add force to the pull on the "science as important and enjoyable" side of the tug-of-war rope.

Written expressly for *Preparing For Reflective Teaching.*

At the same time we do not want to mislead you into thinking that teaching science well is necessarily easy. Teaching science (or any other subject for that matter) requires effort and commitment. The most important commitment you make may be to understanding the science you want your students to learn. We believe that when you understand the knowledge of science, the actual teaching is easier, more effective, and more enjoyable for you and your students.

In the next several pages we will try to sketch out answers to four related questions: Why should we teach elementary school science? What should be taught? How do we teach it? And how do we evaluate what students have learned? We hope that in these answers you will see why we believe that your understanding of science is important.

Why Teach Science in the Elementary School?

Science: A Basic

"Back to basics" has become such a powerful educational slogan that we too frequently neglect to ask questions such as "What are we going back to?" and "What attributes must something possess to be considered basic?" In the most narrow interpretation, "back to basics" implies reading, writing, and arithmetic. How can science be justifiably included in such a basics curriculum? A unifying theme in the three basics is that they provide individuals with intellectual skills that can be used to make sense out of the worlds in which they live. Science fulfills a similar function—knowledge in the various science disciplines (biology, geology, astronomy, meteorology, physics, and chemistry) can be used by individuals to understand the world.

"Is air real?" "Why is the sky blue?" "Why do stars all seem to move together?" "How do you know that the earth is really round and moving?" "How come if you pour hot water on a stuck jar top it comes off easily?" "What is that bird . . . tree . . . insect . . . rock . . . flower?" These and thousands of similar questions are asked by elementary school children every day. They reflect a profound interest (need?) to impose some order upon the world. It is important for teachers to help children to find answers to these questions. But however important this is, it is not enough. Teachers sometimes have to raise the questions, to provide students with knowledge that will allow them to "see" things in their worlds that they would not otherwise see—to cause shifts in their perceptions. To us this is the most important justification for teaching science in the elementary school—the science that students learn is useful in giving meaning not to the adult's world but to the child's world.

Another rationale for teaching science is based upon the role that science plays in American society. We do, after all, live in a world where an understanding of many scientific ideas is essential for making decisions that affect not only the individual but society at large. Individuals need to maintain some role in the processes that shape the society of which they are a part. For instance, decisions about the use of recombinant DNA techniques, if they are to be made by the public, should be made by a public that is literate concerning DNA. How can individuals weigh the pros and cons of nuclear power plants if they do not know something more than the typical newspaper account of nuclear fission, or the concept of background radiation, or the statistical nature of scientific claims? Just as we do not leave decisions about our children's health to used car salesmen who know nothing about health care, we should be extremely concerned about leaving decisions concerning science to individuals who have no relevant knowledge.

There are other justifications for teaching science in the elementary school. For example, several research studies claim that standardized reading scores are better in classes where science is taught. Others argue that elementary school science is prerequisite to understanding junior high and high school science. There is probably some truth to these statements. Yet, of the justifications that we have listed, the first—that science knowledge will help children interpret what goes on around them—is by far the most important. Elementary school science instruction might boost reading skills, prepare students for junior high science, and groom future citizens to be informed decision-makers. But the fact that teaching science links children's interests in the immediate world with knowledge that can help them make better sense out of that world should be the overriding consideration for elementary school teachers.

What to Teach?

Determining what to teach is probably the most important decision that science teachers must make. It is important because as teachers, we want to choose content that will be interesting, understandable, and valuable to students. It is also important because to some extent it determines *how* teachers teach. But let's start at the beginning: What is science all about?

Scientific knowledge describes and explains natural phenomena. The phrase natural phenomena refers to *objects* such as flowers, birds, lakes, rabbits, butterflies, falling balls, magnets, and pendula; *processes* such as erosion, condensation, photosynthesis, respiration, and crystallization; and *events* such as changes from daylight to darkness, fall color changes, the expansion of metal when heated, the collision of moving objects, and the expansion of gases.

There are two major types of science knowledge to be taught: content and process. The content is the actual body of knowledge, and the processes are used to manipulate that knowledge. Another way to look at this distinction is that a teacher teaches students *conceptual knowledge* and the students develop *cognitive skills* that they can use to do such things as observe, describe, and predict.

Conceptual Knowledge

The conceptual knowledge or content of science consists of facts, empirical concepts and laws, and theories. Knowing this can be useful in deciding what to teach. Let's take a closer look at science content.

A Starting Point: Establish the Facts.   Here is a question a student might ask: "When I got up this morning the grass was wet, but it hadn't rained? How did this happen?" The answer should begin with the facts, in terms of the concepts that the student knows. Statements that describe the single occurrence of a natural phenomena are facts. In the present case, let's say that the facts the student knows are:

1. The ground was wet in the early morning.
2. There had been no rain the night before.
3. The morning temperature was much lower than it had been the previous evening.

Establishing the facts provides students with a starting point they can understand and a basis for understanding the new information that will be presented.

Empirical Concepts and Laws Are the Foundation.   Knowing the facts is a start but it is not sufficient. A teacher's next responsibility is to introduce new concepts. Concepts are used to describe and explain natural phenomena, and knowledge of them is necessary for students to understand those phenomena. The empirical (for example, observable) concept "dew point" is important in answering the student's question about the wet grass. The dew point is the temperature at which the moisture in the air as a gas begins to change to a liquid. This concept is empirical in that the temperature at which this change takes place can be observed using a thermometer.

Knowing this concept, an empirical law can be introduced that, in conjunction with the facts stated above, provides an explanation for the wet grass. The empirical law says that when the air temperature drops below the dew point, water will form on surfaces in contact with the air. This empirical law is a statement of not only what had occurred on one occasion but of what will occur at all places and times when the facts are similar to those described.

The power of scientific knowledge to enrich the lives of students is evident in this example. The content is simple and refers to observable objects and events. It provides students with an explanation of a recurring and perplexing phenomena. In addition, the same empirical law can be used to explain other events such as the moisture that forms on a glass of ice water or on the inside of automobile windshields during the winter. The knowledge of empirical concepts and laws is most important for students.

Adding Theoretical Concepts and Laws. The student might then say, "Okay, but why does the water as a gas change to water as a liquid?" The answer to this question requires a change in the type of content that is needed. This type of content is theoretical—it refers to objects and events that are too small or too fast to be sensed. In this case the theoretical concept of water molecules is needed. A molecule can be understood as the smallest particle of water. Other statements called theoretical laws are also necessary to describe how a gas becomes a liquid:

1. Molecules of water are always moving.
2. The higher the temperature, the faster molecules move.
3. In a gas the molecules are moving very fast and are very far apart.
4. In a liquid molecules are closer together and moving more slowly.
5. There is a particular temperature for water at which the molecules move slowly enough and are close enough together to be a liquid.

The answer to the student's question is that the temperature overnight becomes low enough so that the molecules of the water as a gas begin to move slowly and closer together until the gas becomes a liquid. This theoretical content provides an even richer, more complete and more powerful description and explanation of the events that the child saw. It refers to objects and events that cannot be seen, however. It is therefore more difficult for students to learn. In fact, it may not be necessary to include very much theoretical content in elementary school science instruction. There are many fascinating natural occurrences that will interest children. Most often their curiosity can be satisfied and their understanding of the world increased by providing the empirical concepts and laws. In any case, it is a necessity that students obtain a sound understanding of the empirical content before theoretical ideas are introduced.

Science Processes

A content background relevant to a particular natural phenomenon is the fundamental tool that a student needs to do some of the things that scientists do—observe, measure, describe, explain, predict, and experiment. These are the scientific processes or cognitive skills that we teach our students.

Let's return to the example: if students know the meaning of the phrase "dew point," it should be possible to teach them how to *measure* the dew point. Elementary school students can learn to place a thermometer in a glass of warm water, add ice, and record the temperature at which water first forms on the outside of the glass. Given that information, it may then be possible for them to *predict* what will happen during the coming night after being told the air temperature will go beyond the dew point. Students also would be prepared to test this prediction by noting the time and temperature at which dew began to form on the grass.

It is important to recognize that the content must precede the process. Students must know the scientific concepts before they can learn the cognitive skills. This is simply illustrated by trying to describe an object or event without using any concepts or to make predictions without using an empirical law. The breadth and depth of the students' content background will determine the sophistication and adequacy of their descriptions and explanations.

It is equally important to recognize that scientific processes are not generalized intellectual skills. Cognitive skills are content-bound and will differ from topic to topic because the content knowledge needed to describe or predict will be different. This is not to say that teaching science processes is unimportant. When students learn to describe, explain and predict the events that occur in their worlds, their lives are enriched and their abilities to function as responsible and knowledgeable people are greatly enhanced.

Selecting Content and Processes

One of the most important teaching decisions you make will be the selection of the science content and processes you want students to know. There are a variety of factors that influence this decision: the value of the content to students and society, student interest, and the importance of the content for future learning. It seems to us, however, that there are two particularly important factors. One is what you know or are willing to learn; the other is what the students know.

Regarding what you know, it seems obvious to experienced teachers, that presenting ideas you do not understand to others is difficult. Yet, teachers are often required to do just that. They are required to take teachers' guides that provide little or no background knowledge and go through instructional activities without really understanding the purpose of those activities. This is unfortunate and often requires the teachers learn the needed science from resource materials.

The other factor that should receive the teacher's attention is the students—their backgrounds and the knowledge they bring to the learning situation.

We too often forget that students, even the very youngest, do not come to our classrooms as blank slates to be written upon. They come as active participants, with a wealth of prior knowledge that they will use to make sense of instruction—in either a discovery or an expository lesson, from a movie, field trip or book. They use that prior knowledge, including misconceptions, to interpret what goes on in the science class. As a consequence, teachers must take every step possible to determine what knowledge students already possess—what relevant conceptions and misconceptions do they have? This is a formidable task, though not an impossible one. After a few years of teaching it will become obvious that, for any age group, there are trends in conceptions and misconceptions. Once these trends have been noted it becomes easier to gear instruction to individuals. It is important to uproot misconceptions before proceeding. The usual result when students use misconceptions as a foundation for interpreting new science content is that the misconceptions "broaden" as students mislearn new content.

The prior knowledge of students is the most important factor a teacher must consider when planning instruction. But we have a few other, more specific suggestions on how to teach science to elementary school students.

How to Teach Science

Although it is not possible to give anyone a set of rules for teaching science that will be appropriate to all grade levels, pupil types, and content areas, there are some general guidelines that could help a good teacher become an even better teacher. Some of the suggestions may seem like just plain common sense. Even so, it has been our experience that these guidelines are very often not followed by classroom teachers. Part of the problem is that the position of teacher involves much more than planning to teach and then executing that plan—it takes a dedicated and imaginative teacher to keep these guidelines in mind when inundated with administrative responsibilities.

Perhaps the best and most general guidelines are summarized in the saying:

Don't tell students what they can easily read.
Don't have them read what they can be shown.
Don't show them what they can do for themselves.

This old adage remains true today. The best advice on how to teach science content is the use of instructional activities that whenever possible provides direct experience with the objects and events students are to understand. The same is true for teaching processes. In short, provide direct experience.

Teaching Science Content

Teaching content always should precede teaching related science processes, so let's begin there.

Generating Facts and Laws. Recall that a fact is the record of a singular event, constructed from concepts, and that an empirical law expresses some regularity among facts. A teacher's objective might be that students will know some law such as when air temperature is increasing the barometric pressure is decreasing or that water boils at $100°C$. How might either of these generalizations be taught? More often than not the air pressure law will be taught by looking at temperature/pressure changes that occur during the course of a week. The teacher might demonstrate to the students that water boils at $100°C$, or in the case of older students, the students themselves might establish the boiling point. It is worth remembering that laws are supposed to have near universal applicability. To establish that as air temperature increases, barometric pressure decreases using only one or two occurrences from the same geographical location may not be sufficient evidence of the law's universality. It might be possible, for example, to obtain weather reports from other cities, countries and years to reinforce the law. Then it is the world speaking to the student rather than the teacher. By generating facts, the students will be given the opportunity to interact with materials and apparatus—a necessity in the elementary school science program.

One possible result of the generation of multiple facts to develop empirical laws is the realization that what is considered to be a universal generalization only holds under very idealized conditions. For example, water does not always boil at 100°C; in fact, it would be very unusual to find a liter of tap water that would boil at 100°C. The universal generalization that we teach students (although we would not begin to teach youngsters any differently) only applies under certain conditions; the water must be pure and the boiling must occur at sea level atmospheric pressure. In the course of letting students discover facts for themselves, we can begin teaching them about idealized conditions. But the point remains that allowing students to generate their own facts is an important part of science instruction, especially at the elementary school level.

Teaching About the Theoretical World. Helping students develop empirical generalizations, although challenging, is easier to accomplish than the teaching of theoretical knowledge. Empirical generalizations contain only concepts that can be directly sensed. Theoretical laws, however, are often explanations of events or processes in terms of underlying, invisible microphenomena. Since we can't show students the actual microphenomena, what should instruction about theoretical ideas be like? Since theoretical ideas are the most difficult to teach to children, they should be reserved for either older elementary children or students who have good grounding in supporting empirical knowledge.

When teaching about the theoretical world teachers have but one recourse—the use of physical models. Whenever possible it is preferable that these models be dynamic rather than static or pictorial. For example, when modeling an osmotic system in which a liquid (often water) moves through a semipermeable membrane from the area of highest to lowest H_2O concentration, the model could be static—a series of diagrams on a chalkboard indicating various time-slices of the system as it moves toward equilibrium. However, it would be possible and more meaningful if a dynamic model were used. Crepe-paper strips could be hung from ceiling to floor to represent a porous, semipermeable membrane. Individual students could represent individual water molecules. By starting with unequal numbers of students on either side of the model membrane and by giving each of them a set of directions for moving (take four steps, turn to your left, take eight steps, and so on) the unequal system will eventually reach equilibrium. We would urge teachers to consider their curricular objectives very carefully and to make sure that for each lesson that includes theoretical terms the students are provided with models, dynamic ones whenever possible, to make the learning more meaningful.

Teaching Science Processes

Why do teachers take the time to teach their students conceptual science knowledge? The answer to this question is that conceptual knowledge can be used to interpret or make sense of the world (for example, through descriptions, explanations, and predictions). If teachers actually expect students to be able to use their knowledge in novel ways or situations, however, they must provide them with many opportunities to do so. Teachers cannot expect the use to flow automatically from knowledge. The processes of observation, description, classification, explanation, and prediction must be made many times. The path to creative knowledge use is the same as the path to Carnegie Hall—practice, practice, practice.

In having students practice processes such as explaining particular natural phenomena, two things are required: the prerequisite conceptions and specific examples. Aldo Leopold in his book *A Sand County Almanac* gives us some guidance: "The weeds in a city lot convey the same lesson as the redwoods; the farmer may see in his cow pasture what may not be vouchsafed to the scientist adventuring in the South Seas. Perception, in short, cannot be purchased with either learned degrees or dollars; it grows at home as well as abroad."

The important point here for teachers is that the major science laws or conceptions are much like a stageplay. The play, in all of its renditions, is very much the same. From performance to performance, however, one set of variables may change dramatically—the actors. The same is true in science. Assume that the intent of instruction is to teach students to describe and explain energy flow in an ecosystem. To accomplish this, such concepts as energy source, producer organism, consumer, decomposer, herbivore, carnivore, food chain, and food web need to be developed. In addition, there are certain generalizations or laws, such as those about energy pyramids or about pyramids of biomass that would be included in the unit. But how the concepts or generalizations are illustrated is variable. Our recommendation would be to select locally meaningful examples to be described and explained rather than focusing on the spectacular, such as the Serengheti lions or tidal pool ecology from a land-locked Iowan view. All of the ecological interactions in the tidal pool have their midwest counterparts, which can be found in a locally accessible pond or stream. Not only will locally occurring examples be potentially more meaningful to students, but the likelihood that they will use their knowledge to interpret new situations may be enhanced.

What Did the Students Learn?

At the end of each marking period, parents and school personnel will want to know how well each student is doing in class. There are a couple of questions to be considered: What type of information should be provided? How should that information be gathered? Let's take these questions one at a time.

What to Say About What Students Learned

Donna was eighth in her class in science.

Donna correctly answered 77% of the questions on all tests and homework.

Donna understood that air pressure increased as the air temperature dropped but did not understand that this was related to molecules moving more slowly and farther apart.

Each of these statements could be made regarding Donna's performance, yet each says something quite different. The first indicates how one student's learning compares to that of other students. The second implies that the student has learned 77% of what she was expected to learn. The third explicitly indicates what the student knew and did not know.

Which statement should a teacher be able to make? Certainly the last one. That statement provides the most explicit and useful information about what the student has learned. It indicates not only the area in which the student was competent but also an area where additional instruction might be needed. In addition, this type of descriptive statement is needed in order for more general ones to be made. It would be difficult to ascertain that a student was eighth in her class or had been successful 77% of the time without first knowing what the student knew and did not know.

How Can the Needed Information Be Collected?

Probably the most important factor in making adequate evaluations is an awareness of what students were supposed to have learned. There probably were particular cognitions (concepts, empirical laws, theoretical laws) or cognitive skills (science processes such as classifying plants or predicting how air pressure might change) that guided instruction. These objectives should also guide evaluation: teachers are obligated to evaluate students on what they expected them to learn. To do otherwise would be unfair.

Once it has been determined what the students are to learn and instruction has been provided, there are many ways to collect evidence about the student's performance. The most common are multiple choice, true-false, short answer, problem solving, or essay tests. In each of these evaluation procedures tests should be constructed so that there is a direct correspondence between objectives and test items. However, in science there is another method of evaluating students that is effective.

This procedure is to provide students with an actual event or object, then ask them to formulate a description, explanation, or prediction related to the event. For example, students could be asked to describe and explain what is happening when they are shown a glass of ice water that has water (dew) forming on the outside. Such a test could be administered in a variety of ways. A demonstration might be conducted for an entire class and a written response required. For younger students the written response might include drawing or completing pictures. Alternatively, students could be interviewed individually or could do the activity as part of a learning center and tape record their responses to one or more questions.

The major advantage to this type of assessment is related to the range of possible student responses. Students are not restricted to selecting an answer predetermined by the teacher as in the case of multiple choice tests. All students have a chance to respond, and their statements can range from simply providing the facts they observe to more sophisticated theoretical explanations. In this way a teacher can better understand the depth and breadth of a student's understanding. If in their response students correctly use the science concepts and generalizations that were included in instruction, each can be identified. If they use incorrect ideas those too can be identified.

On the basis of such responses a student's correct, incorrect, and missing conceptions can be identified so that additional instruction can be provided. In addition, students can be compared, or the proportion of the content they learned can be determined. Most importantly, though, students, parents, and school personnel can be adequately informed regarding what the students have and have not learned.

Conclusion

We have attempted to construct a general framework for thinking about four important areas of elementary school science:

Why should science be taught in the elementary school?
What science should be taught?
How should it be taught?
How should student learning be evaluated?

While this framework is incomplete, we hope that it does raise some issues that an elementary school teacher will consider.

In the final analysis, teaching science in the elementary school is well worth the commitment in time and energy that it takes to be successful. One observation of the enthusiasm that elementary school children have for well-taught science should be enough to convince any conscientious teacher that science is an important part of the elementary school curriculum.

Thoughts About Teaching Elementary School Mathematics

M. Vere DeVault
University of Wisconsin
George M.A. Stanic
University of Georgia

As one of their many responsibilities, most elementary school teachers spend part of each day trying to help children see the world through the eyes of mathematics. The following introduces some fundamental ideas that might help teachers as they attempt to carry out this difficult task. These ideas are presented in five sections. The first two sections include suggestions for organizing learning experiences and selecting instructional materials. The last three sections focus on specific issues (uses of technology in the classroom, problem solving, and basic skills) that are controversial issues within the mathematics education community and within society as a whole. Although these five sections represent neither all that is accepted nor all that is disputed in elementary mathematics instruction, the ideas presented should be helpful to classroom teachers who must make many important decisions as they interact with the children in their classrooms.

Written expressly for *Preparing for Reflective Teaching*.

A Basic Framework for Mathematics Instruction

Readiness, introduction, development, practice for mastery, and maintenance—these five steps represent the ideal sequence of instruction for
topics in elementary school mathematics. Making experiences sequential
for learners is a continual task of the classroom teacher and has been a
major concern of curriculum theorists for many decades. John Dewey
wrote extensively about the need to begin instruction with ordinary life
experiences; the task of the teacher is to organize these experiences so
that the child eventually comes to understand subject matter as it is
known by the mature person. It is this link between ordinary life experience and organized subject matter that forms the basis of the five step
instructional sequence just presented. It is appropriate, then, that instruction begin with a readiness phase.

During readiness, a teacher capitalizes on the many and varied experiences that each student brings to and finds in the classroom. A child's
life in and out of school is filled with experiences that can potentially
serve as readiness activities; the key is whether or not the teacher takes
advantage of such ordinary life experiences. In order to do this, a teacher
must be able to think ahead about where certain experiences can lead.
For instance, even children in kindergarten may be informally introduced to the concept of division. In planning a field trip to the zoo, a
teacher may ask a class of twenty-five children, "If each car will hold
five of you, how many cars will we need to take to the zoo?" Real world
situations may never work out so clearly (for example, there may be
twenty-three children, perhaps each car does not really hold the same
number of children, and so forth). The children should consider such
real world "dilemmas" as they arise.

The second step in the sequence is the introduction stage. This
marks the movement from the informal readiness stage to the point
where a particular skill or concept is formally introduced to the children. Most of what is typically thought of as formal instruction from a
teacher or a textbook is part of the introduction stage. The concept or
skill informally discussed during readiness is now formally identified
and explained, and children are made aware of what is expected of
them in terms of their own performance and understanding. For instance, after children have encountered numerous division readiness
experiences such as the one described earlier, the concept of division
may be formally introduced in grade three.

Following closely behind the step that introduces a concept or skill
is the development stage. Readiness, just before introduction, and
development, just after introduction, are, perhaps, the two most neglected aspects of mathematics instruction; yet each is vital. A good
teacher recognizes that a child cannot be expected to master a concept

or skill immediately after it is introduced. Children need time to develop both their understanding and their skill. The concept of division may have been formally introduced, but children still experiment with various ways to solve division exercises. They may, for instance, solve division exercises using repeated subtraction:

$$29 \div 7 = ? \qquad \begin{array}{r} 29 \\ -\ 7 \ (1) \\ \hline 22 \\ -\ 7 \ (2) \\ \hline 15 \\ -\ 7 \ (3) \\ \hline 8 \\ -\ 7 \ (4) \\ \hline 1 \end{array} \qquad 29 \div 7 = 4 \ R1$$

As the children experiment with various ways to solve division exercises, they come to appreciate the efficient technique introduced by the teacher:

$$\begin{array}{r} 4 \ R1 \\ 7\overline{)29} \\ 28 \\ \hline 1 \end{array}$$

It is important to remember that the link with the real world should continue throughout development. The formal computational technique is just another way to express such a link; it should not reflect a break with the experiences the children have had. Children should be encouraged in the development stage to use real situations and concrete objects to maintain that vital tie. It is during the stage of development that the majority of the movement from an informal to a more formal organization of subject matter actually takes place as the children become more comfortable with the formal representation. With reference to the real world constantly maintained, the children move from an informal readiness to a formal introduction, to a developmental period during which the relationship between the informal and formal levels of understanding are recognized and brought together in a consistent and coherent whole. It is at this point that the practice for mastery stage begins.

During this mastery stage, the children develop competence in the particular concept or skill. Standards of this competence are established with the children. These standards will take various forms depending upon whether children are to master a computational skill or a concept not necessarily associated with computation. If the children are to become competent at division with one-digit divisors, a teacher may establish standards of both accuracy and speed. What exactly should those standards be? How many exercises must a child solve correctly to be considered, competent? Is 100% too stringent a standard? Is 80% not stringent enough? How important is speed? Teachers deal with groups of children that present a stimulating range of unique characteristics. Can there be an ultimate standard that will apply to all of them for all the things they learn? How should standards differ for different children? These are important issues that must ultimately be addressed by each teacher in every classroom.

The task is not complete with the attainment of a specified level of mastery, however, for two main reasons. First, mastery is maintained only through periodic review. Second, the skills and concepts that have been mastered must not be looked upon as ends in themselves, but as the basis for further growth and development through their use in various applications. As Dewey said, "[One] must constantly regard what is already won not as a fixed possession, but as an agency and instrumentality for opening new fields which make new demands upon existing powers of observation and of intelligent use of memory."[1] Maintenance activities for the computational technique with a one-digit divisor, for example, continue throughout the rest of the elementary grades. The computational skill serves as the basis for a number of other skills, from division with two-digit divisors to division with decimals. What has been learned about the division concept is eventually related to fractions; to ideas of ratio, proportion, and percent; and to the algebraic manipulation of mathematics sentences. A topic can be considered "mastered," but maintenance never ends—either inside or outside of the school.

Instructional Materials

Teachers must continually make decisions about what instructional materials to use, and how and when to use them. The basic framework described above can help guide such decisions. As children move from readiness to mastery experiences, they are also moving from concrete to abstract representations of mathematical ideas. In the division example above, children begin by actually "living through" an exercise in division; they "divide" the class into various groups for the trip to the zoo. Later, when division is formally introduced, children may use blocks, counters, or other "manipulatives" to represent a real world situation. Finally, when a skill is mastered, the mathematical idea is represented by its most abstract form—the efficient computational technique.

This movement from concrete to abstract can be shown in another way, in the context of developing children's understanding of basic numeration ideas. An egg carton with two holders cut off can be used as a "ten tray." In order to show "23" concretely, two ten trays are filled and three single counters are placed next to the ten trays. After working with these ten trays for a period of time, children soon use an empty ten tray to represent one ten (that is, they no longer have to place ten counters in the tray in order to see it as representing one ten). This is a first step in abstraction. As a final step, of course, children write and understand a numeral without aids of any kind.

The movement from concrete to abstract representation of ideas has important implications for the use of textbooks. Above all, it must be remembered that textbooks are not enough. With the busy and often hectic daily routine of the elementary school teacher, sole reliance on the textbook becomes a real possibility. While this response to daily pressures is understandable, it is also most unfortunate. A program that consists only of a textbook and paper-and-pencil activities is inadequate, and it misrepresents the vital link between mathematics and the everyday experiences of children.

Uses of Technology in Mathematics Instruction

Much of the debate surrounding the use of technology in the classroom is centered on the need to defend and even to improve the humanistic quality of classroom environments; many people expect that humanistic quality to be eroded through the introduction of more technology into the school.[2] Though there are many efforts underway to develop instructional programs that use the technology now available, there is little agreement about what that technology should be designed to do and how it should be integrated into classroom environments. As usual, when there is a lack of professional agreement on an issue, individual teachers will have much to say about the uses of technology in their own classrooms. It would seem, then, that our responsibility as teachers is to understand as thoroughly as possible the potential uses of technology so that each of us is in a strong position to make decisions about its use or nonuse in the classroom. Though many examples of technology could be discussed, two are focused on here: the hand-held calculator and the microcomputer.

Hand-Held Calculators.   The hand-held calculator has recently been the subject of much debate and experimentation in the elementary classroom. Opinions range from those who believe the calculator should be used at all grade levels in a variety of ways to those who believe that, especially in the lower grades, there should be no use of calculators because of a fear their use will be detrimental to the development of computational skills. Available research results[3] at this time seem to support the use of the hand-held calculator. The evidence generally shows that children who used calculators were as good as or better in computational skills than children in control groups. There is little evidence that their understandings or attitudes differ from those of children in control groups.

Calculators have been used by children to check their work, thus increasing their experience in estimating, approximating, and verifying answers. Their use in games is designed to provide practice in mathematical applications and for motivation. Calculators used for computation make it possible for children to work with word problems and other types of problem solving that are more realistic and of more interest because of the size of the numbers and the number of calculations that can be made with the calculator in a short period of time. An additional consideration for teachers, school districts, and parents is that the minimal cost of hand-held calculators makes them readily available to almost all children.

Microcomputers. Microcomputers can be used to provide *Computer-Assisted Instruction* (CAI) or *Computer-Manager Instruction* (CMI). There are several specific kinds of CAI uses of microcomputers in mathematics instruction. Probably the first and most frequently used mode is drill and practice. Programs designed to provide drill and practice typically include a management system that stores information about the progress and computer experience of each student. Each time students sign on, they are greeted by their first name, and usually a comment is made about what they had completed when they were last working in the program. From there, the computer might present a few computational examples for review before providing new computational drill material. While at the terminal, an individual student reacts to enough exercises to develop mastery of the skill being practiced.

In a tutorial mode, the microcomputer is used to present new content to learners. And here again, as in the case of drill and practice, the microcomputer has the potential to provide this instruction to students individually. In the past the tutorial mode in radio, film, and television technology has failed to capture the hearts of classroom teachers. Can the microcomputer do better? Until more creative programs become available, that question cannot be answered, but there does seem to be a potential for the tutorial mode in serving as an interactive agent in the development of mathematical concepts. Just as the teacher may use a set of manipulatives in the demonstration of mathematical ideas before an entire class, so the microcomputer can invite the student to arrange and rearrange visual images of these manipulatives in ways that enhance understanding of the mathematical idea. As an instructional service to the individual student, the number and variety of situations presented can be made dependent on the needs of the individual. Because the microcomputer serves the individual rather than the entire class and because it provides interactive capability for the learner and computer to respond to each other, there is reason to expect that the fate of instruction with microcomputers may differ from the fate of earlier technological aids to education instruction.

As a tool in problem solving, the microcomputer may serve instruction in two ways: by providing computational power, making it possible to work with problems that are more realistic and more interesting because number size need not be a limiting factor and by providing experience in computer programming. Computer programming is a continuing series of problem-solving experiences that focuses on the determination of the logic involved in the nature of the problem and the communication of that logic to the machine and to users.

Computer-Managed Instruction (CMI) is designed to keep classroom records of various kinds. In traditional classrooms, recordkeeping is usually thought of as including grades and attendance. These are the visible records, but, in reality, the teacher keeps many other kinds of information as each day progresses: how a student's performance today compares with yesterday's performance, what success certain materials generated with certain children, what resource materials are in the classroom, what level of achievement each child has attained in each of the major content areas of the curriculum, and what instructional materials are preferred by individual students. To be sure, all of this information places a heavy load on the teacher, busy with the minute-by-minute happenings in the classroom. Information is forgotten; appropriate resources go unused; student preferences are ignored; continued work is required of children after they have demonstrated mastery; and both remedial and maintenance assignments are inconsistently made. CMI may not solve all of these problems, but many educators believe it can help.

Problem Solving

Problem solving is frequently discussed today. Many questions have been raised about the nature of problem solving and the extent to which traditional kinds of word problems are adequate. If one accepts the following definition of a "problem," there are a number of consequences for classroom instruction: A problem exists when a person is motivated to seek an answer to a question but has no readily available strategy that will guarantee a correct solution.

The two main elements of this definition are worthy of clarification. The first is the part that declares: a problem exists when a person is motivated to seek an answer to a question. The emphasis here is on motivation, for there is little likelihood that problem solving will occur without it. The second is the part that suggests that a problem exists when the person has no readily available strategy that will guarantee a correct solution. This means that if the student knows specifically how to proceed, there is no problem. What is a problem for one person, therefore, may not be a problem for another person. Similarly, what is a problem for a person at one time may not be a problem at another time.

Four types of problems can be identified. The first type consists of traditional word problems or story problems. Based on the above definition, they may or may not be adequate examples of "problems." Too often, what is called a word problem is nothing more than a practice exercise. Practice exercises have their proper place, but one should not confuse practice exercises with problem-solving experiences. Though many textbook word problems are in quite simple format, when made more complex (that is, when larger numbers are used and more steps are involved), they do represent challenging problems to learners.

A second kind of problem is represented in the way teachers present new ideas, either in teaching computational skills or mathematical concepts. Late in the second grade or early in the third, for instance, children learn to add and subtract two-digit numbers when renaming or regrouping is required. Consider the following example:

$$\begin{array}{r} 37 \\ + 25 \\ \hline \end{array}$$

This can be presented to children in either of two ways. On the one hand, it can be presented in a direct tutorial mode with the teacher explaining how the numbers can be renamed into tens and ones; how the ones and then the tens can be added; and how, finally, the tens and ones can be renamed again.

$$\begin{array}{ll} \begin{array}{r} 3\text{ tens }\;7\text{ ones} \\ +\;2\text{ tens }\;5\text{ ones} \\ \hline 5\text{ tens }12\text{ ones} \\ 62 \end{array} & \text{or} \quad \begin{array}{r} 30 + 7 \\ +\;20 + 5 \\ \hline 50 + 12 \\ 62 \end{array} \end{array}$$

On the other hand, in a problem-solving mode, it is assumed that children have learned to add two-digit numbers that do not require renaming and that they are used to exploring mathematical ideas; so when presented with an addition example or question, they find their own method of determining the sum. As individuals or groups of children, with help from the teacher, seek to find the answer—one that seems reasonable—they are solving a problem as we have defined it. At first, they may use unique and varied ways of solving the problem. Later, they learn there is a regular or standard way of solving this kind of example; and when confronted with further examples, they perceive them not as problems to be solved, but as computational tasks to be accomplished. The way we introduce new ideas, then, determines whether such experiences qualify as examples of problem solving.

The distinction between these two ways of presenting new material can be viewed as the relative position of teacher instruction and independent exploration time. In the first example, the teacher tells children what is to be done, and then the children work independently to practice what they have been told to do. In the second example, the children begin their independent work immediately, and after this exploration, the teacher helps the children share with one another and to talk about what they have learned before they proceed to another stage of independent study, this time, practice.

These first two problem types have been taken from typical textbook/classroom instruction. The first consists of the word problems found in the texts, and the second is concerned with the sequence of teacher-student activities associated with the introduction of a new topic. The third type of problem is frequently found in supplementary materials outside of the regular mathematics textbook and is represented by a host of mathematics situations that draw heavily on patterns, geometry, or number theory. Consider the following examples:

1. What numbers should be placed in the blanks in each sequence?
   1, 1, 2, 3, 5, __, 13, 21, __, 55, __
   1, 3, 2, __, 3, 5, __, __, 5, __, 6, __, 7
   2, 3, 5, 7, __, 13, 17, __, 23, __, 31
   Find the smallest numbers with 6 divisors.

2. Cubes formed from unit blocks are hollowed out so that only the outside blocks are left. How many blocks are hollowed out of 3 × 3 × 3 cube, a 6 × 6 × 6 cube, and a 12 × 12 × 12 cube?

3. Two straight lines may intersect once. Three straight lines may be drawn so that there are three points of intersection. What is the maximum number of intersections when four, five, or six straight lines are drawn?

Though such problems are increasingly found in textbooks as enrichment activities, they are not typically a part of the regular mathematics curriculum. Other sources of these activities range from workbooks to the special interest and knowledge of the teacher.

Finally, a fourth kind of problem is represented by mathematical applications in subjects other than mathematics. Science, social studies, the arts, physical education, and the language arts all provide abundant opportunities to use mathematics in a problem-solving mode. In science, study of the relation between variables requires substantial use of mathematics. The relationships between temperature and air pressure, light and plant growth, weight and distance from the fulcrum, speed and distance, and pressure and depth under the water represent problems of interest that can be solved in a variety of ways—all using mathematics. In the arts, perspective drawing provides experiences in geometry, and in social studies, one can make comparisons among the productivity, income, travel, and history of particular people. All of these investigations require a variety of uses of mathematics.

If problem solving should be a major goal of instruction, these four types of problems provide a view of curriculum in which problem solving may permeate a large portion of the mathematics children experience. Because there is not clear agreement on the nature of problem solving, on what problem-solving skills are most essential for young learners, or on the extent to which problem solving should permeate the curriculum, individual teachers have considerable freedom and responsibility in determining the emphasis they place on this aspect of the mathematics curriculum.

Basic Skills

Discussions in the popular press and in professional circles repeatedly focus on the need to improve basic skills of students in mathematics. It appears that the present debates over this recurring theme are more persistent and insistent than those of the recent past.

At least two different positions have been taken by proponents of improved basic skills instruction. One group has a limited view of basic skills and speaks of improving computational competence in the four operations with whole numbers, fractions, and decimals. A second group defines basic skills in a larger sense and calls for improvement in problem solving, applying mathematics in everyday situations, being alert to the reasonableness of results, estimating and approximating, acquiring appropriate computational skills, mastering geometry and measurement, reading, interpreting, and constructing tables, charts, and graphs, using mathematics to predict, and gaining computer literacy.[4]

Classroom teachers are faced with conflicting messages. On the one hand, they are told to consider the benefits of new advances in technology and to focus on problem solving. On the other hand, they are urged to focus on teaching basic computational skills. Though no one would argue against computational competence as a reasonable goal, there is potential danger in overemphasizing a limited view of basic skills. Teaching mathematics means teaching a unique way of looking at our world; knowing how to compute is only one small part of that. There is considerable variation among teachers, even within the same elementary school, as to how they view the basic skills. Individual teachers are left, therefore, to define their own views of basic skills, and those views are reflected in the practices they implement in their classrooms.

A Concluding Thought

In the first part of this discussion, a five-step instructional sequence was discussed as an appropriate way to view mathematics instruction. In a similar way, becoming a teacher can be linked to those five steps. The experiences gained as a student in elementary, secondary, and higher education can be viewed as a part of the informal readiness for teaching. The first course in education provides a formal introduction and methods work with associated observation and participation in the schools is a developmental stage. It is not until student teaching and even the first years of full-time teaching, however, that major practice for mastery occurs. Finally, through inservice workshops and university courses, teachers take part in maintenance activities that revitalize and expand their commitment and skills. Throughout the entire sequence, each person must reflect on the fundamental problems and issues of instruction in the classroom, some of which have been introduced here. The fact that the most important issues are so difficult to resolve requires a significant commitment on the part of teachers; it also makes teaching the exciting and rewarding experience that it can be.

Notes

[1] J. Dewey, *Experience and education* (New York: Collier Books, 1938), p. 75.

[2] G. T. Fox and M. V. DeVault, "Technology and humanism in the classroom: Frontiers of educational practice," *Educational Technology* 14 (1974): 7-14.

[3] J. F. Weaver, "Research on calculators: Implications for classrooms of the 1980s," in *Mathematics education research: Implications for the 80s*, ed. E. Fennema (Alexandria, Va.: Association for Supervision and Curriculum Development, 1981).

[4] National Council of Teachers of Mathematics, *An agenda for action: Recommendations for school mathematics of the 1980s* (Reston, Va.: National Council of Teachers of Mathematics, 1980).

Many teachers avoid dealing with art in any depth, claiming that they are "unartistic" or untrained in art appreciation. In the next article, Beyer challenges you to reexamine the way art is usually viewed in schools. Viewed in the way Beyer advocates, art can and should have a very meaningful place in any classroom.

What Role for the Arts in the Curriculum?

Landon E. Beyer
Knox College

One of the persistent problems within the curriculum field is how to determine what knowledge is most beneficial, worthwhile, or valuable, and thus worthy of inclusion in a school program.[1] Out of a virtual universe of possibilities, we must select those disciplines or areas of study, and those specific topics within them, which are most educationally appropriate. Criteria must be developed to allocate both time and resources within the school so that the curriculum reflects what is most educationally viable from that universe of possibilities. While the search for definitive answers and unquestionable criteria is probably futile, reminding ourselves that the process of curriculum making is a necessarily selective one may serve to bring into sharper focus the question of what (and *whose*) ideas, values, and perspectives we ought to embody as teachers.

The problem of deciding upon what disciplines and topics to include within the school's curriculum is not totally explicable as a process of rational decision making. Whatever content areas we seek to incorporate within the curriculum do not arise solely through a process of reasoned discourse but come to us already filtered and distilled in ways that we may be only partially aware of. This process of filtering and distilling is in a large part the result of whatever traditions and perceptions surround our understanding of these areas. The view we have of any discipline will be affected by what we perceive or assume that field to be: what are its central tenets, ways of proceeding, and special insights. Such perception—accurate or not—will in turn color how we regard that discipline as a possible ingredient in the school's curriculum. Our attitude regarding the desirability of a natural science curriculum, for instance, will rely upon whatever perceptions and traditions accompany our understanding of the sciences. And not just our own personal view,

Written expressly for *Preparing for Reflective Teaching.*

but the larger, more generalized societal perspective on the natural sciences will play an important role in this regard. This is of some significance for determining curriculum practice and policy. We may condone certain sorts of natural science curricula—or specific topics or areas within such a curricula—while rejecting, down-playing, or simply remaining unaware of others because of our understanding of what constitutes this area. This same understanding will be useful in deciding the overall constitution and shape of the school curriculum: what subjects ought to be given more and less emphasis, how they ought to be organized, and so on. Our sentiments about what content areas to include in the curriculum, and the relative value of any one of them, is affected by our sense of the possibilities and limitations inherent in any given discipline. It is important, then, to consider how a subject area is peceived and valued within a society, and by those within our educational institutions, in analyzing what knowledge to include as a part of the school curriculum.

Frequently it is suggested that a society's traditions in painting, literature, music, architecture, and so on, mark the supreme achievement of that society or age, that the various art forms make a central contribution to the "good life" (however that is defined). Within our own society, it is often alleged that our greatest works of art do indeed represent at least important manifestations of our culture; we spend vast amounts of money to purchase particular works of art, especially paintings, while the investment of time and energy in artistic appreciation seems to be on the rise.[2] All of these tendencies lend support to the view that the arts are an important thread in the social fabric. At the same time, however, we must recognize the very real ambiguity that marks the position of the arts in contemporary society. For while certain tendencies as noted above appear to foster the social status of the arts, there are countervailing tendencies as well. Artists are often viewed with some suspicion, as living on the fringes of respectable society, occupying less than laudable social and occupational roles. The "fine arts" (especially opera, ballet, and certain forms of classical music) are frequently viewed, with some scepticism, as the province of a snobbish elite, and the claim that artistic endeavors are "impractical," play-full, quasi-leisure (and thus not totally serious) activities is commonly heard. Each of these assertions expresses doubt as to the importance and viability of the arts in American society.

Similar contradictions regarding the place and value of the arts operate in schools. We speak in praise of teaching as "an art form," hoping to provide an alternative posture to our overly technological profession; we promote various artistic productions (concerts, plays, art and craft shows, literary creations, and so on) as evidence of a school's commitment to excellence, and offer art classes out of some fundamental (if vague) commitment to developing "the whole child." On the other hand, we devote comparatively little time to curricular areas dealing with the arts;[3] we offer a number of art classes as electives, while other subjects are required; we schedule music, art, and drama classes as "specials" (for example, "non-basics") to be fit into the school week almost as an afterthought. It is precisely such areas that are mentioned as "frills," representing subjects that may be justifiably cut back or eliminated altogether in times of budgetary crisis such as the one we are now in.

In and out of schools, we commend the arts with one hand while using the other to keep them at arm's length, provide rhetorical support for their expansion while undercutting substantive involvement, heap praise upon their alleged accomplishments at the same time we curtail future possibilities. How can we account for these apparent contradictions of dualisms? Is there any way to make sense of this "manic/depressive" state in which the arts are held captive in our schools and in our society at large?

To understand the predicament of the arts requires an analysis of something I mentioned above: the specific traditions that stand behind our understanding of the arts and aesthetics.[4] Only by looking at such traditions will we understand why we are caught in a kind of artistic and aesthetic schizophrenia and what we might do to overcome it.

While the traditions within the arts and aesthetics that have shaped our contemporary understanding are numerous, there are four particular ideas or concepts that have had a profound and lasting affect on our understanding of art. These concepts include: 1) aesthetic disinterestedness, 2) psychical distance, 3) aesthetic perception, and 4) aesthetic formalism. Even though these four areas are closely interrelated in our experience with the arts, I will deal with each of them individually so that the major characteristics of each may be clearly delineated.

Aesthetic Disinterestedness

To be *dis*interested (or to act in a disinterested way) is not the same as being *un*interested in something. This concept does not ask people to be lackadaisical, apathetic, or uninvolved. Rather, to be disinterested is to make and act on decisions without concern for their effects or consequences. To be disinterested is to value some decision or action not as a means to some external end but on the basis of the inherent correctness of that action itself. An example here may clarify what is involved in this concept. If we are presented with an ethical dilemma that demands some decision, say whether or not we should repay a debt that the lender has forgotten about, we would either withhold or make the appropriate payment without considering the consequences of our decision one way or the other. Instead we would focus on the inherent correctness of our action, in taking a disinterested perspective. In general, to be disinterested is to take a nonutilitarian perspective on our actions and ways of thinking.

To be aesthetically disinterested, therefore, means that we should only pay attention to the poem, painting, or piece of music we are concerned with, and not worry about the consequences it may have for us after we have finished our appreciation of it. In this view the possible impact of the work of art is limited to the actual time we spend on it. Its affect on us outside of this encounter is unimportant and irrelevant.

To be disinterested in this way requires an important sort of selflessness. As a contemporary spokesperson for this point of view has remarked, "perception cannot be disinterested unless the spectator forsakes all self-concern and therefore trains attention upon the object for its own sake."[5] In a significant sense, our enjoyment of a work of art must be impersonal since its impact on us is limited to the actual time we spend attending to that work.

Psychical Distance

This component of our aesthetic heritage is concerned with another sort of separation of art from our thoughts and interests. Rather than putting physical distance between ourselves and a work of art, we are instructed to distance ourselves psychologically from it. Basically this involves putting art "out of gear" with our other activities and experiences, so that art is not connected with our "practical concerns." The classic essay dealing with this phenomenon suggests that even a potentially dangerous situation—being engulfed by a fog while on a ship at sea—can have an aesthetic effect:

> Abstract from the experience of the sea fog, for the moment, its danger and practical unpleasantness; direct the attention to the features 'objectively' constituting the phenomenon. . . and the experience may acquire, in its uncanny mingling of repose and terror, a flavor of such concentrated poignancy and delight as to contrast sharply with the blind and distempered anxiety of its other aspects.[6]

The appearance of fog for a ship's passenger is a cause for practical alarm since it diminishes visibility, thereby increasing the risk of collision. Yet even this potentially perilous situation can be aesthetically pleasing if we psychologically distance ourselves from the fog and its dangers. Paying attention to the fog itself—its moving, nebulous outline and shapes, the cloud of mystery and suspense it symbolizes, and so on—becomes a possibility only if we put our practical concerns, worries, and fears to one side. It is this conscious disavowal of the practical side of our lives that "psychical distance" is designed to achieve.

Aesthetic Perception

The two previously discussed notions—aesthetic disinterestedness and psychical distance—reinforce and extend each other in various ways. In developing the sort of disposition that follows from these ideas, a particular kind of perception is necessary. The aesthetic perception that results may be distinguished from our more usual, everyday perception in many ways. While we are usually preoccupied with a concern for accomplishing objectives, meeting expectations, and realizing aims, aesthetic perception requires a different outlook. Instead of thinking about art as a means to some end or goal, it is the object "in and of itself" that ought to guide our response to an art work. In *Aesthetic and Philosophy of Art Criticism*, Jerome Stolnitz notes that, "On occasion we pay attention to a thing simply for the sake of enjoying the way it looks or sounds or feels. This is the 'aesthetic' attitude of perception."[7] The type of experience that results from this sort of perception is of particular interest. Such an experience, Stolnitz continues,

> . . . seems to isolate us and the object from the flow of experience. The object is being admired for itself, is divorced from its interrelations with other things. And we feel as though life had suddenly been arrested, for we are absorbed wholly in the object before us and abandon any thought of purposive activity toward the future.[8]

The act of implementing this aesthetic perception produces its own context, a context separated from everyday social interactions and thoughts. Both the personal, practical interests we have as people, and the historical and social context of the work of art, are to be disregarded. Aesthetic perception is thus an attempt to dislocate the painting, play, or poem, and the person experiencing it, so that the resulting experience is severed from other people, experiences, and contexts. It is an experience that is almost totally autonomous.

Aesthetic Formalism

The preceding ideas lead inevitably to a focus on the internal qualities of the art object. Since we are to focus attention on the work of art itself rather than any consequences it may hold for us as art appreciators, distance ourselves psychologically from the art object, and isolate our perception from practical, everyday concerns, the only arena left as a focus for our attention is the realm of the inherent qualities of that object or event itself. These are often called the "surface qualities" of the art work and refer to such things as the pitch, tempo, and rhythm of music; the color, shading, brush stroke, and symmetry seen in paintings; and the camera angle, sequence of shots, and relationship of sound to visual image contained in film. As a result we have focused on the "looks of things" as the primary element in aesthetic experience. As one writer has expressed this, "If a thing looks to have a characteristic which is a desirable one from another point of view, its looking so is a proper ground of aesthetic appreciation. What makes the appreciation aesthetic is that it is concerned with a thing's looking somehow without concern for whether it really is like that; beauty we may say, to emphasize the point, is not even skin deep."[9] It is the arrangement of an object's "surface qualities" that becomes the center of attention in our appreciation of art works. An abiding concern for the form of the work of art is thus generated.[10] This is what is meant by aesthetic formalism as one of the dominant traditions that has shaped our contemporary understanding of art.

The concepts of disinterestedness, psychical distance, aesthetic perception, and aesthetic formalism can be seen as contributing to the development of what is known as a "presentational aesthetic." Only those qualities or features actually *present* in the art work form the basis for our experience with works of art. The effect of such ideas is to abstract the work of art from our more usual or common experiences, providing it a life, purpose, and value of its own.

It has often been concluded, as a result of this approach to aesthetic experience, that "*aesthetic experience is an experience which is valued intrinsically*, an experience which is valued for itself."[11] In addition to isolating the arts from any social or historical context and removing the personal ideas of those involved with the arts, this approach also restricts what is to count as aesthetic *value*. The only value that the arts can have is to be found precisely in the interrelationship of those surface qualities that are the focus of attention. The appreciation of a poem's structure, use of metaphor, and rhyme scheme, or of a painting's use of color, shading, placement of figures, and so on, becomes the substance of aesthetic value.

To emphasize and even isolate the surface qualities of art works is not always a bad practice, of course. Pointing to how the features of a painting are related, how they work together to produce some effect, and so on, may well be helpful in understanding what that work is about. But this approach to the arts places them outside the realm of other, allegedly more pressing, concerns. As a result, the arts may be regarded as the ephemeral, pale offspring of more central, fundamental issues and concerns. Within such an orientation the arts serve primarily a decorative or ornamental function, cut off from any personal or social activities in which we are engaged.

The influence of these traditions on our understanding of art, both in society generally and in school in particular, has been substantial. Recall the contradictions in our treatment of art noted earlier: the tendency to see art as potentially enlightening, to celebrate artistic productions in society and in schools, and to see the arts as contributing to the enhancement of "the whole person" and to the realization of the "good life;" while at the same time we frequently view artists with some disdain, regard the arts as a kind of leisure activity, designed for a snobbish elite, and regard art classes in the public schools as frills. We recognize, however vaguely, the power of art at the same time that we are suspicious, even fearful, of it.

The four aspects of our traditions in aesthetics discussed above directly contribute to this unhappy state of affairs. We have separated art from life, providing it a special domain or universe, divorced from the commitments, ideas, and activities that motivate other aspects of our lives. In focusing attention exclusively on the surface qualities of a poem or piece of music, we limit its impact and value: it can only be significant for the time we actually read or listen to it. Any impact the art work may have on us in our more usual, day to day activities is outlawed. Within such an approach, art has little chance of being seen as a central, vital concern. In removing art from other concerns, we have overprotected it, thus insuring its impotence. It is little wonder that we regard the creative artist as somehow different from other workers and builders. He or she may become socially ostracized because the realm of artistic production is conceived as fundamentally different from other work activities.

It is also not surprising that we regard the arts as occupying a less than totally serious domain, even as creating leisure-like activities. Since a rather wide gulf has been fixed between artistic and other endeavors, with the former being removed from our typical day to day concerns, how can the arts be regarded as totally serious? Their very essence is, in this view, tied up with their lack of practical utility. Separating the arts from our personal concerns and involvements virtually guarantees they will be taken less seriously than areas that directly relate to our needs, convictions, and commitments.

Given this characterization of what art is, we should be able to see more clearly why the arts play a relatively minimal role in the school curriculum; why art classes are normally thought to comprise some nebulous domain of "specials" within the jargon of school people; and why they frequently fall victim to the budget cutter's axe. The traditions we have inherited and that tend to further secure the position of the arts as "second class citizens."

In the remainder of this discussion I want to briefly sketch how we might recapture the power of art that has been concealed by the dominant traditions discussed above. In so doing I will also indicate some alternative traditions in the arts that, when drawn out, may provide us with some clue as to the potential of art in contributing to the "good life." These alternative traditions may serve, then, as the basis for a revised conception of the arts, a conception that may foster an alternative view of the role of the arts in the curriculum.

The dominant traditions that have influenced our contemporary understanding of art have removed it as a possible catalyst for ethical deliberation and personal involvement. Our experience with works of art, thus concerns "the realm of appearance enjoyed for its own sake, (and consequently) demands no commitment to action."[12] In the more specific question of the relationship between the arts and moral conduct, we are told that "it is naive to believe that art cannot endanger morals. It can if the viewer is unable to perceive art objects aesthetically, and the untrained perceiver is likely to have this infirmity."[13] Moral considerations are thus not only irrelevant, given the notions of aesthetic disinterestedness, psychical distance, and so on, which dominate our treatment of art, but such considerations amount to an "infirmity." It is this demarcation between the arts and ethics that I find most troubling. The alternative tradition that might replace the prevailing ideas in the field and form the basis for an alternative curriculum in the arts, must overcome this separation of art from moral reasoning, ethical conduct, and social life in general. How might this be done? Let us look initially at the question of moral reasoning itself.

We act out of moral considerations only in situations where we believe there is a correct or proper course of action to follow, for example, where it is required of us as moral persons to act in a particular way. We feel compelled to attempt the rescue of a drowning person, for instance, because we have a sense of value for human life, a sense of duty to fellow human beings, and so on. In cases such as this our actions seem intimately related to various moral guidelines, based on ethical deliberation and judgment of some sort. In this and similar situations we have some sort of (usually unwritten) "moral code" that helps us decide what to do in those circumstances. From time to time, of course, this code may change if we come to see that we have not fully considered, whether from a theoretical or empirical perspective, all the relevant facets of a given situation. For example, our view of the moral propriety of programs of "affirmative action" may well change given additional information about the history of women and minority groups, their exclusion from certain social and economic positions, etc. Again, our position regarding the morality of abortion may be altered given previously unexamined considerations concerning the quality of life, possibilities for self-fulfillment and development in conditions of material scarcity, and so on. In short, our moral considerations are to some extent fluid, subject to reconsideration and refinement.

The process of rethinking and reconsidering our moral positions can occur when we reflect upon our aesthetic experiences as well. When an art work affects our thoughts and feelings in a profound and significant way, it also affects the way we feel and think about the issues raised or the subject matter presented in the piece. Consider as an example the recent film, *Apocalypse Now*. At one level of appreciation—one consistent with the dominant traditions surrounding the arts examined earlier —we may consider and extrapolate the formal, presentational features contained in this film; elements such as camera angle, the sequence and interrelationship of scenes, lighting techniques, musical elements and their relationship to these other features, and so on, become important within this approach.

But the meaning of this film goes beyond such a recitation of the object's formal qualities. Films such as *Apocalypse Now* also say something that is of more personal significance to their audience. Specifically in this case we may come to understand something of the nature of war in general and the Vietnam War in particular, the capacity of human beings under certain circumstances to inflict pain and suffering on others, and so on. This film may add another dimension or level of meaning to our attitude toward or way of looking at these and related events in society. And such changes in attitude, in ways of seeing and feeling, can also influence what we consider to be appropriate or desirable conduct. By becoming ethically engaged with the film, the moviegoer may well be led to think and act differently about events related to the nature of our society and the effect of its military interventions. This process of rethinking and reevaluating moral questions and issues reconnects the arts with precisely those human concerns and issues that are excluded by the view of art discussed above.

Works of art present us with situations, events, and people, whether real or imagined, that can affect our thoughts, feelings, and judgment outside the face to face contact with that work. They can disclose to us something about our own life situations that might otherwise go unnoticed, unrecognized, and unappreciated. In treating a particular subject matter from a new perspective or vantage point, works of art can reveal to us something about the subject depicted which in turn helps us see both it and ourselves differently.

There is a connection between art and moral responsibility that is subtle and often overlooked in many discussions of the relationship between art and morality. This is the connection between the moral responsibility of the observer and the moral implications the work of art may have, between the scheme of morality we choose to subscribe to and the moral pronouncements suggested by the work of art. When participants are moved by a work of art to look at some situation from a previously unconsidered perspective, to view the subject matter of the piece in a fresh, new, or lively way, they may change their beliefs and opinions about that subject. If these changes in patterns of thought are of a certain sort and intensity, a change in moral attitudes and corresponding behavior may result from the artistic encounter that the viewer has undergone. We might, after watching and thinking about the meaning of *Apocalypse Now*, reconsider the nature of military involvement of the type represented, and our own personal involvement in future such wars.

Perceiving aesthetic objects can make a genuine contribution to our knowledge of the world in which we live and work and can provide us with alternative conceptions of different, divergent "worlds." Aesthetic objects can, in brief, move the viewer to enlightened social action. As D. W. Gotshalk has put this point, "we act largely on the basis of what we value and cherish. And if the fine arts at their best refine these bases of behavior, making our capacities more able and our values more wide and discriminate, they constitute a discipline in decency and a modification of character from which decent social action can spring."[14] Ultimately, I would suggest that the best artistic encounters have meaning because they tell us something about our world and allow us to see both it and possible alternatives to it in a way that fosters social action that is informed, responsive, and ethical.

To return to the problem of the contradictory status of the arts with which we began, we should see more clearly now at least part of what is necessary in order for the status of the arts to be elevated. It is not "merely" that present fiscal constraints threaten to diminish the potency of the arts; it is that we have inherited ideas and practices that tend to discount the power of art to affect our actions and involvements outside the isolated aesthetic encounter. To actualize the power of art in contributing to the "good life," we must span the gap between art and life that we have inherited.

What is required, in sum, both within schools and in the wider society, is a kind of politicization of personal and social meaning in aesthetic experience. We must acquaint our students with the power of art, its ability to change the nature of human life and existence, rather than merely concentrating on whatever surface qualities works of art possess. We must narrow the distance between "the world of art" and the "world of action" if the arts are to acquire a more central role in the school curriculum.

Notes

[1] In writing previous versions of this paper, and thinking about the issues raised, I have benefited from discussions with Mike Apple, Don Crawford, Carl Grant, Shirley Kessler, and Dan Liston.

[2] See Landon E. Beyer, "Aesthetics and the Curriculum: Ideological and Cultural Form in School Practice" (Ph.D. dissertation, University of Wisconsin-Madison, 1981).

[3] In many elementary schools, for instance, instruction in the arts takes place once or twice a week, for less than a full hour. While artistic activities may take place apart from formal art classes, these activities are often secondary, incidental, and connected with "play" or "leisure" activities.

[4] Throughout this chapter, I will employ "aesthetics" to refer to the study and analysis of issues dealing with the creation and appreciation of works of art. Thus an "aesthetic experience" is an experience that brings us in contact with a work of art, either as creator or (more often) appreciator.

[5] See Jerome Stolnitz, "On the Significance of Lord Shaftesbury in Modern Aesthetic Theory," *The Philosophical Quarterly* 11:43 (April, 1961): 107.

[6] Edward Bullough, " 'Psychical Distance' as a Factor in Art and an Aesthetic Principle," originally published in the *British Journal of Psychology* V, 87–98; reprinted in *Aesthetics: A Critical Anthology*, ed. George Dickie and Richard J. Sclafani (New York: St. Martin's Press, 1977), p. 759.

[7] Jerome Stolnitz, *Aesthetics and Philosophy of Art Criticism* (Boston: Houghton Mifflin Company, 1960), p. 34.

[8] *Ibid.*, p. 52.

[9] J. O. Urmson, "What Makes a Situation Aesthetic?" in *Contemporary Studies in Aesthetics*, ed. Francis J. Coleman (New York: McGraw-Hill Book Company, 1968).

[10] For an example of formalism in the theory of art appreciation, see DeWitt H. Parker, *The Principles of Aesthetics* (Boston: Silver, Burdett, and Company, 1920).

[11] Stanley S. Madeja with Sheila Onuska, *Through the Arts to the Aesthetic* (St. Louis, Mo.: CEMREL, Inc., 1977), p. 7.

[12] Harry S. Broudy, *The Whys and Hows of Aesthetic Education* (St. Louis, Mo.: CEMREL, Inc., 1977), p. 7.

[13] Harry S. Broudy, *Enlightened Cherishing: An Essay in Aesthetic Education* (Urbana, Ill.: University of Illinois Press, 1972), p. 48.

[14] D. W. Gotshalk, *Art and the Social Order*, 2nd edition (New York: Dover Publications, Inc., 1962), p. 213.

I spend a great deal of time listening to my students and raising questions with them. Usually when I have asked them to give me a definition of social studies, they do a fair job—but only a fair job. One will say, "Social studies is history and geography." Someone else will chime in, "It's world cultures and current events." Another student will

say, "It's a study of the family and the community." But these definitions of social studies are restrictive rather than comprehensive.

In the following paper by Gay and Cole you will see how comprehensive social studies can be, but before you read it, you might try writing your own definition. After your analysis of their article, read the
article by Cobbin and Thomashow and see how they use their communities as social studies laboratories. In these two papers, we see that
social studies is more than the material contained in a textbook or a
newspaper; it is alive and exciting, something that kids will remember
and not forget. Pay attention to how and why Cobbin and Thomashow
selected certain experiences and activities for their students.

Civic Socialization: Instructional Agenda of Social Studies

Geneva Gay
Purdue University
Bernadette Cole Slaughter
Seattle Public Schools

It's 10:30 A.M. Room 112 is dark, except for the light projecting on
the wall screen. As we enter the room the credits (for example, produced by, directed by, written by, narrated by . . .) appear on the
screen, signalling the end of the filmstrip. For the last twenty minutes
the students have been watching an audiovisual presentation on "To be
a Citizen." To the hum of the machine's cooling off, the lights are
turned on, and we overhear this conversation:

Teacher: Well, how do you feel about what you have just seen?
Student A: I had thought being a good citizen was just voting and obeying
the law.
Student B: I can accept that. But, I don't understand what being able to
communicate my thoughts and feelings have to do with citizenship.
Student C: What does owning a Cadallic have to do with citizenship? If a
person can afford to buy it why shouldn't he or she have it?
Student D: I don't know. All those people who lived long ago, those starving
children in Cambodia, and those men who went to the moon
mean nothing to me.

Written expressly for *Preparing for Reflective Teaching.*

Student E: It was a nice flick but that's all I have to say.
Student F: Why do we have to learn this stuff anyway? Doesn't being born
             in the U.S. automatically make you a citizen?
Teacher: As we discussed last week, good citizenship means many different
             things to different people. Now we can see that it can be . . . .

The conversation we have just witnessed, or some facsimile, is not
an uncommon occurrence in social studies classes. Teachers frequently
are called upon, by students, parents, the public, and other colleagues
to clarify and defend their subjects and to justify the importance of
what and how they teach. Obviously, then, teaching social studies, or
any subject, involves much more than merely transmitting knowledge
about that subject. It also includes diagnosing student needs, selecting
instructional materials, planning and coordinating learning activities,
managing classrooms behaviors (of both one's self and the students),
and translating one's own philosophy of education. Teachers must do
more than just pass along factual information about social institutions
and events to their students. They also need to deal with feelings,
attitudes, values, and actions related to social issues. It will not be
enough merely to have students learn who the Pilgrims were, why they
came to the New World, and where they settled along the Atlantic coast.
Nor will it be sufficient for students to memorize the names and locations of the member nations of OPEC. Of equal importance will be the
need for them to examine the principles of freedom and responsibility,
separation of church and state, cause-effect relationships, and how early
settlement patterns may affect present-day population distributions.
They also will need to explore the world-wide consequences of any
decisions made about oil trade by the OPEC nations, the concepts of
supply and demand, scarcity and interdependent globalism, as well as
their feelings and reactions to how world nations use political, military,
and natural resources in power negotiations.

Social studies teachers are not the only ones who must frequently
explain and defend their subject area. Other teachers have to do likewise. This need becomes even more important in times like these when
money is scarce, when attitudes are conservative, and when the competition among subjects for top billing in school curricula intensifies.
Therefore, being an effective classroom teacher requires that, at least,
one knows his or her own subject well, is familiar with some basic
principles of teaching and learning, views teaching as encompassing
more than knowledge transmission, knows a little about the other
subjects taught in schools, and understands how different school subjects fit into the overall system of teaching and learning. The following
discussion is designed to acquaint you with two basic notions of teaching a subject as they relate to social studies: what is the content body

of social studies, and how does social studies fit into the total school curricula.

The Name

Unlike some other subjects in the school curricula, social studies is not a simple one to define. Its definition is complicated by its unique nature of having "many subjects within a single subject." History, geography, economics, sociology, and government, individually and collectively, are called "social studies." One can say "social studies" and mean "history"; or "social studies" can mean several different subjects in history, such as Russian history, American history, world history, history of the Middle East, Renaissance history, and ancient history; or it can even mean five or six different subjects (for example, comparative politics, social psychology, women studies, civics, world religions). Despite the confusion over its definition, social studies does have some commonly agreed upon components. It is primarily concerned with knowledge, values, and skills about the social existence of human beings. Its interest in developing value commitments, rational thought processes, civic sensitivity, and practical social application skills make the purpose and place of the social studies in school curricula unique. Its instructional agenda is the "civic socialization" of youth.

Other subjects are concerned with socialization, too. But, only social studies has the major responsibility for teaching youth the habits, knowledge, values, and skills of effective citizenship in society. Whereas language arts, for instance, teaches reading and writing because these constitute the essence of that subject's substance, social studies uses these as *means* of getting to the body of its content. This content is derived from the principles of democracy embedded in different documents, practices, and cultural experiences of the United States and the world. Thus, the Constitution, the Declaration of Independence, human behavior, social institutions, and critical thinking are to social studies what comprehension, composition, grammar, listening, and effective communication are to language arts. Hence, social studies content is intended to develop understanding of the structures and operations of social systems (for example, governments, families, economies, religions, cultures, etc.) and human behavior in group settings.

Definitions of social studies are plentiful. They cover a wide range of perceptions. Yet, most address human relationships and citizenship education in some form or another. One such definition describes social studies as embracing bodies of knowledge and thought pertaining to relations of human beings—men, women, and children—to one another and to the physical environment in which they live and work.[1]

A notable difference among the many definitions of social studies is how to teach citizenship effectively. Some of them suggest it can be done best by teaching factual information about American history and heritage. Teachers using this approach will emphasize *knowing* the legal and constitutional requirements of citizens, the qualifications for holding public office, the techniques and value of voting, heroes and heroines who are models of good citizenship, and the privileges and responsibilities of American citizens. They believe that accurate knowledge leads to desirable behaviors. Other definitions of social studies recommend action-based learning that focuses on problems and conditions of society, and uses the methods of social scientists, critical thinking, conflict resolution, problem solving, and socio-civic participation as the pivotal points of citizenship education. Consequently, instruction emphasizes analyzing causes and consequences of persistent world crises and recurrent social issues, along with planning and implementing action programs (for example, voter registration, circulating petitions, protesting, political campaigning, and so forth) to redress these problems. Another category of social studies definitions contends that self-knowledge, self-understanding, self-direction, and self-realization are the best ways to prepare youngsters for citizenship in a democratic society and world.[2] Here teachers concentrate on how the individual student acts and reacts, thinks and feels about social experiences and events. They frequently prompt discussions with questions that ask, "What do *you think?*," "How do *you feel?*," "How did _____ affect *you?*," "What would *you* do?," "If *you* were in that person's position or circumstance, how would *you* behave?" The underlying premise here is that a person who better understands how and why the self operates as it does will be a greater benefit to society.

All of these approaches to defining the social studies and achieving effective citizenship education are interesting and challenging. But, most are still rather difficult to use as a practical guide to classroom practice. The description of social studies as "the study of human relationships in a variety of settings"[3] is much more meaningful and easier to translate into practice for many classroom teachers. Instantly, samples of "human relationships," such as the individual with self, groups, society, and the environment come to mind, as do their corresponding social studies disciplines—psychology, sociology, economics, politics, anthropology, geography, and ecology. "A variety of settings" produce images of families, neighborhoods, communities, states, regions, nations, and the world. It also helps us to see how the past, present, and future fit into the description of social studies education. If we accept this definition, we can then understand why first graders learning about the structures and functions of families, schools, play groups, and "neighborhood helpers" (for example, the friendly firefighters, the protective police officers, the concerned doctors and nurses, etc.) are developing knowledge and skills in human relationships and citizenship. So are high school students who are deciphering international diplomacy, social welfare agencies, presidential-congressional relations, and cross-national cultural patterns of group lifestyles. Thus, the "varieties and contexts of human relationships" take many shapes and forms and occur under numerous circumstances. But, they, along with the knowledge, attitudes, values, and skills needed to better understand them, still constitute the most persistent and pervasive organizing framework for planning and teaching social studies curriculum.

The Practice

When planning social studies instruction for several grades, teachers typically use an "expanding horizons," "spiralling structure," or "cyclical arrangement" of topics to organize the scope and sequence of the curriculum. This planning process emphasizes history and geography, and structure and form in studying human relationships and institutional operations. It begins with relationships and institutions closest to the individual (self, family, neighborhood), and gradually moves outward to include larger communities, and more abstract concepts, such as the state, the nation, the hemispheres, and the world. The "expanding horizons" structure is the most common design found in elementary social studies programs.

Secondary school social studies programs tend to use the "cyclical arrangement" of topics and the "spiralling curriculum" to design instruction. An example of this is teaching world history or world cultures in Grade 10 in more detail than the introductory level in Grade 6. Or, teaching civics in Grade 9 and American government in Grade 12. Each of these courses builds upon its predecessor, the first in the sequence being state history/government, which is usually introduced in Grade 4. American history is often taught in Grades 5, 8, and 11, with each subsequent course becoming increasingly more complex and contemporary. Thus, American history in Grade 5 may concentrate on exploration, colonization, and independence; in Grade 8 it may deal with the period from 1800 to World War I; and in Grade 11, the period from post World War I to the present is examined in detail.[4]

It is not uncommon for social studies curriculum designers to overlay topical, thematic, or conceptual emphases onto the standard expanding horizons organizational pattern. An example of this approach is the Scott, Foresman Elementary Social Studies Series. This program develops seven themes or concepts across grades K-7. The concepts are diversity, interdependence, self-identity, choice, power, socialization, and change. Each of the grade level books has seven units, each of which develops one of the themes. Yet, the overall structure of the program is an expanding horizons format, with the possible exception of the Grade 7 book. The following is a description of the textbook series.

Books K-3—Family, Home, School, Community
Book 4—World, including the United States
Book 5—Chronological development of U.S. History
Book 6—World cultures
Book 7—World of adolescents[5]

Scott Foresman also points with pride to the fact that "strong history and geography strands provide sequential development of both knowledge and skill"[6] in the series.

What does all this mean with respect to the practice of social studies education in schools? It seems to support the idea that social studies in practice *is* history, geography, and American government. Whether citizenship skills in these subjects are developed through teaching facts about American history and heritage is more difficult to determine. Such a determination would require a careful analysis of instructional programs actually in use in the classroom. But, when tradition, more than anything else, is used to determine *what* content is taught *when* in the social studies curriculum, it affects *how* that content is taught as well.

Is social studies a relevant subject in school? Is it important to the general education of youth? These questions are not uncommon in discussions of educational priorities, goals, funding, and achievement. Some would have us believe that social studies is a waste of valuable time and resources; others argue that it is indispensable to the general education of American youth. The dissenters may be persuaded by the "intangibility" of social studies goals and by the difficulty in measuring the achievement of its most significant objectives. "Civic socialization" and "effective citizenship" are difficult to define, and even harder to determine when they are happening. The unimpressive performance of students on standardized tests of citizenship skills and knowledge have led others to question the worth of social studies education as presently taught and learned.

On the other hand, social studies advocates give the subject a high rating. They are impressed by its ideological commitments and its close association with the general goals of education. When educators talk about "goals of schooling" they generally mean academic, job, citizenship, and personal adjustment skills that are valued in a society. Social studies advocates agree that its major goal is to teach youth knowledge, skills, and attitudes that promote citizenship in American and global societies. These include institutional structures and functions, social values, critical thinking, democratic principles, and problem solving. Therefore, both education in general and social studies in particular are committed to the socialization of youth into American and world cultures.

The Theory

Many educators have developed desirable as well as practical descriptions of social studies. That is, they are as concerned with what "should be" as they are with what "is." Reviews of textbooks on defining and teaching social studies, and publications of organizations, like the National Council for the Social Studies, reveal striking similarities about what social studies education should be. There is agreement that critical thinking, problem solving, and analyzing values constitute the essence of social studies instruction. These broad goals are supported by more specific ones like knowledge acquisition and processing and participatory skill development. Persistent efforts are made for social studies to attend equally to the cognitive, affective, and psychomotor domains of learning throughout its instructional programming.

In social studies cognitive or knowledge instruction is designed to focus on the "whats" of human relationships and institutional functions. The intent is to teach some fundamental ideas, concepts, facts, and generalizations. Although knowledge acquisition is important, it is not the end-all of social studies instruction. It is more of a means to an end, rather than an end in itself. Social studies educators are much more interested in students understanding *why* things happen than knowing *what* happens. Thus, learning to *use* information to interpret, analyze, evaluate, and apply knowledge about human behavior and social interactions is imperative. We might call these emphases "processing skills" since they include techniques for acquiring information, and the methods of critical thinking, problem solving, and analyzing values.

Analyzing values is an important skill for students to learn because social studies educators believe that attitudes, feelings, and values also are critical to understanding human motivations and behaviors. Furthermore, they believe that thinking and valuing are systematic processes that use similar step-by-step procedures. These procedures include defining the problem, hypothesizing about solutions to the problem, suggesting alternative solutions and exploring the consequences of each, collecting information pertinent to the problem, and testing the accuracy of the hypothesized solutions against the evidence or collected information.[7]

Valuing differs from critical thinking or problem solving in that it is concerned with "analysis and clarification," instead of "solutions" per se. Whereas critical thinking and decision making employ logic and reason to arrive at *the most desirable* solutions to a problem, valuing uses systematic thought to *understand* what values are and their sources and expressions, rather than to discover the "single best value" in a given situation. Hence, a social studies teacher using problem solving to study the Americans captured and held hostage in Iran for 444 days would be primarily interested in students judging the adequacy of the "release provisions," and/or alternative solutions, based on the *rationality and accuracy of the facts* involved. By comparison, valuing exercises on the same issue would require students to examine the whats and whys of *their feelings and attitudes* toward Iran and Iranians. As another example, teachers might have students discover ways to minimize conflicts among different ethnic and cultural groups in the United States. This would be problem solving. Exploring attitudes and reactions toward the civil rights movement of the 1960s, school desegregation, sexism, and euthanasia would fall into the category of valuing. Similarly, knowing the democratic principles of honesty, endurance, and the work ethic is knowledge acquisition. However, trying to determine why some people consider honesty and pleasure of a higher order than property ownership and self-denial is values analysis. Essential to both analyzing values and problem solving is the ability to distinguish factual information from opinions, evidence from propaganda, emotion from reason, what one believes and feels from what is true or real.

The relationship among knowledge, reasoning, value analysis, and action, and their significance to social studies instruction are evident throughout the professional literature. Consider, for instance, the advice of the National Council for the Social Studies that "students must come to understand that for all the importance of evidence, facts alone do not determine decisions, that there are times to suspend judgment, and that many problematic situations have no set answers."[8] Or, James Banks's belief that "What a person does with the knowledge derived from social inquiry depends largely on the values which he or she holds in regards to the decision-problem elements and components,"[9] and "Before individuals can make sound rational decisions and act intelligently, they must be helped to clarify their many conflicting and confusing values."[10] And, John Michaelis's reminder that knowledge, value analysis, and reasoning are basic skills youth must learn if social studies is to successfully teach such value-laden issues as those inherent in the democratic ideals on which the United States is founded. These skills also are necessary if students are to adequately analyze such recurrent societal concerns and world crises as the uneven distribution of resources, pollution, industrial progress and environmental abuse, overpopulation, and war and peace.[11] Finally, developing value analysis skills in conjunction with thinking and problem solving is imperative since, as Banks writes:

> the value problems of youth are intensified by the wide range of conflicting values from which they must choose, and by the contradictions between the values that adults verbally endorse and those exemplified by their actual behavior . . . . Students must be taught a *process* for deriving their values rather than set of values that educators regard as the 'right ones,' . . . few values are functional for all times, places, and cultures, and we have no accurate ways to predict what values will help students to meet the challenges in the world of the future.[12]

Social studies also places a high premium on participatory learning, or what John Dewey called "learning by doing." K-12 programs should seek to involve all students directly in decision-making experiences and socio-civic activities that are meaningful to them. Whether the topic of discussion is the military might of ancient Sparta, the growing inbalance between the natural environment and technological improvements, the threat of nuclear war, or life in the 21st century, the challenge for the social studies teacher always is to move students beyond mere recall and memorization to interpretation and application of information. A list of action-oriented behaviors has been compiled that can be used to determine if teaching and learning are participatory. They include: observing, proposing, organizing, negotiating, compromising, rule-making, voting, debating, and service delivery.[13] Action learning can take many forms. It can be individualized or group, real or simulated, cognitive or affective, reflective or projective.

Action learning as endorsed by social studies epitomizes many of the basic principles of socialization and citizenship for democratic living. It recognizes that individuals must assume responsibilities both as individuals and as members of groups if democracy is to prevail. It accepts the principles of interdependence and reciprocity between individual development and social welfare. It underscores the idea that knowledge *acquired and applied* in classroom situations, simulations, and real life events is the best way for students to *demonstrate* proficiency in citizenship and socialization. It acknowledges that cooperation within the context of group action is essential for democratic living. And, it operates on the belief that students must develop conscientious commitments to social and civic activism—to *be involved* in charting the direction of their lives, and the society in which they live.

The Value

What is the worth of social studies in school curricula when compared to other subjects like science, mathematics, language arts, and the creative arts? Does it receive parity, preferential, or prejudicial treatment with respect to public opinion, resource allocations, and school philosophy? Theoretically, the contributions of all subjects to the socialization and education of American youth should be of equal merit, although differentiated by area of emphasis. Too often this is not the case in school practice. Some subjects emerge as more basic or significant than others. The status of social studies among other school subjects is, at best, equivocal as we have indicated above. Despite this ambivalence, we believe the content and objectives of social studies are critical to the effective preparation of today's youth for constructive citizenship in a complex, and often chaotic, society and world.

All teachers have a responsibility to prepare their students to deal with both quantitative and qualitative aspects of human behaviors, societal institutions, and socio-cultural systems. Social studies teachers in particular must realize the uniqueness of their subject in school curricula and to the general education of young citizens. Traditionally, social studies scholars have acknowledged the significance of the subject by advocating the teaching of concepts, principles, and skills that transcend local and national geo-political boundaries. Some examples are power, interdependence, change, supply and demand, culture, decision making, and value analysis. Social studies classroom teachers must resist the temptations of accountability and "back to basics" trends to teach memory and recall of facts (they are easier to measure, and, thus, easier to translate into accountability terms!) and continue the tradition of emphasizing conceptual understanding and skill development. School districts recognize the significance of social studies in the number of credits required for high school graduation. In most states this number is second only to the credit requirements in the language arts.

Unfortunately, the attitudes, values, and opinions of the public about social studies are not always consistent with the amount of instruction required by state mandates or the theoretical impressions about the importance of the subject. Many educators and members of the public express considerable skepticism about the relevance of social studies and its academic rigor. The dissatisfaction of the public with education in general is even more extreme for social studies.[14] Students often rate social studies content lower in practical use and significance to their lives than other subjects. Even some social studies teachers lack confidence in the importance and intellectual potency of the subject. The results of standardized tests measuring student achievement in social studies tend to be lower than in other subjects.[15] In theory and potential value social studies has first-class status among school subjects; in school practice, though, it is frequently treated as a "second class citizen."

This ambivalence between the theory and the practice, the status and the value of social studies education might very well be the result of our own inability to successfully tap the potential of the subject.

Although the true value of social studies may not be realized for some time to come, this subject does have the potential of contributing significantly to the attainment of the general goals of American education. John Michaelis says it can help students,

> gain *self-realization* through experiences that foster each individual's growth in knowledge, skills, and personal values . . . better understand *human relationships* through . . . the study of various cultures, the development of interpersonal skills, and analysis of intergroup problems . . . develop *civic responsibility* through . . . concepts and main ideas of government . . . legal rights of individuals, and thinking and valuing processes . . . gain in *economic competence* as they explore concepts, attitudes, and skills related to good workmanship, career awareness, and contributions of different workers, and uses of resources . . . sharpen *thinking abilities* . . . *learn how to learn* as they apply reading, study and other skills, . . . engage in independent study activities that emphasize self-direction and self-evaluation . . . and . . . use models of inquiry and processes of thinking.[16]

Conclusion

The value of the social studies, its characteristics and philosophy are well documented by authors of books, articles, and curriculum materials. We agree with them that social studies offers rich rewards for the individual and the society through its goals and objectives. Although a great portion of the potential of social studies is yet to be realized, the school curricula would be lacking without it.

The importance of the *human* factors of life and living cannot be overstated. Problems and dilemmas dealing with human beings in society are often neglected though they are most taxing to the human imagination, or even because of this. Social, political, economic, and educational problems are major issues in our society and the world. Resolutions in these areas require not only skill but creativity as well, especially in the use of human and social resources. Since *human factors* and *social relationships* are the particular province of social studies, it should perhaps become the *instrumental core* of all school curricula. In our view, citizenship and socialization will continue to be the major philosophical purposes and goals of general education, and, thus, the necessity of social studies for all youth will prevail.

Notes

[1] Charles A. Beard, *The Nature of the Social Sciences* (New York: Charles Scribners' Sons, 1934).

[2] John U. Michaelis, *Social Studies for Children: A Guide to Basic Instruction* (Englewood Cliffs: Prentice-Hall, 1980).

[3] *Ibid.*, p. 4.

[4] Irving Morrissett, "The Needs of the Future and the Constraints of the Past," in *The Social Studies*, 80th Yearbook of the National Society for the Study of Education, ed. Howard D. Mehlinger and O. L. Davis, Jr. (Chicago: University of Chicago Press, 1981), pp. 36–59.

[5] Scott, Foresman Social Studies, *Stepping Stones to the World*, advertising brochure (Glenview, Ill.: Scott, Foresman and Co., 1978), p. 2.

[6] *Ibid.*

[7] James A. Banks with Ambrose A. Clegg, Jr., *Teaching Strategies for the Social Studies* (Reading, Mass.: Addison-Wesley Publishing Co., 1977).

[8] *Social Studies Curriculum Guidelines* (Washington, D.C.: National Council for the Social Studies, 1973), pp. 13–14.

[9] Banks with Clegg, *Teaching Strategies for the Social Studies*, p. 26.

[10] *Ibid.*, p. 27.

[11] Michaelis, *Social Studies for Children*.

[12] Banks with Clegg *Teaching Strategies for the Social Studies*, p. 440.

[13] Bryon G. Massialas and Joseph B. Hurst, *Social Studies in a New Era* (New York: Longham, 1978).

[14] Morrissett, "The Needs of the Future and the Constraints of the Past."

[15] Howard D. Mehlinger, "The NAEP Report on Changes in Knowledge and Attitudes, 1969–76" *Phi Delta Kappan* 59 (June, 1978): 676–678.

[16] Michaelis, *Social Studies for Children*, pp. 6–7.

Breathing Life into Social Studies and Language Arts

Jacqueline Cobbin
Texas Southern University
Cindy Thomashow
Keene State College, New Hampshire

The kids' excitement over this program has stirred up the parents. And why not? They've been involved in it, too. The whole community has been involved in one way or another. When kids do other than 'canned' experiences you always get more enthusiasm. They were able to apply their skills to a real endeavor, understanding differences and learning social studies first-hand. The kids found out a lot about their own backgrounds and developed a sense of pride in them this year. They spashed their community on a piece of paper for others to learn from—that meant so much!

Ann Ranta, classroom teacher
Walpole, New Hampshire

Written expressly for *Preparing for Reflective Teaching*.

Students are more eager to communicate their ideas in written form because they know someone their age is going to read it. It (the program) has also brought the class closer together. Education that is multicultural was a new term to the fifth graders. It meant that "I am somebody and so are you." The program provided a realm of education, learning about others, that had not been experienced before. I am sure these student's will remember the experience throughout their school years.

Verna Jones, classroom teacher
Houston, Texas

When children (and teachers) are turned off by social studies texts, is there a more exciting way to teach the subject? How can language arts be made to seem more meaningful to students than by their learning to write friendly letters to make-believe people? Can teachers integrate the study of multicultural issues into the regular curriculum without sacrificing objectives set by the school system for the year? If children don't have opportunities to interact with members of different racial and cultural groups every day, what kind of school experience can foster an understanding of cultural and racial diversity?

Out of these questions grew the Cultural Exchange Program that was piloted this year in two classrooms, one in Walpole, New Hampshire, and one in Houston, Texas. The program was designed to spark some life into daily lessons, to satisfy general educational objectives in social studies and language arts and to integrate multicultural activities into the regular fifth grade curriculum. Combining penpal exchanges, local community study, and innovative communication ideas, the two teachers involved designed a dynamic program in which students participated with enthusiasm and great interest. It broadened the students' experiences with people of different racial and cultural backgrounds and helped to build an understanding of the cultural pluralism and ethnic diversity that exists in the world around them. Teachers and students both found the approach to be a refreshing change from the old texts and lesson plans.

There exist many Walpole, New Hampshire, situations in the country, where children live and attend school in a monocultural setting. Most of them will have few opportunities throughout their school lives to meet and share with people who represent different cultural and racial groups. When geographic isolation limits daily contact with different kinds of people, it is important for children to learn through other channels that there are many cultural elements in our society.

On the other hand, there are also many situations like the one in Houston, Texas. The children in this elementary school attend classes with peers who are from the same racial group. Although they may, at times, interact with people from other cultural or racial groups, a significant part of their day is spent with people who basically share the same cultural and world view. It is important to broaden their awareness of the differences among people by exposing them to other values, lifestyles, and cultural experiences.

With this Cultural Exchange Project, we want to develop in children an understanding of the characteristics ethnic and racial groups have in common, the unique status of each group, and why ethnicity is an integral part of our social system. From this exchange, the students learn facts and concepts that help describe differences among cultural and racial groups, and they connect personally with students who come from varied backgrounds.

Our purpose in doing this project is to help facilitate education that is multicultural in the classroom. The information that is communicated between the two classrooms focuses on the cultural similarities and the differences of the children who are involved in the exchange. Exchanges include children who are from the same age and grade level and yet live in dramatically different environments and have different cultural heritages or racial backgrounds. The Houston-Walpole exchange is between an urban and a rural environment. One group is made up of predominantly southern, black Americans and the other, of New England, white Americans.

Another basic goal of the project is to develop pride in the children about their own cultural heritage and their local community. The project increases the use of the local environment (cultural distinction, lifestyle, architecture, geography, etc.) in each classroom and highlights the value of community resource people (for example, oral histories, local crafts, photographers, businesspeople) in a curriculum that focuses on multicultural issues. Activities are designed to improve the students' knowledge of and concern for their own cultural environment and community as well as that of the class with which they are exchanging.

Parents are drawn on as resource people, as well as locally known "experts" in history and story telling. The community becomes the field of study in that local libraries, historical societies and residents are used as resources by students and the character of each community is studied. For example, in order to show the Houston children their town, the Walpole students created a 'walking' tour through the town by recreating the town on a map. They mounted pictures of buildings on wooden blocks that could be placed on the appropriate location. Each block also bore a description of the use and history of the buildings as well as some comments on local color and legend.

Studies of one's own background are dynamic and meaningful teaching activities. They are exciting, familiar, and accessible to children. Relating larger concepts of cultural heritage, intragroup and intergroup racial and ethnic experiences, and the realities of our social system to the everyday experiences of a child results in a clearer and more immediate understanding of those concepts. We feel strongly that the information learned by the students should be shared from the perspective of their age group. The children select the subjects of interest to share with the participating classroom and relate it to others in their own language through auditory tapes, video tapes, photographs, drawings, and written correspondence. Both groups organize the information they find in creative ways in order to share their heritage with each other. For example, the Walpole students learned to do oral histories by interviewing people from the local area, taping them and editing the text to be sent to Houston. They did gravestone rubbings and collected epitaphs of historical figures, researching what contributions each person had made to New Hampshire history. They staged a mock Town Meeting that was attended by area Selectmen to discuss issues relevant to the governance of the town. A tape of the meeting and reports explaining the procedure were sent to Houston. A survey of the ethnic background of each student was compiled and graphed for Houston. Houston followed up on this by sending back a videotape in which students created skits that traced the cultural characteristics (food, clothing, folktales, etc.) of each ethnic group mentioned on the graph. The Houston projects focused on the urban character of Houston and on black culture. In studying the economic base of Houston, the students sent reports on the oil and cattle industry, recreation and businesses based in Houston. On a map of downtown Houston, flags marked locations important to the lives of the students. A visit to the Barbara Jordan Archives resulted in a study of famous black people who had been raised in Houston. A pictorial essay about these people was sent to Walpole. Walpole reciprocated with a videotape of skits performed based on local historical figures from New Hampshire's past.

The classroom teachers involved in this project developed curricula that was grounded in and extend from a child's own experiences with his or her community. Teachers devised creative activities and collected resource materials to help students develop a sense of self in relation to their community and their cultural heritage. Teachers readily admit that their students find school texts boring because they lack a clear relationship to the student's life experiences. One solution is to involve the students in experiences that bring to life some of the facts and concepts normally covered in class activities and texts. The exchange of information, participation in multicultural activities, and study of the local community are integrated into several parts of the curriculum including social studies, the arts, language arts, and many others. The style of integration depends on the teacher's creativity and the willingness to experiment with traditional curricula.

Ann Ranta in Walpole used the historical facts gathered by students in math word problems. (For example, in 1802 the fort in Bellows Falls was erected. It burned in 1846. How many years did the fort stand?) In Houston, the children used their knowledge of black historical figures to stage a play on the subject of pride for the rest of the school. The play included original musical compositions.

The learning that is possible through this exchange goes far beyond the content of traditional subjects to include an awareness of local community history, an increased awareness of multicultural issues, the development of a sense of social responsibility, the clarification of children's values, and the development of a sense of pride for locally unique and distinct characteristics of the community and its people. The correspondence component offers a motivation for the development of communication skills (expository writing, use of audio and visual media, expression through crafts and artistic medium, the use of music to define culture).

The comparative treatment of culture and lifestyle described here should not be confused with that of the traditional social studies curricula, although it might complement that curriculum. The emphasis here is upon the child's own subjective evaluations and comparisons of culture and lifestyles through their letters, conversations, and contact through other means of expression. This approach helps children come to see other cultures and groups as composed of individuals with differences and similarities just as they may find in their own setting.

The exchange differs from other penpal correspondence programs with which we are familiar. One primary difference is that the communication is organized around subject matter, the study of the local community and multicultural issues. Not only does this help the students to focus the content of their writing, but it also offers topics that fall within the student's own experience that they feel they can express to others with some confidence and interest. A second important difference in the exchange approach is that several different media are used in communicating about environments.

Numerous benefits result from the opportunity of one group of students from one particular place to correspond with a peer group from a different place. The students develop specific skills from the study and communication of local environments and cultures: inquiry skills, problem formation, analysis and synthesis of information from asking questions about cultural and environmental matters; and independent investigation, observational and perceptual skills, graphics and research skills used in answering questions.

The students know that communication will continue throughout the year and progressively build an image of what the other community is like in terms of its people, places, language, culture, racial, and ethnic character. For this reason, they are challenged to express themselves in great depth considering that their correspondents have no other means of learning about their culture except through their communication efforts.

Teachers of the fifth grade classrooms in Houston and Walpole are working with the Teacher Corps, a federally funded program, on the project. After an initial telephone conversation between the two teachers, a time line was set up to determine when and how correspondence would take place between the classrooms. The teachers encouraged students to pursue the study of similar themes like recreation, lifestyle, geography, employment, urban-rural differences, environmental characteristics, local crafts, and other topics. By choosing similar themes to share between both classes, the connection between them was organized and comprehensible to the students. A project was worked on by students for about four weeks and then mailed to the other classroom. Between each mailing, the teachers spoke with each other to discuss and plan the next project and to evaluate the success of the previous one. A total of five projects in each classroom were completed and exchanged by the end of the school year.

This particular exchange ended with a visit by the Houston children to Walpole, New Hampshire. The students themselves raised the money to finance the trip. They initiated the idea of the visit after having corresponded with Walpole for five months. The level of excitement and the interest that was generated in the project is obvious in the motivation of these students to organize a live meeting between pen-pals. The visit was structured by the two teachers and the Teacher Corps projects to reflect the learning that the children gained throughout the year of the two communities and focused on bringing to life the cultural and racial differences between the two groups. The success of the project was recorded in the eyes and smiles of each child as they met for the first time and in the warm embraces that ended their visit.

Next time you are in a school, sit in a classroom for two or three hours if possible and pay attention to what is being taught. Also, look through the materials that are being used and see what ideas and concepts they contain and whose perspectives they embody. If you have time, interview the teacher, and ask why he or she selected to teach the particular things being taught and how he or she would evaluate the materials being used. Then ask yourself some questions:

What else could have been taught?
What kind of world view was this teacher presenting?
What would you yourself have selected to teach, and why?

This process can help you begin to analyze critically the curriculum and instructional materials in schools and can prepare you to design and teach a curriculum that is in harmony with your own philosophy of teaching.

Chapter 4

Instruction and Classroom Management

Many factors go into becoming a reflective teacher. One important factor is the ability to reach all of the kids you are teaching. Reflective teachers know how to adjust their instruction to the learning styles of their students. A reflective teacher, by my definition, is one who can successfully teach any child. He or she is a student of the process of teaching.

Think of classrooms you have been in as a student and think about your reaction to the instruction you were receiving. Was it exciting and challenging? If not, how could your teachers have changed the instructional process so that it would have been more beneficial to you? How could they have found out your reactions to their teaching so that they would have known what changes would have been appropriate? Now imagine yourself as a teacher. How can you find out how to make your instruction beneficial to each of your students? The articles that follow analyze and discuss the instructional process from the points of view of particular groups of students you may have.

For the Prospective Teacher: Strategies for Success in the Inner-city

Robert Saddler
Chicago Public Schools

Teachers, to be effective, must have faith in the techniques they employ in their work. This faith, if it is strong enough, will make their teaching vibrant and alive—their enthusiasm will shine through. To increase effectiveness, the teacher must understand the possibilities of accom-

Written expressly for *Preparing for Reflective Teaching.*

plishment and also the limitations created by the class and by external conditions. Accompanying this understanding of conditions should be certain principles that serve as a working basis, principles that evolve from definite methods of approach, from objectives to be accomplished, and from the types of students being served.

All too often, however, the inexperienced teacher is tossed into a new teaching situation without much introduction to existing class-room realities. Thus, specific objectives and principles, and the accompanying faith and enthusiasm that they can engender, are pushed aside in the hassle of just trying to exist, to make it through another unit, another week, or, at worst, another day.

While the vast majority of us who teach do so because of an initial faith and enthusiasm, a desire to convey learning, we need guideposts based on reality and commonsense to aid us.

While this paper cannot hope to eliminate all uncertainties for the teacher approaching a new situation, perhaps it can provide a beginning, an anchor. With that aim in mind, the following overview discusses seven areas that seem to be vital to successful teaching: traditional educational psychology precepts, influences of life style, reciprocity in relationships, discipline, teacher expectations, language, and relationships with parents and community. Although much of what will be stated here is directed specifically to the prospective teacher who will be working in a poor, minority, urban setting, each of these elements actually applies to all students in every type of school setting and needs to be kept in mind and reinforced by all educators, especially now when schools seem not to be succeeding as much as would be hoped.

Traditional Educational Psychology Precepts

By this time in your general and educational psychology courses, you will surely have learned the essential maxim that in spite of obvious physical differences, people have more basic similarities than differences. All have the same fundamental needs, motivations, and drives, although no two people have them in the same proportions or express them in exactly the same way. This is especially true for children. All children need an environment that helps them grow physically and mentally to their fullest potential, the security of being loved, cared for and accepted by parents and friends, and opportunities to learn and to be rewarded by a sense of accomplishment. Each child, however, needs them in different and constantly changing degrees.

Thus, in our efforts to provide for the whole child, educators must consider the role of individual differences, realizing that pupils learn at different rates and in different ways. To allow for varying degrees of maturation, the effective classroom curriculum has to be tailored in order that the same information can be presented in different ways. Effective curriculum also must be patterned so that when student readiness (the characteristic needed for the child to profit from a learning experience) does exist, it will be strengthened through immediate feedback and positive reinforcement. Further, we must remember that isolated skills development does not constitute mastery of knowledge; only through the ability to transfer learning does true intellectual development occur. Finally, these academic precepts can be fostered only when certain basic and sometimes conflicting needs of the children are satisfied. These include needs for affection, role models, approval by authority, approval by peers, discipline, independence, and competence and self-respect.

To accomplish all this must seem like an awesome task to the prospective teacher; in fact, it is an impossible one. Such a statement may seem defeatist and unsuited to this article, but good teachers recognize this fact. Good teachers, like good parents, realize that they are merely human and that although they will give their utmost they will not always achieve their goals nor always act correctly. Further, good teachers realize that it is not necessary for them to be absolutely perfect at all times; it is only necessary that they have the intelligence, the genuineness, and the enthusiasm to enable their students to respond to them and to learn from them. With this awareness, teachers will be able to set and achieve realistic goals.

Influence of Lifestyles and the Minority, Urban, Poor Child

While the traditional educational precepts are the same for minority children in a poor, urban setting as they are for other children, the prospective teacher needs to be aware of some by-products of the lifestyle in such an urban environment that affect learning. Poverty affects the achievement of many minority children in specific ways. Basic needs for food, clothing, and shelter often go unsatisfied, and it is difficult for children affected in this way to achieve in school. Poverty also prevents many minority children from having the kinds of experiences that support the instructional efforts of the school. Trips to cultural facilities, books in the home, educational toys—in other words, all the objects and services that are commonly part of the experiential background of middle-class children and that satisfy educational needs outside of school—cost money, and many minority families cannot afford them.

Also, while some educators have erroneously concluded that a poor, urban environment is unstimulating, it is in fact often over-stimulating.

That is, children living in noisy, overcrowded conditions, surrounded by activity are so bombarded by sensory stimuli that they learn to block them out. This habit sometimes hinders them in school because they can shut out the instructional stimuli presented to them by teachers.

Further, this lifestyle often generates a value system that is in opposition to the value system of the school. For example, children of the urban poor usually tend to value aggressiveness over intellectualism, because aggressive behavior fits into a survival pattern; intellectualism seems to generate few immediate benefits. This is why minority children generally do not like to be touched by teachers in a stress situation; the youngsters are apt to interpret any physical contact, even the middle-class "pat on the back," as an aggressive act.

Probably because of the negative factors almost inherent in the life of the poor, urban, minority child, this youngster often possesses a sophistication in coping with daily existence, an ability to develop life survival skills. Too often such skills and their importance are not recognized by the teacher, for students can use these abilities to wreak havoc in the classroom. If properly channeled by the teacher, however, the same skills can be used to help students to achieve. For example, the child's relationship to the peer group is usually an extremely close one, and the child will go to great lengths to "save face" in front of the group. The child who is placed in an embarrassing posture before the group will usually use disruptive behavior as a cover-up. But the teacher who realizes the nature of the peer-group relationship can seek out ways to provide the child with opportunities to "shine" before the group in some area of strength and, therefore, reinforce positive behavior.

This section has touched on only a few of the lifestyle factors applicable to the minority youngster. Prospective inner-city teachers are advised to read as extensively as possible on the subject and, later, as they begin teaching, to mesh this theoretical knowledge with their own observations and experiences. In order to be effective educators, we must be aware of the influence of the culture in which children are raised.

Reciprocity in Relationships

Emerson said that the secret of education lies in respecting the pupil. We could better say that the secret of education lies in mutual respect between youngsters and their teachers. Such reciprocity generates the continuous flow of communication without which learning is impossible. But, reciprocal respect is difficult to achieve when the teacher is ignorant about the way students live. Teachers need to foster their understanding of and sensitivity to students' lives, teach if the goals of equal educational opportunities are to be realized. Merely reading and talking about them in college classwork, or practicing dealing with them in student teaching experiences, has serious limitations. Reading and talking may result in a degree of intellectual understanding, but these processes have little effect on the attitude of the teacher. The student teaching experience usually fails to involve the student teacher with the out-of-school life of students.

It is incumbent upon the teacher to use opportunities for learning about children's lives outside of the classroom. For example, participation in extra-curricular activities and involvement with the parents and the community offer excellent means for attaining deeper awareness of a youngster's whole life.

For prospective teachers who protest, "But I won't have the time" or "But I'm afraid," the immediate response must be that lack of commitment and fear have no place in the emotional baggage of the inner-city educator. Certainly, commonsense and appropriate caution are necessary, but fear, distrust, scorn, or pity of those we teach must be eliminated from our psyches. Such negative attitudes will definitely be felt by the students, for young people are amazingly perceptive to character. If they sense an easiness, the hope of educating them will be diminished.

Discipline

To be successful teachers, we must always remember that understanding and lack of discipline are not synonomous; in fact, they are very much the antithesis of each other. It is axiomatic that young people need, want, and respect reasonable, fair, consistent discipline. Yet, often teacher candidates express more apprehension about discipline than about any other aspect of the teaching-learning process.

It is important here to cite some working definitions of discipline. Discipline is the state of organization or control within an individual or group that propels the individual or group toward positive goal achievement.[1] Classroom discipline is a condition where pupils use their time in educationally desirable ways. The teacher who cannot establish this condition cannot teach. Yet, good discipline does not always require every student in place, every pupil silent, everyone focused on the teacher. In such a classroom the listeners may still be learning nothing. Discipline has not failed when six eager children burst out with an idea at once, so long as they are willing, at some point, to listen to each other. The test of discipline is whether or not the behavior of the group permits everyone to work effectively.

Persistent disorder or confusion within the classroom means that the majority of the students do not know what to do, or how to do something, or do not want to participate. If this is so, the teacher needs to re-examine the teaching goals and the students' understanding of those goals. Sometimes students rebel when goals are unreasonable. Other times, the goals are reasonable but have been poorly explained to the students. If so, the teacher should find out what the pupils are trying to do and explain where they are on the wrong track or should clarify the limits of allowable behavior.

Even if the goal is reasonable and understood by the students, they may still not do what is required. One cause of this is boredom; monotonous and repetitive tasks are an invitation to mind-wandering and trouble-making. Thus, teachers need to arrange work that permits students to satisfy noncognitive needs while learning. Fear of failure is another reason why students may not do what is required. Pupils who are baffled and expect to remain baffled will prefer any diversion. In this case, the teacher needs to set goals that can be reached and to make the work clear.

A search into the teacher's own personality might also reveal blocks to classroom discipline: the frequent sarcastic remark, a temper that is difficult to control, the occasional fit of moodiness, a chronic detachment from the group, phlegmatism, or a consistent gravitation toward ego involvement—all of these would be harmful when projected on a class. The underlying reasons why certain classes fail to reach a desired state of inner control may be no further away than the instructional leader. Conversely, the teacher who possesses a firm knowledge of subject matter, a secure personality, enthusiasm, respect for the students, and a willingness to modify actions while always retaining ultimate control, should be successful in maintaining good classroom discipline.

Teacher Expectations

Another aspect of maintaining good classroom discipline is for the teacher to have high expectations of the students. High expectations of the students encourages the teacher to create and establish a classroom that will encourage goal achievement. The teacher works to help the students to fulfill worthwhile educational goals, and the students work to satisfy their teacher's expectations. The expectations become a source of motivation.

This whole process sounds like a continuous self-generating cycle precisely because that is what it is, a self-generating cycle, a self-fulfilling prophecy. Unfortunately, however, this self-fulfilling prophecy also acts in reverse; poor teacher opinions of students can breed poor achievement. The negative aspect of this self-fulfilling prophecy, so widely discussed in educational literature in recent years, was perhaps most succinctly stated by Kenneth B. Clark in *Dark Ghetto* when he wrote that black children

> by and large do not learn because they are not being taught effectively and they are not being taught because those who are charged with the responsibility of teaching them do not believe that they can learn, do not expect that they can learn, and do not act toward them in ways which help them to learn.[2]

It should be noted here that while we, as educators working in the inner-city, are primarily concerned with teachers' expectations as they relate to poor, minority youngsters, variance in a teacher's expectations can exist even within a single inner-city classroom composed of only black children. Since degrees of poverty exist, differentiation in a teacher's expectations can be formed on the basis of students' attractiveness, dress, and, especially, the teacher's perception of students' family income levels.

The self-fulfilling cycle is apparent when children in the same school and at the same grade level in two separate classrooms are taught differently by the two teachers. One teacher feels that these youngsters are not capable of mastering difficult material and, therefore, "watersdown" the curriculum and presents it in a lackluster manner. The other teacher believes that the students can achieve, and handling of the subject matter reflects this belief. This teacher is enthusiastic and confident, and the children know it which motivates them to learn. In both cases, the teachers' expectations predict a large degree of the students' success.

Language

An important facet of teacher expectations reflects itself when educators hear the dialect of the English language spoken by most black, urban, inner-city youth. Too often, educators equate the use of this dialect, which I will refer to as black English, with the inability to learn. When hearing black English spoken many people question the competence and intelligence of the speakers. This happens because many people, including educators, assume that this black dialect is the result of careless, unstructured pronunciation and grammar and a meaningless vocabulary. Yet, research reveals that black English is actually a highly structured language having deep historical roots. Knowledge like this is extremely important for teachers who work in inner-city areas, because it makes them discard the fallacy that this dialect is inferior to standard English.

Many urban, inner-city, black youths have become unreachable because the educational system has alienated them by scorning their language habits. Such alienation begins early with the massive failure of public schools to teach large numbers of children to read. Many children speaking standard English often have difficulty learning to read, and children whose speech style is different from the writing style in text books have even greater difficulty in mastering reading skills.

At the start of his or her formal education, the poor, black child learns to feel stigmatized. They experience difficulty doing what is expected of them and as a result develop feelings of inferiority. Such feelings are often reinforced by standard I.Q. tests that the youngsters cannot understand because the tests are given in standard English. Youngsters who fail I.Q. tests are placed in a low track, often learning to fear verbalizing. They eventually lose interest in their school work and, too frequently, drop out of school as soon as possible.

A blatant error has been committed with these students, for mastery of standard English and true intelligence are not necessarily related. Sadly it is only the students whose educational achievement is high who seem, while still retaining numerous features of Black English in their speech, to have also learned to use standard English effectively. These students are expected to succeed. It is a vicious cycle. They are more able than others to adapt in standard English settings; they are considered brighter; they are placed into higher levels of classes; they *do* learn more because they are exposed to more; and they learn to value educational success. Usually these are the students who achieve upward social mobility.

Often, such students are cited as exceptions to most black children, who are believed to come from highly deprived, non-verbal homes. However, the assumption that verbalizing is not highly valued in the black community is nonsense. First, although many parents may seem non-verbal when they visit an alien educational setting, they are quite verbal at home. Second, verbal ability is often highly prized in the peer group, and peer group relationships are important in language development. Among young men, for instance, a "dude" is admired for his "smooth rap." Also, most inner-city high school students can be beautifully creative in compositions, once they are taught to use their imaginations and to let their words flow.

A teacher can gain more informative and fascinating insight into black English by researching some of the literature on this subject. Since a major challenge for teachers of black, inner-city youngsters is to teach standard English while not giving these students the impression that their dialect is inferior, and since most formal education courses do not provide prospective teachers with the tools to do this, the matter rests with us.

Relationships with Parents and Community

Just as we, as educators working in inner-city areas, must continually seek new avenues for communicating with our students, so too must we earnestly strive to improve our relationships with those students' parents and, through them, with the community's viable organizations, agencies, and community leaders. Actually, establishing and maintaining mutually rewarding and satisfying relationships with parents is one of the best ways to learn about our pupils and to express our genuine interest in them. Such involvement is a prerequisite for those of us who aspire to be truly effective teachers. But, we need to be aware of barriers that exist to parental involvement in the school.

Usually in poor, urban communities the reality of situations does not foster wide community support as in other communities. When people's lives are consumed daily with the looming spectre of poverty, when they must scuffle to get jobs, even poorly paying ones, or worry about stretching welfare checks, little energy is left for actively participating in their children's daily education. In this type of situation, people are not usually anxious to become involved in the schools—so many other things seem like high priorities.

Poor parents often have subtle attitudes that also inhibit their participation in the school. For example, parents frequently view their children's school as an unfamiliar, alien, and even hostile environment in which they cannot hope to make themselves heard. Many parents feel that the school is a closed system in which they are outsiders. Others are fearful that if they register a complaint or make a suggestion to the school their child may suffer some type of discriminatory action. Still others recall unpleasant memories of failure in the school setting and are threatened by the thought of reentering an arena where they might again feel inferior.

To compound all of this, we, as educators, too often further impede parental participation by the very types of relationships we attempt to establish with parents. We seem to be steeped in the traditional concept of the school as an information giving body where we talk about the child's attendance, grades, behavior, personality, everything that we think we know about him or her, and the parent listens to this primarily one-way flow of information. In other words, parents are usually on the receiving rather than the participating end of communications about their children. Yet, if only we would listen, there is so much that parents could tell us about their children that would help us to teach them, to really communicate with them. In fact, there is so much knowledge that we could gain from each other—parents and educators together—if we would relate to each other in a mutually effective manner.

Like it or not, the initiative for action in establishing such reciprocal relationships lies with the school and with us as individual teachers. First, we must sincerely understand that most parents do deeply want their children to get an education to better their lot in life, but they are sometimes so hampered by their own problems or inadequacies that they are unable to do, on their own, what is best for their children. As professional people, teachers should take an understanding attitude toward the parent's problems as well as the children's. In condemning a parent, the teacher only widens the gap between home and school and makes effective communication and resulting cooperation difficult to obtain.

Next we must change the traditional encounters with parents. As Daniel Safran of the Center for the Study of Parent Involvement in Oakland, California contends,

> Teachers must learn to elevate communication to a more human and productive level. . . . An adult relationship must be established with parents. Too often, many teachers forget this and treat parents like kids.[3]

Above all, we must work to establish an atmosphere of mutual trust and respect between parents and teachers. There need not be a question of who controls the community's schools—a fear too prevalent among educators—for meaningful parental involvement does not portend control at the expense of teachers' rights; rather, it signifies a school community unified enough to accomplish what is necessary to educate its youngsters. Never for a moment doubt the powerful force exerted by administrators, teachers, parents, and community working together. I have seen just such a combination dramatically turn a school around in only five years. Of course, the greatest effect is achieved when all elements of the school community work together, and the best place to begin is with the school administration and its endeavors within the community. But even in the absence of all else, an individual teacher can begin to make things happen.

Conclusion

Surely, this article cannot claim to have given prospective teachers who will be working in a poor minority urban setting—or, for that matter, any inexperienced teachers—a manual for successful teaching. Nevertheless, I hope it has provided a beginning, a realistic guide that sincere, caring teachers can use as they approach their task.

Such teachers will find, I believe, that teaching is more than a task, more than merely a decent job. It is a rewarding, satisfying, often joy-filled experience if only one can move beyond the narrow confines traditionally prescribed for educators and exercise the multi-faceted, self-directed, committed, responsible, and responsive instructional leadership so necessary in working with, in truly teaching, young people.

It is obvious that, although teacher training institutions and those who train teachers are talking more than ever about the need for defining and using behavior patterns rather than isolated skills for competency-based teacher education and teacher evaluation, most institutions have not yet developed programs sufficient to meet these needs. Thus, at present, it rests with us to teach ourselves in these vital matters.

In all of this, communication is the key; if we cannot communicate with our pupils, we cannot teach them. And real communication can arise only from mutual respect and understanding flowing between teachers and students. It is up to us, the adults, to take the first step.

If we are competent teachers who are humanistic in our approach to education, aware of realities and proficient in techniques and skills, our likelihood of obtaining desirable educational outcomes is great. By establishing an academic environment in which pupils can achieve, usually we can be successful—not always, for some failure is inevitable—but certainly far more successful than many of us have been. Reaching these goals in educating our children is neither easy nor impossible; in truth, it is both difficult and possible.

Notes

[1] Gail M. Inlow, *Maturity in High School Teaching* (Englewood Cliffs, N.J.: Prentice-Hall, Inc., 1963), pp. 338–339.

[2] Kenneth B. Clark, *Dark Ghetto: Dilemmas of Social Power*, (New York: Harper and Row, 1965), p. 131.

[3] Daniel Safran, *Community Participation in Education* (Boston: Allyn and Bacon, Inc., 1979), p. 105.

Mainstreaming and the Classroom Environment

Christine E. Sleeter
Ripon College, Wisconsin

When teachers hear the word "mainstreaming," they often have at least one of the following reactions:

- I'm all for it, since kids with handicaps need to be with their peers just as much as any other kid.
- I have a hard enough time coping with 30 regular kids—how can I be expected to teach a student who needs a lot of special attention?
- It's a fine idea, but I don't have enough training to work with handicapped children and so I'd be hesitant to have any in my room.

Implicit in many regular education teachers' reactions to mainstreaming is the idea that special education students are very different from regular students and therefore require a very different kind of teaching. This is seen as particularly true of students with educational handicaps, since these are the students whose handicap is directly tied to failure in regular classrooms.

The purpose of this paper is to help you think about mainstreaming students with mild educational handicaps. The first section of this paper will discuss why they are classified as being handicapped, and what role the school in fact plays in actually making them handicapped. The second section will present some questions and concerns teachers and student teachers often have as they attempt to adapt their classroom environment to these students.

Mild Educationally Handicapped: What does That Mean?

Educationally handicapped refers to a characteristic of a student that inhibits learning within the traditional classroom environment. A student who is educationally handicapped is classified as severe when the student has great difficulty learning not just academic material but also basic knowledge for survival in this society. Severely handi-

Written expressly for *Preparing for Reflective Teaching.*

capped students are rarely mainstreamed for any length of time into the regular classroom. A student who is mildly educationally handicapped has characteristics that inhibit the student's academic success in a traditionally-run regular classroom but does not limit the student's ability to learn basic knowledge and skills for personal survival. Mild educationally handicapped students include those who have learning disabilities, educable mental retardation, and emotional disturbance. Let us briefly examine each of these.

Glen is classified as being learning disabled because he has an exceptionally difficult time learning to perceive, interpret, and produce language—usually written language—accurately. This difficulty is a problem for him in an environment that stresses reading and writing, and sometimes in one that stresses oral communication with little concrete or pictoral reinforcement.

Marsha is classified as being educable mentally retarded because she learns many things—especially academic concepts and skills—very slowly and has difficulty learning abstract concepts. Marsha functions with reasonable success in a non-academic environment, such as at home or on the playground, and learns some non-academic school subjects like art or music quite successfully. For this reason, there has been continuous disagreement between people in the school and people in the community and home regarding the extent to which Marsha has a problem that can be thought of as handicapped.

Charles is classified as being emotionally disturbed because he does not behave in a socially accepted manner in certain situations. In Charles's case, this includes behaviors such as fighting, hitting, and moving about considerably more than others. Withdrawing from adults and peers are behaviors of other students classified as emotionally disturbed. Such "deviant" behavior is most noticed in socially crowded environments such as classrooms because it disrupts the social order that facilitates the group's working together. This behavior is also often linked with poor academic work on the part of the student, which contributes to its being seen as a problem.

The classroom environment is a key factor determining the success or failure of students such as Glen, Marsha, and Charles. In fact, given a classroom environment that supports their strengths without penalizing them for their weaknesses, these students need not be seen as handicapped. To see in more detail the relationship between classroom environment and characteristics of mildly handicapped students, let us take an imaginary journey into two quite different environments—Mr. Miller's classroom and Mrs. Jackson's classroom. In each classroom, we will focus our attention on Glen, Marsha, and Charles. While this is a fictitious journey, the characters are not entirely fabricated—they are composite sketches of mild educationally handicapped students I have taught, talked with, and observed in classrooms, and of teachers and classrooms we have all seen and experienced.

Mr. Miller's Classroom Environment

First, let us visit Mr. Miller's classroom. Mr. Miller believes that all students should learn essentially the same material but recognizes that students learn at different rates and with different levels of proficiency. Therefore, he has determined which things all students need to know and teaches them these things at different rates. Mr. Miller has classified skills work—reading, writing, and math—as a "need to know" area and has divided the class into ability groups based on their proficiency level in these skills. Each group can then move through the curriculum, structured by a basal reading series and math series, at its own rate. The things students should but do not need to master, in his estimation, are taught to all students at the same time so each can absorb as much as he or she is able. Mr. Miller expects some students to acquire the knowledge in greater depth than others but believes all should be exposed to the same content. Much of this instruction is through reading or lecture, although Mr. Miller conscientiously brings in films, invites speakers, and does demonstrations to maintain student interest and provide something for his poorer readers.

As Mr. Miller is orienting you to his classroom, he points out three students who have been identified as being handicapped: Glen, Marsha, and Charles. They will be removed from his classroom for special help part of each day starting next week. You spend the day observing in Mr. Miller's class, during which time you "shadow" each of these students, starting with Glen.

Glen and Marsha make up the lowest reading group. As you observe reading instruction, you notice that most of the time is spent laboriously drilling on reading skills, and on slow oral reading from the basal. Afterward, you ask Glen how he feels about reading.

"I hate it," he replies. "It's boring. The book is boring, and the worksheets are boring. I wish reading had never been invented." Unfortunately for Glen, social studies, and science instruction are based largely around reading. Today in social studies there is a filmstrip, which Glen operates, and then a worksheet about major concepts in the filmstrip. Science instruction consists of several pages to read from the science book, with questions to answer. You again ask Glen how things are going for him in class today.

"I feel like the only thing I'm good at around here is running the projector and watering plants. At home I have an aquarium and I've learned a lot about fish from watching them, asking people about them, and reading about them in some books my mom got me. But in here, you have to be able to read and answer questions or you don't learn much. I'm not saying it's Mr. Miller's fault because he tries to help. He usually has me read with someone, and he helps me with the worksheet. But he makes almost everyone else do the work on their own, so I feel dumb having special help. And some kids make fun of me and call me "dummy" because I'm always needing extra help to get the work done. I wish science at school could be like the way it is at home —interesting and fun."

Marsha responds to your question about reading somewhat differently. After watching her diligently but slowly complete her workbook assignment, you ask her how she feels about reading.

"I don't mind it," she says. "I gotta learn to read. I just wish there were more kids in our group. The bigger groups get to read plays and do fun things like that. Maybe if I work hard I can catch up and be in a group with more kids."

Marsha's response to reading characterizes her approach to everything else she does in class: she works slowly but diligently, and she usually works alone unless Mr. Miller is helping her. At the end of the day you ask what she has learned.

"Well, I don't really remember anything about the science lesson, but I learned a lot about our state capital from the filmstrip. When my family lived in another state, we visited the capital. It looked different from this one—more modern. The building was square, with a statue on top. This building is round. I like drawing pictures of different kinds of buildings."

Having noticed Marsha working and playing alone most of the day, you ask her if she ever works with other kids in class. "No, they mostly just leave me alone. I try being nice and sometimes they are nice back, but they don't talk to me much. Mr. Miller is nice—he talks to me and helps me when he has time."

You then reflect on Charles's day in Mr. Miller's class. Charles spent part of the day in the office for shoving other students as he came into class. When he returns, you ask him about it. "I know I'm not supposed to hit people, but they were calling me names, and I didn't know what else to do. I just get really mad when people call me names. Some kids in here think I'm a real dope. It seems like I'm always getting yelled at."

Charles sits down and starts his science assignment. After about ten minutes he pokes the student in front of him with a pencil. Mr. Miller immediately asks him to stop. Two minutes later Charles stretches and yawns loudly. Several people look at him and Mr. Miller frowns. A few minutes after that Charles goes to the pencil sharpener and hits a girl on the head along the way. "Quit it," she says.

You ask Charles about his behavior. "I just can't sit still for that long and do that work. I can read the book OK, but it's boring to sit that long. The only times when I don't get in trouble a lot are when I'm playing football, when I'm working on cars, and when I'm building electronic things at home. I like being active and I like working with my hands."

Mr. Miller's classroom is an environment in which three students are failing academically: Glen because he cannot read and therefore learns much less than he is capable of learning, Marsha because she needs more help than Mr. Miller can give in order to finish the work, and Charles because he cannot sit still long enough to finish the kind of work Mr. Miller gives him. These three students are also failing socially: they are viewed by their peers as dumb or bothersome and are either teased or ignored. In Mr. Miller's classroom, all three are mildly handicapped.

Mrs. Jackson's Classroom

Now let us visit the classroom of Mrs. Jackson. Mrs. Jackson believes that a wide variety of things are worth learning and that there is a variety of ways in which people can learn. If you walk into her classroom almost any hour of the day, you would find a hub-bub of activity, with different students doing different things. You would also usually find a helper or two—since Mrs. Jackson can't instruct or help several different groups and individuals at once, she brings in parent volunteers, school specialists, and paraprofessionals. She also encourages students to help each other and periodically has training sessions for adult and student helpers to increase their effectiveness. Mrs. Jackson also spends a considerable amount of time in basic skills instruction, but she structures as much of it as she can through projects the students are working on, and provides individual and small group instruction in specific skill areas while her classroom helpers are available to supervise other learning activities.

Let us imagine Glen, Marsha, and Charles in Mrs. Jackson's room. Mrs. Jackson explains that she has had Glen and Marsha classified as learning disabled and educable mentally retarded respectively in order to obtain the help of the special education teachers in the school but comments that she does not view these students as being handicapped in her room. In fact, she has tried to structure the work so that *all* her students benefit academically, grow socially, and feel competent.

Early in the day Glen's special education teacher comes into the room and gives Glen individual instruction in reading skills. Then Glen joins a small group of classmates who are reading mystery stories. Today they read to each other in pairs and then discuss the story as a group, using a list of questions they developed under Mrs. Jackson's guidance. Glen participates actively in the discussion. Then Glen joins another group that is working on a project about sea life. They will be presenting their work to the class next week. Since Glen is knowledgable about fish, he acts as group leader; his task is to coordinate the project, make a mural about sea life, and deliver part of the oral presentation. Other group members complete library research and construct a food chain diagram.

How does Glen feel about school work in this environment? "I'm learning a lot. I want to be able to read better, and I'm getting reading help. I don't hate reading any more. Mrs. Jackson suggested I read with the mystery group because I like mystery stories—even though I can't read every word and I need help, I don't mind because the stories are so good. Besides, Mrs. Jackson has talked with us about how we all have strengths and weaknesses. I didn't know this before, but several other kids in the class go to specialists or take special lessons or buy special equipment for problems they have. Like, Mary has to do eye exercises every night, Joe goes to the orthodontist because his mouth doesn't close right, and Mike is colorblind. So no one teases me about my reading this year. Anyway, I can do lots of assignments in here on my own because there are usually choices about how the work is to be done."

Marsha's reading activities are similar to Glen's except Marsha is in a different interest-reading group. Marsha is also in a group that meets about three times a week with Mrs. Jackson. In this group, the students learn and practice social skills. Mrs. Jackson explains, "Someone like Marsha, who learns slowly anyway, has not had much of an opportunity to learn social skills since her peers usually ignore her." Marsha is also working with three students on a social studies project about the relationship between environment and life styles. The students read, view films, and discuss questions under the guidance of an older student from another classroom; based on this information they are preparing a picture-and-tape presentation for the class on this topic. Marsha is the artist for the group. As the class leaves for recess, Marsha is included in a game with students in her group.

Later she tells you, "Mrs. Jackson is teaching me how to let people know I like them. She taught me to smile and say something nice to people even if they don't say anything first. So I tried that with Jody. Jody has been in my grade for a long time, but she always left me alone. Now, working on this social studies project, we've gotten to be really good friends. Jody also helps me in math, and I'm going to teach her how to make chocolate chip cookies this weekend."

How does Charles fare in Mrs. Jackson's room? Since there is always some noise and movement, Charles's constant activity does not stand out. Furthermore, Charles frequently has an opportunity to work with his hands as he learns. He takes you over to the counter and shows you a model of undersea life he has constructed. He explains, "I didn't used to know anything about the sea, but Mrs. Jackson suggested I try building some models of fish. She gave me some books and a box of junk and told me to see what I could do. Now, this is a white shark. . . ." and Charles proceeds to explain the habits of each species in his undersea model.

Mrs. Jackson has provided an environment in which each student is unique but no student is handicapped. By teaching to the strengths and interests of her students, Mrs. Jackson is maximizing the success of each. Weaknesses are also recognized and attended to, often with the help of specialists, but weaknesses are seen as only a part of the total student. In addition, cooperative group work is frequently used in order to help students develop social skills and friendships, as well as to encourage students to learn from each other. Those whose social skills are poor are provided special social skills instruction, just as those whose reading or math skills are poor are provided special help. Furthermore, Mrs. Jackson openly discusses human differences with her students and makes sure that her curriculum includes a wide diversity of people. The underlying message of her curriculum is that diversity is normal.

But What About . . .

You may be saying to yourself, "I see the point, but—" In order to provide an environment that accepts a wide range of differences among students, there are some questions and issues you must deal with. Those most commonly voiced by teachers include the following.

I teach high school—this discussion doesn't apply to me, does it? Yes, it does! As a former high school teacher, I have tried many of the things advocated in this paper in a regular class and witnessed the effects of "traditional" classrooms on special education students whom I also taught. Many people think that the curriculum and the teaching strategies at the secondary level cannot be diversified without sacrificing academic excellence. It is more likely that the real reason there is less diversification within the classroom is that most secondary teachers simply have not had an opportunity to learn how to diversify their teaching without sacrificing excellence.

Isn't a classroom like Mrs. Jackson's deemphasizing the basic skills that are necessary to function in this society? That depends on how the teacher views basic skills. It is true that a classroom environment could be structured so that students used only their strong skills. It is equally true that such an environment would ill-prepare some of them for a world that expects all citizens to be able to read, write, and use arithmetic. But there are differences among methods of teaching. You can: teach to strengths while building up weak skill areas; teach to individuals' strengths and ignore their weak skill areas, or expect all students to learn through reading and recitation (which usually happens in school). Without deemphasizing the value of reading, writing, and arithmetic, alternative skills and learning modes can be given more value so that weaknesses do not always become roadblocks to success.

If ability groups tend to segregate students with academic problems from their other classmates, how do I teach them skills on their level without isolating them? You can group students for skills work on their level, but remember that during the day you can group students in a variety of different ways for other instruction. You can group students in a way that brings together a variety of different talents for the production of a single project. Grouping by interests, heterogeneous grouping for tutoring, and grouping friends together are also useful. You need not limit yourself to one or two kinds of groupings. What isolates children is remaining in the same group all day or working alone most of the day.

If I restructure classwork to improve students' social relationships, won't that interfere with the academic progress of all students? Not necessarily. A teacher like Mrs. Jackson does not teach everything through heterogeneous grouping. For example, there are skill groups for basic skills instruction, as well as individual projects in which students can pursue areas of learning in depth according to their own capabilities. In addition, there is no ceiling placed on what can be done by each student in small heterogeneous group projects.

I'm supposed to follow a set curriculum and so the only thing I can vary is the rate at which I teach it. You must decide how sacred you believe a set curriculum you are supposed to follow actually is. While modifying the content of your curriculum in no way entails throwing it away, it does mean that you will need to select what is worth teaching, and what could be replaced with content that relates to the interests and strengths of your students. If you deviate from prescribed curricula you feel you are expected to follow, carefully monitor your students' basic skills scores and keep track of what they are learning. If they are not falling behind in the basic skills, and if some are excelling where they were not before, it will be hard to dispute the modifications you have made in the curriculum in order to make it more meaningful to students.

It sounds like you are advocating getting rid of educational handicap classes—but these classes have been so beneficial to some students. Let us look at what has made them beneficial. The main factors include teachers trained to target instruction to individual students, teachers who genuinely like and appreciate "problem" students, and small class size. Most teachers can and should learn to teach and enjoy a wide diversity of students, but they need not take sole responsibility for the instruction of each and every student. In addition, there should be specialists who have additional training to help the regular teacher and to provide extra instruction to some students as needed.

If I only had fifteen students, I could do all that, but with a large class size, I simply don't have time. A few teachers are able to manage teaching and supervising a wide variety of learning activities by themselves. Many, however, learn to use help, since a cadre of helpers can multiply teaching time available for each student in the room. Help can come in the form of other students, parents, paraprofessionals, and specialists. You may also want to become politically involved in issues affecting class size. Volunteer some time to campaign for a school budget that allows for smaller class size. Talk to people about why class size should be reduced.

I just don't have the resources to get a lot of different things going. Accumulating resources takes some time, and even if you are a preservice student, you can start now. Label several boxes with broad subject areas or interdisciplinary topics and then keep your eyes open for interesting resources you might be able to use. Whenever you buy something, however, keep the receipt—it is tax deductible. As a teacher, find out if there are any budgetary resources available to you; ask your principal, your special education colleagues, or a supervisor you might have. Sometimes there are funds available that you can use but that are not well advertised. Find out if there are unused books in your school or recycled materials in your school district. Additionally, ask parents to contribute such things as old magazines, scraps of fabric, etc. Volunteer to try out materials for book companies or for university professors. Once you have established a network, finding resources will not be much of a problem for you.

I don't have the skills to teach a wide variety of kids or to manage a lot of different projects. If you are a preservice student, you are in a good position to prevent this from becoming a problem. Seek out experiences that will prepare you to structure your classroom in a variety of ways so that you can adapt your room environment to your students. Take courses that help you increase your skills for teaching a variety of students. If you are currently a practicing teacher, visit some classrooms of teachers who are doing successfully what you lack skills in doing. You may be able to learn what you need from them (for example, an efficient management system for keeping track of student work), or learn exactly what additional training would benefit you (for example, a particular inservice course in mathematics).

Conclusion

To teach "handicapped" students successfully requires more than making a few adjustments to the traditional classroom curriculum. It requires some major changes in what is taught and how teaching is structured. But you need not be in the dark as you attempt to make the necessary changes—there is a rapidly growing body of literature providing guidelines for planning a classroom that integrates a diversity of students, and a research base that supports the effectiveness of most of the suggestions listed here. By following these suggestions and wrestling with the issues involved, you cannot only integrate mainstreamed students into your classroom but can also prevent some students from coming to be seen and classified as "educationally handicapped." You can create a learning environment that positively supports all your students.

There are many different kinds of rewards you will receive for adapting your instruction to each of your different students. The following poem from a parent of a child with a learning disability is a moving example.

Ode to an LD Teacher

Blanche LeBlanc

> You took my child,
>   He was failing.
> You took my cries,
>   I was hurting.
> You took my cares,
>   There were many.
> Life was one of constant fear.

Reprinted with permission from the author.

You taught my child,
and he's learning.
You heard my cries,
and I'm smiling.
You soothed my cares,
and they're lighter.
Now it's clear.
You changed our life,
and I know it.
But I've neglected
to show it.
Please forgive me,
I'm no poet.
Thank you, Dear.

Thus far we have thought about instruction from the standpoint of how students learn best. Instruction also needs to be considered from the standpoint of what kinds of people it is encouraging students to become. In the following article, Wynne questions whether traditional methods of instruction focus too much upon competition and not enough on working together or team learning.

Team Learning: Bringing Virtue to the Classroom

Edward A. Wynne
University of Illinois

There is increasing concern among educators about how to improve the character of their pupils. Some of this concern is directed at preventing bad or wrong conduct, with maintaining discipline. Some of it is directed at encouraging students to become ethical or to be actively good citizens. Although there are diverse ways to deal with this, most of the approaches have an important element in common: they invite students to talk,

Reprinted with permission from the *American Educator*, Summer, 1981.

think, and write about the practice of ethics. They do not invite or compel the students to *do* ethics.

This current focus on discussing virtue instead of practicing it is distressing. Indeed, as far as the practice of virtue goes, many teachers, in the management of their classes, actively (albeit accidentally) encourage their students to engage in selfish and inconsiderate conduct. Given this prevalence of selfish practices among pupils, talking about virtue tends to be academic—in the worst sense.

Many teachers, for example, grade students solely for showing that they have learned their particular academic lesson. If students want to do well, they understand that concentrating on their own work and disregarding their classmates is the way to win teacher approval—as evidenced by grades. If students choose to spend time helping other pupils (assuming they are not cheating), such assistance will often not help their own grades at all. Indeed, it may even lower the final grade of the helping students, since the helpers will have less time available for their own studying, and if the students helped become better, their improvement may cause the teacher to raise standards for the whole class (including the formerly successful students).

The troubling themes I have just expressed are reflected in a joke a college student recently told me:

"How many pre-med students are needed to change a light bulb?"

"Three! One to change the bulb, and two to pull the ladder out from under the changer."

The joke is apocryphal but based on persuasive evidence. In this student's comparatively prestigious college, there are well-documented instances of pre-med students destroying each other's lab experiments so that the comparative class standing of the destroyers will be raised.

Of course, the rigorous competition pervading some pre-med work is more intense than that which exists in many classrooms. Indeed, some classrooms may even have too little competition. Still, the principle underlying the pre-med anecdote is pertinent to all levels of education. Students, quite properly, see grades as rewards, issued by prestigious adults—their teachers. These rewards, in general, are granted to students who do their own work and do it better than others. Such grading systems provide few or no incentives to students to be solicitous to others or to wish their fellows—their competitors for recognition—well. This process is epitomized in the pre-med stories, where students who are learning to help the sick first learn to get ahead by undermining their future colleagues.

Some of the effects of such policies are suggested by the observations —including those of many teachers—that many pupils seem to become more self-centered and ill at ease as they become older. These changes are often attributed to developmental patterns. However, such personality traits are not commonly found among young adults in many other cultures. Some researchers have argued that the distressing traits that we see as sometimes typical of adolescents are largely due to the particular social environments in which our society places them. The traits are not inherent in all young persons everywhere. We, the adults in the United States, maintain policies that cause them to develop. I believe that one cause is our school grading systems, which become steadily more individualistic as pupils progress through school and college. After being exposed to such systems for, let us say, ten years, it's not surprising that pupils do not expect much from their peers and are reluctant to give much of themselves. Indifference such as this is what helps students to earn good grades.

Of course, not all pupils earn good grades or make grades their paramount goal. Even inadequate students, however, are influenced by the process I have described. Some poor students keep striving and thus adopt withdrawn attitudes, even though they do not receive good grades. Other students (some of whom may even have academic potential) reject the grade race and withdraw into peer groups that are anti-academic in their orientation. Sometimes such groups drift into antisocial conduct, since the structure of school rewards provides them with few legitimate outlets for collective efforts.

This system also creates barriers between students who earn good grades and many other students. The implicitly selfish conduct of many good students generates various forms of interstudent resentment, which either lowers the academic motivation of some potentially good students or diminishes the solicitude of the good students toward their less able peers.

The harmful effects of modern grading systems have intensified over the past fifty years. Pupils are staying in schools for more years and are attending school more days each year. As more pupils aim for college, individual grades, and test scores become more important. Schools and colleges have become larger and more departmentalized, and it is harder to shape healthy interpupil relations in such environments. The increasing segmentation of the school process—in some communities we now have preschool, elementary school, middle school, junior high school, high school, junior colleges, and four-year colleges—has also handicapped the vitality of helping attitudes.

It is difficult to teach students about ethics or morality in this environment. All important research about learning, as well as a vast well of traditional wisdom, has stressed the importance of practice as the key to comprehension. The idea of effectively teaching about doing good in classrooms in which pupils routinely ignore each other's problems is a solecism. Indeed, such an approach may generate a sort of adolescent pretentiousness; students judge the morals of real or hypothetical presidents, mayors, businessmen, and characters from novels while not even considering or acting upon their own personal obligations to each other. The judgments of others who are remote to students are probably unduly harsh because we first learn perspective by examining our own conduct.

Many teachers and administrators have recognized that unethical attitudes may be stimulated by devil-take-the-hindmost competition and have attempted corrective measures. Some of these are sound, others are questionable.

For younger students and self-contained classes, teachers establish climates that stimulate both application to individual learning and concern for fellow classmates. Sometimes such climates are related to grading systems, which focus on both academic performance and classroom conduct; sometimes, even when grades are the sole focus of academic work, the teacher communicates the importance of pupil-to-pupil solicitude through words and conduct. Teachers (and administrators) also establish various nonacademic responsibilities for students (for example, tutoring, monitors, messengers), which require pupils to engage in unselfish acts of immediate helpfulness to others.

Other measures to moderate destructive competition are less admirable. Sometimes the pursuit of excellence by pupils is ignored by teachers; thus, no one cares about doing well. Sometimes teachers and professors assign projects to teams of students so that interpupil cooperation is encouraged. Not all team assignments are designed properly so that the appropriate effects are attained, however.

I routinely survey my college pupils about the team assignments they have been given in college or in their precollege work. In particular, I ask how they were graded for such work. In most cases, they simply were given whatever grade the total team effort earned or received the same grade for their team work that they were individually earning in their other classwork. Both grading systems are counterproductive. When all team members receive the same grade, both the workers and the loafers (and we all know that not all students want to work hard) get the same grade. This equivalence leads to its predictable effect. One reasonably able high school student once told me he wasn't going to work hard on his assignment since "it is a group project." In other words, he felt that, even if he didn't apply himself, some ambitious student would do the work for the team in order to protect his or her own grade. Similarly, when all team members simply get their individual preteam grades, there's no incentive for any of them to work at all.

When a teacher assigns a task to a team of students, we cannot assume that the team will really "work together" unless the teacher establishes a reward system congruent with this end. Otherwise, the assignment may simply encourage various forms of exploitation or indifference.

Several researchers have developed systems of grading an assignment that deal with the problems I have portrayed. Essentially, the systems provide for grouping students in relatively heterogeneous teams and giving them projects that are done on a collective basis. The grading and assignments involved stimulate intergroup effort. Some of the grading systems make provision for different grades among the team members based on their different contributions. The systems can be adopted either by groups of teachers or in individual classrooms and can be applied to various subjects. Some of them are adaptable at a college level.

Teachers do not need extensive training to use them (the inservice training time for one system runs from two to four hours). Considerable research has demonstrated that pupils taught by such systems do as well —or better—on objective academic tests as pupils taught by traditional methods of grading and assignment. Furthermore, the team systems are popular with pupils, and the quality of interpupil relations in such classes—especially across races—is much higher than in traditional classes.

These team-learning systems, in effect, require the participating students to practice virtue—and not just talk about it. The students practice virtue since they are under pressure to pay attention to what their team members are doing and to try and help them do better. As we realize from our own lives, it is not always pleasant or easy to be helpful to others—after all, if such conduct was always fun, virtue would not be precious. Of course, the "problems" for students of being virtuous to their peers are not insurmountable. In well-designed team learning, the challenges are akin to other constructive learning problems; they are mildly demanding, provide some novelty, are relevant, and can be surmounted with a genuine effort.

Many of the questions teachers have about team learning are not about the details of structure but about the larger intellectual framework into which the new system fits. These objections may go something like this:

- Team learning is not good because life is competition, not cooperation. As a result, it can teach students unrealistic attitudes.
- Team learning is not fair because in team situations individual students' grades may be affected by the conduct of other students who are beyond the affected students' full control.
- Team learning is not good because students will be unprepared for it (due to their previous individualistic learning) and too much stress will result.

Here are some answers, however, to these objectives:

Adult life includes both competition and cooperation. It is the class-room, not life, that is abnormal, since it gives such stress to individualistic competition. To illustrate this, allow me to recount a meeting I had with a corporation president. As we talked about modern education, he remarked that he received many appeals for money from his prestigious undergraduate school. He said that he felt obligated to donate to the school but did not "trust" what was going on in its regular academic programs; he felt that too many college graduates did not have healthy attitudes toward work life. The only activities he felt he could justi-fiably support with contributions were competitive team sports—he believed that such activities taught students the appropriate attitudes for work life.

In other words, healthy adult life is not lived alone but with friends, spouses, coworkers, and neighbors. And, among all the jobs adults can hold, teaching is perhaps the most isolating. Maybe this isolation handi-caps teachers in appreciating the high level of cooperation that prevails in most adult work. This isolation may also cause them to overvalue in-dividualistic competition rather than encourage student teamwork.

Human beings are always affecting each other, but it is usually simplistic to talk about "control." All relationships require us to consider the attitudes and conduct of those around us and shape our own acts and words to attain appropriate effects on our associates. The only way to escape such pressures is to live in cells or physical isolation. Too many classroom students tend to become emotionally isolated, even though they are surrounded by others because of the reward structures schools establish. For educators, the appropriate response to this problem is not to praise and maintain such isolation but to devise new structures that better prepare students to influence—and to be appropriately influenced by—others.

Students have a variety of experiences beyond living and working in highly individual classrooms. They are members of families, usu-ally have groups of friends, and may be involved in a variety of other cooperative activities. Thus, cooperation is not totally foreign to them. Unfortunately, some important types of youth cooperation are not desirable, including "gangs" and other forms of group delinquency. Probably one cause for the formation of such delinquent groups is the failure of adults—often educators—to recognize the healthy need of the young to engage in cooperative activities. A wiser response would be to harness this important force through the development of team-learning systems so that young persons are encouraged to work together under the supervision of responsible adults for constructive ends.

A final objection to using team learning is one that I never hear uttered but that I believe is still quite important. Too many teachers want to be Big Daddy—or Mommy—to their students. They want their students to see them as the ultimate source of authority and wisdom. Team learning conflicts with this aim, since such learning stimulates higher levels of student-to-student interaction and leaves the teacher as the overall guide rather than the personalized mentor.

A coach, for example, is an important person to team members. The coach tries to shape relationships within the team by a variety of devices and has many one-to-one contacts with players. A team would not be a "team," however, if its members looked largely to the coach for relationships or even to learn skills. Most of the players' contacts are with fellow team members.

In well-run athletic teams, the general level of intensity—and learning—is higher than in most classrooms. In effect, the coach (or, if we choose, the teacher) enlarges the instructional pie by bringing more people into the action. Because of this enlargement, all participants—including team members or students—have more responsibility. Thus, in team-learning situations, teachers and pupils, too, will all have more "pie." Unfortunately, some teachers seem more concerned with having larger proportions of the pie. For this reason, they resist team learning since such an approach requires them to share the sun with others—their students.

Sometimes this resistance is defended by teachers who argue that individualization would be sacrificed. In practice, this individualization often only means that most students are isolated from each other and that a few of them hold the attention of the teacher. It is just statistically impossible for a teacher—regardless of class size—to relate to most of the pupils in any class on a personal basis. (This is especially true in departmentalized schools and classes.) In the end, the wise teacher or professor must be concerned with fostering good pupil interaction through approaches such as team learning. Without such a collective focus, a teacher may only have a few engaged students who may end up as pre-med students who go around destroying each other's experiments.

Let us take the concept of team work advocated by Wynne into an area that is often the number one concern (unfortunately) of teachers— discipline. In too many schools the criteria for determining a good teacher centers upon the teacher's ability to control the students. I frequently hear teachers voicing a we-they relationship with their students when it comes to discipline, instead of a "we-ness." Seymour Sarason provides an illuminating discussion about how and why teacher-pupil support in the classroom is established. And Curwin, Mendler, and Culhane offer suggestions for working out effective classroom relationships.

The Teacher: Constitutional Issues in the Classroom

Seymour Sarason
Yale University

Constitutional Issues

Almost all teachers meet a new group of pupils on the first day of school. The beginning phase of the school year certainly extends beyond the first day, but by the third or fourth week a routine is established and teacher and pupils have, so to speak, sized up each other; the rules of the game by which everyone will be governed are fairly well known. How does this come about? How do teachers present and explain these rules of group living? Are these rules discussed? Are they for children only? What role do pupils play, if any, in the formation of rules? These questions and others comprise what I like to call the constitutional questions because in each classroom there is a constitution, verbalized or unverbalized, consistent or inconsistent, capable or incapable of amendment, that governs behavior. Constitutions tell us a good deal about history, tradition, and conceptions of human behavior.

We did an informal observational study of six classrooms, two each in grades 3, 4, and 5 in a suburban school system. In each of these six classrooms we had an observer who sat in the classroom for the first month of school beginning on the first day. The task of the observer was to record any statement by teacher and child that was relevant to "constitutional issues." The results were quite clear:

1. The constitution was invariably determined by the teacher. No teacher ever discussed why a constitution was necessary.
2. The teacher never solicited the opinions and feelings of any pupil about a constitutional question.
3. In three of the classrooms the rules of the game were verbalized by the end of the first week of school. In two others the rules were clear by the end of the month. In one it was never clear what the constitution was.
4. Except for the one chaotic classroom, neither children nor teachers evidenced any discomfort with the content of con-

Taken from *The Culture of the School and the Problem of Change*. Allyn and Bacon, Inc. Boston 1982.

stitutions—it was as if everyone agreed that this is the way things are and should be.

5. In all instances constitutional issues involved what *children* could or could not, should or should not, do. The issue of what a *teacher* could or could not, should or should not, do, never arose.

On a number of occasions I have presented these findings to groups of teachers with the question: How do we explain them? In every group the question produced silence. In one group a teacher responded in a way that I think verbalized what most teachers were thinking: *What* is there to explain? I would then follow my initial question with another question: What do we have to assume to be true about children and teachers in order to justify these findings? These discussions were by no means easy or pleasant, and understandably so, if only because the teachers had never been called upon to make explicit the conceptions and values upon which these practices were based. But what were some of the assumptions that teachers could, after prolonged discussion, recognize and state?

1. Teacher knows best.
2. Children cannot participate constructively in the development of a classroom constitution.
3. Children want and expect the teacher to determine the rules of the game.
4. Children are not interested in constitutional issues.
5. Children should be governed by what a teacher thinks is right or wrong, but a teacher should not be governed by what children think is right or wrong.
6. The ethics of adults are obviously different from and superior to the ethics of children.
7. Children should not be given responsibility for something they cannot handle or for which they are not accountable.
8. If constitutional issues were handled differently, chaos might result.

If one does not make these assumptions, which is to say that one thinks differently about what children are and can do, one is very likely to think differently about what the role of the teacher might be. In this connection it is instructive to note that as I pursued the issues with the groups of teachers, and the assumptions could be clearly verbalized, *many of the teachers found themselves disagreeing with assumptions they themselves recognized as underlying their classroom behavior.* Equally as instructive was the awareness on the part of a few that if one changed assumptions one would have to change the character of one's role, and this was strange and upsetting, as indeed it should be because they realized that life in the classroom for them and the children would become different.

The problem we are discussing goes beyond the classroom, and its generality hit me with full force during one of these discussions with teachers. That it hit me with such force in this particular group was in part due to the fact that several of the teachers were quite adamant in maintaining that young children had to have their lives structured for them by adults because they were too immature to participate in and take responsibility for important decisions governing classroom life. *What I became aware of during the discussion was that these teachers thought about children in precisely the same way that teachers say that school administrators think about teachers; that is, administrators do not discuss matters with teachers, they do not act as if the opinions of teachers were important, they treat teachers like a bunch of children, and so on.* And should not these analogies be extended to include the way in which school personnel regard community representatives in relation to participation in educational policy? Elsewhere, I have emphasized the significance of power, and people's view towards it, in understanding relationships within the school culture and between those within and without the school setting. The failure of efforts to introduce and sustain educational change have foundered largely because they have not come to grips with the power aspects of existing relationships, and by coming to grips I obviously do not mean change by fiat or appeal to people's good will or to token gestures that everyone recognizes as a degrading charade. Readers will recall that one of the major findings of Berman and McLaughlin was that successful educational change required the serious and active participation of the classroom teacher. Similarly, Cowen (Cowen et al., 1975), whose program in the Rochester schools is the most long-lived successful intervention that will be found in the research literature, emphasizes the centrality of the classroom teacher in planning and implementation. Unlike most proponents for change, Cowen altered the teacher's accustomed feelings of powerlessness, a change that had remarkable effects on the teacher's motivation, creativity, and industry. The point that must not be overlooked, however, is that teachers tend to regard children in a way that arouses hostility and lowers motivation in teachers when others regard them in that same way. The use and militancy of teacher organizations have a complex history, but one of the most important factors was the unwillingness of teachers to be governed by a tradition in which they had no part in decisions and plans that affected them. During the turbulent sixties and early seventies, a period during which teacher militancy dramatically increased in strength and consequence, there was a similar militancy on the part of pupils (largely in middle and high schools) centering around dissatisfaction with the powerlessness of students in regard to life in schools. Students were no longer content to be the traditional students—passive receptacles of learning. They clamored to be regarded as capable of participating in and taking some responsibility for their formal education. Just as teacher militancy was perceived as a threat to the decision-making power of administrators and boards of education, and just as the militancy of community groups was perceived as a threat to the power of educators, so was the militancy of students perceived by school personnel. The creation of alternative schools has to be seen in the context of the different power struggles that were going on.

One should not overlook the fact that what was going on in the public schools was also going on in the college and universities: students were challenging their accustomed role of powerlessness in the classroom. A constitutional change seemed to be occurring. The amending of constitutions has been and always will be accompanied by strong conflict for two reasons: there are differences in conception of what people (teachers, students) are, and it is recognized that what is at issue is what life in a school is and could be. The conflicts wax and wane depending on what is happening in the larger society. The issue of power has long been the basis for competing educational theories, but it requires sea-swell forces in the society to illuminate dramatically the practical significances of these competing theories for institutional change. To change the quality of life in a classroom, especially when that change involves changes in power relationships, involves no less than a basic change in the culture of the school. It is not a change that can happen quickly. It is certainly not a change that can take place only from within what we traditionally call a school system. It is a change, in whatever degree, that will occur through alterations in the transactions between school and society.

It is not my purpose, except in a very secondary way, to say how things should be. The primary purpose is to describe some of the important regularities in the culture of the school and to relate them to the conceptions and theories that "justify" these regularities. In order to do this I have tried, wherever possible, to contrast these existing relationships with the ever present but neglected universe of alternatives of conceptions from which derives a universe of alternative actions. This tactic not only serves to make one aware how the weight of habit and tradition can obscure the difference between what is and could be, but it also helps force those who want to introduce changes to be more precise about what it is they want to change. The "constitutional problem" is a case in point. I have known many teachers, principals, and school administrators who pride themselves on their adherence to democratic principles and feel strongly that the needs and rights of children have to be taken into account. In addition, these same people can point to colleagues whom they label as authoritarian or restrictive, with the implication that these characteristics are antieducational in spirit and effect. Without denying in the slightest that these differences exist, I have also to say that, constitutionally speaking, the differences are not all that great; in terms of how and on what basis the classroom constitution is determined, the "democratic" and "authoritarian" teacher are not as far apart as one might think.[1]

In both cases I have been impressed by three things: constitutions are for children and not teachers, complete power is retained by the teacher, and children passively accept the constitution developed for them. Those who wish to change life in the classroom are dealing with constitutional issues and not, as is too frequently the case, with high-sounding slogans whose conceptual underpinnings remain unexamined with the usual result that there is a discrepancy between what is said and what is done.[2]

As a reminder, in this chapter we are attempting to understand the relationship between what teachers do (or do not do) and how they think about children and themselves, to understand the "theories" of teachers—not their feelings or values, but their conceptions of what people are. And teachers, like the rest of us, have such conceptions, which, again like for the rest of us, are usually implicit rather than explicit.

Notes

[1] This conclusion is similar to that made by Jules Henry (1963), based on his observations of life in the suburban classroom. Henry is one of the very few anthropologists who has directly studied the classroom. His description and discussion of life in the classroom are illuminating and provocative. Given the emphasis in anthropology on foreign and so-called primitive cultures, it is not surprising that this important discipline has not focused on the classroom in our society (e.g., Spindler (ed.), 1963).

[2] The constitutional issues, as well as others to be raised in this chapter, could be regarded as relevant to, or subsumed under, a theory of instruction. This would be a matter of indifference to me were it not that theories of instruction do not deal with constitutional issues, but rather focus on the cognitive characteristics of the individual child, and on how these characteristics develop and could be taken account of in curriculum building. As often as not the theory talks about *a* child, and not a child in a group of children. Any theory of instruction that does not confront the reality that the teacher does not instruct *a* child but a group of children is not worth very much, to teachers at least. Even where the teacher intends to instruct a particular child, it takes place psychologically (for the child, teacher, and

the other children) in the context of being part of a larger group and set of relationships. I quite agree with Jones' critique (1968) of Bruner's (1966) theory of instruction; that is, his overemphasis on cognitive skills and curricular skills and underemphasis on the affective. Jones comes close to including the constitutional question in his theory of instruction, but it is far from as explicit as I think will be found to be necessary. This may be because Jones, in reacting to Bruner's overemphasis on the cognitive side, gets riveted on the expression of the affective side, and what tends to get sidetracked are the constitutional arrangements between teacher and class that maximize such expression. Depending as Jones does on Freud's and Erikson's conceptions about individual development, he cannot develop what is needed: a truly social psychological theory of instruction. These objections aside, I consider Jones' book a distinct contribution.

Kids and Teachers Discipline
One Another

Richard Curwin and Barry Culhane
National Technical Institute for the Deaf
Allen Mendler
Rush Henritta School, New York City

Few sane people would pick a fight if they were outnumbered 25 or 30 to 1; yet that's close to what most teachers do when they adopt a traditional plan of classroom discipline. The guiding "them against me" philosophy guarantees a no-win situation.

It doesn't have to be that way. Discipline can be a shared, even-handed responsibility developed and administered as part of a classroom social contract. Such a contract is produced through a process called Three-Dimensional Discipline, which is based on prevention, action and resolution. The social contract consists of three kinds of rules and their consequences, all of which are generated, discussed, tested and refined by members of the class:

1. The teacher develops rules for the students and proposes consequences—not "punishments"—appropriate for violations of the rules.
2. Students develop rules for the teacher and consequences for violations of those rules.
3. Students develop rules for themselves and consequences for violations of those rules.

Reprinted by special permission of LEARNING, *The Magazine for Creative Teaching*, February, 1980, © 1980 by Pitman Learning, Inc.

The process is time-consuming and can at times be tedious. But the product—a statement that reflects the needs of all persons in the classroom—is well worth the effort. The contract saves time in the long run because it tends to be a guide to civil behavior—and a means of preventing bad behavior—rather than a mere schedule of violations and penalties.

The First Rule: Make Good Rules

Make your rules as specific as possible. A detailed list of rules about things that really matter is more effective than one global rule whose vagueness masks many areas of doubt and confusion. Make your rules positive by stressing acceptable behavior. For example, "Settle disputes by talking rather than by fighting" is a better rule than "No fighting."

Also, by distinguishing between *punishments* and *consequences*, you ensure that students understand the relationship between a violation and what follows. Punishments are designed merely to "get even" or to hurt the offender; they have little to do with the behavior involved. For example, traditionally, if Johnny throws paper on the floor, he is punished with some form of silent detention. Experience indicates that such punishments do not produce long-term changes in behavior. Consequences, on the other hand, are designed to correct rule-breaking behavior quickly and directly. Consequences for throwing paper might be picking up the paper, apologizing to the teacher and the class for the specific misbehavior, and possibly—if the offense warrants—tidying up the classroom still further. It is particularly important for students to understand that consequences are not a matter of the teacher "getting even," but rather a group's way of "undoing" inappropriate behavior.

Teachers Make Rules for Students

The teacher brainstorms a comprehensive list of rules as part of the raw material from which the social contract will be developed. These rules must, of course, fit under the umbrella of existing federal, state, local, and school regulations. Within those bounds, the teacher should try to draft rules about matters that are personally important as well as rules to meet the needs of the class as a whole. Examples of such rules are: "Homework must be turned in on the day it is due," and "Students will be on time for class." Achievement—how much and how fast students learn—is not a proper subject for general rule making, but the teacher's rules should otherwise cover every aspect of classroom behavior and study habits. Bear in mind that these rules will be understandable and enforceable only if they are specific. If general rules leave room for doubt and interpretation, discipline is likely to collapse.

After establishing clear, specific rules, the teacher must develop consequences for violations of each rule. Students should know that there will be no allowance for mitigating circumstances (for example, the teacher will not overlook the violation even if Mary forgets her homework for the first time ever or when John acts up after coming back from three days sick in bed). Exceptions to the rules invite manipulative behavior, excuse thinking and the whining "I didn't mean it" that teachers of young children have grown to dread.

The teacher, on the other hand, should not box herself in with a short list of unjustifiably harsh consequences. A range of alternatives, with at least one that falls in the warning or stop-and-think category, can help the teacher avoid this problem: Within a range of alternatives, any one consequence can be implemented at the teacher's discretion. Or a posted hierarchy of consequences can make clear what will happen each successive time a rule is violated; for example, for violating the rule, "Students will arrive for class on time," the consequences might be:

- The first infraction results in a teacher-student conference.
- The second infraction results in the student attending an afterschool class to make up the lost time.
- The third infraction results in a parent-student-teacher conference to find ways that the student can get to class on time.

Such a sequence offers the teacher less discretion, but the consequences are uniform, and everyone knows in advance exactly what will happen each time a rule is violated.

It may be helpful to have a system of positive consequences (free time, preferred activities, reduced homework, etc.) for students who consistently follow the rules. Some teachers, fearing that this practice creates an environment in which good behavior must be "bought," feel that it is wrong to reward expected behavior. Providing positive consequences, however, can prevent good students from developing the attitude that "the only way to get attention is to act out."

Students Make Rules for the Teacher

Rule making offers students a chance to express their feelings about the range and the limits of the teacher's behavior. It enables them to feel that they have at least some control over what happens in the classroom.

Student rule making for the teacher will vary depending on the students' age, grade and the kind of classroom—single subject or self-contained—in which they work. The teacher may choose to start the social contract process by reading a list of proposed rules and consequences for students, carefully explaining how each one helps maintain a supportive, productive classroom environment. The teacher might then present examples of two or three kinds of rules students can make for the teacher before inviting students to compose a full complement of policies.

The teacher might also choose to reverse these steps, encouraging students to develop rules they think should be obeyed by a fair and supportive teacher before introducing the teacher-made rules.

In either case, students' proposals, like those of the teacher, must be consistent with existing federal, state, local and school rules. This safeguards against the listing of such rules as "Students can smoke in class whenever they want" and other equally unrealistic measures. Students will accept this limit more easily if they understand that the teacher's rules follow the same guidelines.

Have students generate their rules by brainstorming. They should feel free to propose any rule that seems important and that does not violate existing laws and regulations. Help create an atmosphere in which everyone is comfortable making suggestions. Students should not fear that their ideas will seem silly or impractical to the teacher or to fellow students.

Students might make the rule, "The teacher must give all homework for the upcoming week on the Friday before so that students can plan their weekly work schedules." They would impose one of the following consequences, written specifically for this rule, if the teacher committed a violation:

- The teacher can give only four days of homework, none for the weekend.
- The teacher cannot give any homework that week.
- All homework is optional for extra credit.
- Students can choose their own homework assignments for the week.

Students Make Rules for Themselves

The students, who by now should be well acquainted with the process, develop a list of rules and consequences that define acceptable and unacceptable behaviors for themselves.

For violating the rule, "Name calling, use of four-letter words and use of putdowns are *not* allowed," possible consequences might be:

- The student must make a public apology.
- The student must write a letter of apology.

Violation of the rule, "Permission must be asked of others and granted by them before anyone can borrow items that belong to them," might result in one of the following consequences:

- The borrower must return the borrowed item.
- The borrower must loan the student something of the student's choice for one day.
- The borrower must pay rent, but no more than 25 cents a day.

Working for Concensus

All efforts up to this point involve production of raw materials from which the social contract will be forged. The first step in evaluating these raw proposals is to make sure all students understand the implications of the rules and their consequences and how these implications might affect classroom life. Role playing different rule-violation situations is a good way to demonstrate the relationship of rules and consequences to an orderly, functioning classroom.

The social contract is made up of rules and consequences endorsed by either the whole class or a great majority of it. During final negotiation of the social contract, the teacher may serve as "the authority" or as an equal group member. The role of group member—maintaining control only to see that the decision-making process works effectively—is obviously more attractive. The teacher, however, will ultimately have to live by the contract and be responsible for its implementation; so if there are rules and consequences that the teacher cannot accept, and must veto, they should be dealt with at the outset of the class discussion. The fewer vetoes exercised the better, though, for mutual trust in the process is greatly influenced by the teacher's willingness to go along with the rules and consequences that are agreed to by the class. Announce that the contract will be "on trial" for a month or so and that modifications and changes can occur at the end of that time. Because an inappropriate rule of consequence can be eliminated on the basis of real data at that time, the teacher is able to avoid vetoing proposals that will clearly prove to be unworkable. Test as many rules and consequences as possible in the classroom.

Final agreement on the rules and consequences of the social contract is best reached in three stages:

1. Seek unanimous consent. Some rules and consequences will be readily accepted by the whole group the first time the class goes through the list.

2. For all remaining rules, try to obtain a consensus through debate and discussion. Many more rules and consequences will be approved this way. A second opportunity for a consensus decision may be evident when discussion ebbs and differences appear minimal. The teacher may then say, "I can see that most of you want this rule, and I wonder if anybody who does not would really object to trying it for about a month to see what happens." If strong objections reappear, a consensus is not possible.

3. Vote to determine inclusion or exclusion of the remaining rules. The suggested models are the U.S. Senate treaty-ratification vote or the U.S. House of Representatives impeachment vote, either a two-thirds or three-fourths majority, to ensure that most students will abide by the rule or consequence.

Testing for Commitment

Some of the prime reasons that students break rules are that they do not understand them, they do not know they exist, or they "play ignorant." Extensive discussions help ensure that each student understands all the rules and consequences proposed and makes intelligent, informed choices. One additional step can make certain that real or "play" ignorance is not a cause of discipline problems. A written test will measure whether or not students understand the social contract. Like any other test, it should match the age and abilities of students. Either a perfect or a near perfect score is required for students to pass the test.

The final step in the social contract process is the designing and displaying of a poster or bulletin board presentation that clearly states each rule and consequence—preferably signed by all students and the teacher.

Most teachers who have implemented social contracts report significant decreases in the amount of instructional time that they spend attending to discipline problems. Although the social contract process may be initially time-consuming and sometimes tedious, it is likely to be worth all the time and energy put into it. The social contract is a vehicle for making classroom rules explicit and for inviting students to become part of the process. The teacher, then, is not the only person in the classroom dealing with discipline problems; all discipline problems are shared by everyone in the class and resolution occurs through participation. Such shared responsibility is a good way to tackle, and to subdue, the discipline problems in any classroom.

The previous article offered some practical suggestions for developing a classroom code for discipline. But, before you "grab on" to different practical suggestions you will get along the way, you first need to recognize the implications of your own teaching philosophy regarding classroom discipline. The article by Newton that follows offers a framework to help you do this.

Models of Schooling and Theories of Discipline

Robert R. Newton, S.J.
University of San Francisco

Part of the educational philosophy of every professional educator is a position on the aim and practice of discipline in schools. Though the primary and immediate goal of schooling may be cognitive development, no teacher or administrator is unaware of the idea that the socialization of a young person is a concomitant and necessary outcome, essential not only to prepare the student to live in society but also to insure an atmosphere which is conducive to learning during the school years.[1]

A theory of discipline colors how students and teachers relate and interact in a school. In schools where discipline is severe and rules are inflexible, the student-teacher relationship is formal and distant. Where rules have been replaced by guidelines and reprimand by rapport, the teacher-student relationship tends to be casual and informal. Underlying these diverse approaches are conflicting assumptions about how students grow and about how rules, authority, and punishment advance or retard that growth.

Different approaches to discipline are also one of the most frequent sources of conflict between teachers and administrators as well as among teachers. To some faculty members, discipline is perceived as too loose, a thing of the past, and not supportive of the intellectual climate that they are trying to build. Other teachers in the same school see discipline as too repressive, mistakenly focused on punishment, and ineffective in producing self-discipline. What is at issue is not so much perceptions of discipline as basic assumptions about the educational process, about models of schooling, and how education takes place. A

From *The High School Journal*, Volume 63, No. 5 February 1980. Copyright 1980 The University of North Carolina Press. Reprinted by permission of the publisher.

position on the role of discipline in the process of growth derives from and depends on answering more basic questions on the purpose of schools.

An explication of the educational models that underly attitudes towards discipline can create a better understanding not only of the various options available to educators but also of the reasons for conflict and confusion in this vital area of school life. In the analysis which follows, four educational models are described; then the implications of these models for discipline are explored and explicitated. The aim is to promote a greater awareness of the theoretical assumptions which motivate different attitudes toward discipline, and—as a consequence—to provide a more solid basis both for understanding and for intelligent action.

Four Educational Models

A. Individual Fulfillment

One model of schooling is the humanistic or Individual Fulfillment approach.[2] Starting with the optimistic assumptions about human nature that are the basis of humanistic or third force psychology, the Individual Fulfillment model emphasizes student initiative and self-direction as the heart of the educational process. What the student discovers for him/herself is what is really important. Growth takes place through the natural 'unfolding' of the student's unique capacities rather than through pumping outside knowledge and skills into the student. At the core of the educational process is learning-to-be-a-person, the development of a deep understanding of self; this personal self-realization then becomes the core around which all other learning takes place.

In such a model, the teacher's role is helpful and supportive rather than instrusive and directive. The teacher stands back and encourages, provides resources, interprets, and clarifies. The curriculum emerges out of the natural curiosity of the child placed in a rich educational environment. The school is structured around the concept of openness—physical, intellectual and affective—aimed at releasing and encouraging the powerful, deeply personal, but often untapped, desire of the student to know and to become.

B. Scholarly Discipline

A second model of schooling is the Scholarly Discipline or subject-oriented approach.[3] It focuses on knowledge and intellectual skills as the aim of schools. Its contemporary impetus came from scholars who were concerned that schools had lost their academic focus, and, as a consequence, were not producing graduates who were both knowledgeable and had the capacity to advance knowledge. The curriculum is composed of the enduring concepts and ideas which have emerged in the various disciplines through centuries of intellectual effort. If the material of the disciplines is properly translated and organized, it is assumed that students at any level can absorb the methods of inquiry and the important ideas of a discipline and their interrelatedness (the structure of the discipline). In a real sense the student becomes a beginning practitioner of the discipline—a fledgling historian, biologist, etc.

The role of the teacher in this approach is that of a model, a scholar who has chosen to communicate the substance and ways of knowing of a discipline to the next generation rather than to produce new knowledge. The school focuses around the 'traditional' pursuit of knowledge as it is contained in the time-honored approaches to understanding the world—the disciplines.

C. Educational Technology

The third approach to schooling is the behaviorist or Educational Technology model.[4] Deriving its basic insight from the work of the behavioral psychologists, the Educational Technology model concentrates its attention on educational outcomes. Learning is defined as change in behavior; schooling is the process through which precisely defined behavior changes are made to occur in students through the proper arrangement of activities and contingencies of reinforcement. The major force in shaping behavior is the environment.

The student is seen as a highly adaptable individual who is capable, if properly reinforced, of achieving the most complicated performances. The curriculum is an experimentally designed behavioral strategy which can produce learning more efficiently than any other less scientific approach. The teacher in this model becomes an expert in diagnosis, prescription and evaluation, a professional capable of adjusting materials and reinforcement to the needs of the individual student. Objectives have been carefully determined; evaluative methods are equally precise.

D. Social Reconstruction

The final model of schooling, the Social Reconstruction, interprets the goal of schools as social change and improvement.[5] The school itself is conceived as a miniature society where students learn the realities of political activity and where they are sensitized to the vital social issues which confront the human race. In the process, students develop not only the intellectual/political skills to enable them to effect change but also absorb a system of values which will motivate them to be active in the reform of unjust or dehumanizing social structures.

The curriculum in this model is adapted to include—wherever possible —explicit treatment of ethical issues implicit in every subject worth serious concern. The school environment provides an experience of life in society and of the importance of personal participation in the political process. The graduate emerging from such a school has developed critical intelligence which he/she will apply to the vital social problems of our civilization. The ultimate goal of the school is advancement/reform of society through the dedication of well trained, morally sensitive individuals.

The following chart serves to summarize and compare these four models of schooling on the important aspects of schooling.

Models and Schooling and Discipline

As noted initially, models of schooling—as perspectives on how students learn and grow—'spill over' into theories of discipline. In the following discussion, the implications of the four models as they bear upon discipline are explicitated.

A. Individual Fulfillment

Consistent with the basic premises of the Individual Fulfillment model, the aim of discipline in this approach is the development of self-direction by each individual. Just as the educational process in general relies primarily on the initiative of the student to direct his/her own learning, so the student in the Individual Fulfillment school is trusted to develop internal control of his/her behavior.

The basic principle which the school seeks to implement is the right of the student to exercise responsibility for personal behavior. Adults may provide the general context in which decisions are made, but the student should not be deprived of the right to decide for him/herself.

The rules which the school articulates for student behavior take the form of guidelines rather than specific regulations that govern every possible contingency. These guidelines provide opportunity for the exercise of freedom by the 'room' which they permit to students; they encourage rather than discourage initiative and responsibility.

The role of the adult members of the school community is to pro-

Table 1

Four Models of Schooling

	Aim of Learning	First Principle	Teacher	Student	Curriculum	Evaluation	Advocates
INDIVIDUAL FULFILLMENT	to be, to become	unfolding of nature	guide, helper partner	ultimate source of initiative and direction	curriculum with minimum structure	highly individual and personal; no uniform outcomes	open educators, liberals, radicals
SCHOLARLY DISCIPLINE	to know	accumulated wisdom of the disciplines	mediator	beginning practitioner of the disciplines	guided tour through the disciplines	knowledge of traditional content; ability to use scholarly tools, methods	academic community
EDUCATIONAL TECHNOLOGY	to do	systematic development of potentialities; from simple to the complex	implementor of an experimentally validated strategy	highly adaptable sophisticated respondent to reinforcement	scientifically developed sequentially arranged behavioral strategy	attainment of precise behavioral objectives/changes	behavioral psychologists, scientific managers
SOCIAL RECONSTRUCTION	to change to reform	school as an agency to change society	socially sensitive/responsible person	potential change agent	intellectual skills needed to reform society; ethical dimensions of subjects	knowledge, skills; ethical/social attitudes and value orientation	social reformers, political activists

vide a supportive environment in which students can exercise responsible self-regulation. The teacher is a non-directive counselor, allowing the student to be his/her own project, to mold his/her own behavior.

Authority or justification for this approach is founded in a basic trust of the natural processes of growth, as emerging naturally from the student's perception of the world and the natural sense of what is right and wrong in a particular situation. As Maslow suggests, the child, if given true freedom, can be trusted to choose what is really right for him/her. Rather than imposing a code of conduct from the outside, the rules for behavior are perceived, generated, and imposed by the student.

Punishment and reward are self-imposed and individual rather than a set of standard punishments for standard offenses. The student is allowed to make his/her own mistakes, put in contact with the consequences of those mistakes, and encouraged to learn from them.

In general the attitude of the faculty toward students is one of trust. They are given the benefit of the doubt, supplied freedom rather than controlled, and counselled rather than punished. Through such a process, a graduate who has personally internalized both the values and the practices of productive behavior will emerge from the schooling experience.

B. Scholarly Discipline

The Scholarly Discipline model of discipline unfolds from more traditional premises. The aim of discipline in this approach is to demonstrate the importance of right order and the observance of rules in any society. Respect for legitimate, hierarchical authority is the foundation stone, and it is both expected and demanded.

Authority is seen as external to the student. It is a natural part of the societal context of which he/she is a part. Regulations are established by adult authority and are predicated on the assumption that they are integral to the accomplishment of the goals of the school. The right of the faculty to establish these regulations is taken for granted.

The student is expected to cooperate willingly with the regulations and to offer his/her conformity and obedience in the interest of preserving good order in the school; he respects proper authority. The right of the school and its faculty to command respect is an extension of the respect and obedience owed by the young person to parents. Faculty members emerge as authority figures who are seen as originators and monitors of the rules for life in the school. Their status is taken for granted and is not subject to questioning: any faculty member has the right to command and it is the student's obligation to cooperate. Insubordination is the most problematic of all student behaviors.

The rules and regulations are specific, addressing the typical disciplinary problems and specifying not only the behavior that should have been manifested but also the consequences for the violation of the rule. Regulations are enforced fairly and equitably for all students. Punishments are public and uniform and follow virtually automatically upon the determination of a breech of discipline. Failure to enforce rules would eventually erode the authority on which they are based.

In general, students are regarded as junior members of a society which is governed by adults who are also role models. The expectation is that the student will not only recognize his/her experience but will also accept this subordinate status as the natural order for someone who is growing toward adulthood rather than being already there. By learning to accept authority and live cooperatively with others under authority, the young person gradually is prepared to be a cooperative member of the larger society.

C. Educational Technology

The aim of discipline in an Educational Technology school is to establish those patterns of behavior which will assist students and teachers in the achievement of learning outcomes. It is assumed that the most efficient disciplinary patterns can be identified and described, and, with the proper reinforcement, shaped in the learner.

The rules aim at encouraging and rewarding proper behavior rather than monitoring and punishing breeches of discipline. Underneath this strategy is the belief that behavior change is the result of approval rather than disapproval and that right patterns of behavior are established through positive rather than aversive reinforcement.

Authority for right behavior derives from and is a function of the need to create a productive learning environment. The rules are instruments to attain the discipline necessary to achieve behavioral learning outcomes, and—by virtue of this function—are legitimized. The set of rules that emerge are the result of a careful analysis of the proper behaviors and a systematic strategy designed to produce them.

The role of the student in an Educational Technology discipline system is that of an adaptable respondent to reinforcement. The student will, in the long run, be happier if he/she is able to establish the behaviors that will provide for a smoother integration into the existing social order.

The role of the faculty in this model is to provide the appropriate reinforcing environment and not only to specify the kind of behaviors that are desired but also to identify those means by which the desired behaviors will be rewarded. The discipline program is a carefully designed, low key behavior modification program.

In general, the student in the Educational Technology model of discipline is seen as a respondent to environmental forces which can shape his/her behavior in the proper direction in a satisfying, rewarding fashion and thus avoid the demeaning and negative effects of punishment-centered discipline. It is a scientific approach to designing and implementing a happy learning environment.

D. Social Reconstruction

The aim of the Social Reconstruction model of discipline is to give the student the experience of participating in the formation of the society of the school. The school, as an agency which prepares young people to live in and to improve society, must provide the student with an initiation into the realities of life in a democratic society.

The basic principle of discipline in a Social Reconstruction school emerges from the concept of the school as a society complete in itself, governed by those who populate it. Social rules and norms, both the generation and implementation, are the responsibility of the participants. The regulations that are enacted provide good order and allow the society of the school not only to function but also to address the important moral/ethical issues which are at the heart of any organization.

The source of rules is the democratic group process. Authority derives from the "consent of the governed;" its exercise is subject to critical review in terms of its efficacy in preserving and improving the society and promoting the welfare of its members.

The student is an active participant in the political and democratic process which generates rules and norms. The voice of students is not only accepted but also given influence, authority, and power in determining how the school is operated as well as how its goals are pursued. Faculty are participants in this political process, adding their opinions and voices to the decisions which emerge in the political process.

The punishment/reward system is based on group decision. Enforcement of rules, as their generation, is for the most part in the hands of the citizenry of the society—the students.

In general, the Social Reconstruction model envisions the student as an active, responsible participant in the formation of the society of the school. Discipline is a function of the democratic process and is basically the group's own self-regulation. The rules of good order enable the school society to pursue the goals for which it is organized: learning. The students as a group are trusted to govern themselves wisely.

The following chart summarizes the role of discipline in each of the four models.

Table 2

Conceptions of Discipline in Four Models of Schooling

	Aim of Discipline	Basic Principle	Type of Rules	Source of Rules
INDIVIDUAL FULFILLMENT	the development of student self-direction	the right to be responsible for his/her own behavior	guidelines which permit freedom, encourage responsibility	adults provide the context; student determines own behavior
SCHOLARLY DISCIPLINE	demonstration of the importance of right order to the attainment of organizational societal goals	legitimate, hierarchical authority as the key to any society/organization	regulations derived from organizational values/principles	determined by responsible authority (principal/faculty)
EDUCATIONAL TECHNOLOGY	establishment of the most efficient disciplinary patterns to achieve the desired learning outcomes	behavior shaped by the appropriate rewards	behaviors/outcomes which are most effective in producing an efficient learning environment	carefully devised by behavioral analysis, engineering
SOCIAL RECON-STRUCTION	participation in the generation of a just society	life in the society of the school; social rules/norms determined through a responsible political process	principles/regulations for good order determined by participants	determined by democratic group decision

Table 2 (continued)

	Nature of Authority	Role of Student	Role of Faculty/Administration	Punishment/Reward System	Attitude Toward Student
INDIVIDUAL FULFILLMENT	internally perceived and imposed; emerging from the best instincts of the student	source of regulation; responsible agent	helper/guide/creator of the environment/opportunity for responsible action	self-imposed; students allowed to suffer consequences of misbehavior and learn from mistakes	trust in the ability of the student to regulate self
SCHOLARLY DISCIPLINE	implicit in the traditional understanding of a good society	willing to cooperate with legitimate authority; conform to societal rules of good order	authority figure who monitors and enforces uniform rules	traditional punishments specified for offenses	expectation of cooperation with legitimate authority
EDUCATIONAL TECHNOLOGY	a function of the outcomes of the instructional process	an adaptive respondent to positive reinforcement	specifier/reinforcer or proper behavioral patterns	emphasis on positive reinforcement rather than punishment	capable of developing appropriate social behaviors given proper reinforcement
SOCIAL RECONSTRUCTION	emerging from the consent of the group; its exercise subject to the critical review inherent in the democratic process	an active participant in the creation of good order	participant in the generation of rules to govern the school society	group influence/pressure; group determination of punishments and their mode of imposition	responsible participant of a social group

Conclusion

As with any theoretical framework, each of the models presented above can both promote understanding and also be the springboard to further insight and future activity. Each model has its strengths. The Individual Fulfillment model of discipline is committed to the proposition that real growth must take place in an atmosphere of freedom and risk-taking. Self-direction rather than obedience to outside authority must be the goal of any disciplinary system if it is to have a lasting effect on the student's life. The Individual Fulfillment model focuses attention on self-development from the very beginning.

The Scholarly Discipline follows a traditional model which seems to flow out of the natural order of man in society. The family, the school, the nation, etc., all require the establishment of legitimate authority. The young person, finding his/her way in so many aspects of life, should be dependent on adult authority and guidance during the formative years.

The Educational Technology model offers the most scientific approach to discipline. As behavioral psychologists so often note, the behavior of students is shaped by the reinforcement they receive from adults and the environment. Why not take a more rational approach to creation of an environment and disciplinary patterns which will mean a more productive learning environment both for the student and for his/her classmates?

Finally, the Social Reconstruction model proposes an approach which supplies not only the experience of life in a society but also develops the skills for critical appraisal of social/ethical issues emerging out of social interaction. The student learns to be a member of a group and to see his/her behavior and conduct implicated in the larger group through which he/she achieves identity, to which he/she must contribute, and to whose norms he/she owes observance.

While there is an obvious overlap in these models, they are distinct viewpoints—separate and competing approaches to discipline. Experienced educators should be able to interpret past or present conflicts over discipline within the framework provided by the four models.

Each of these models contains a fundamental insight, both about human nature and also about discipline: the self-determination of the Individual Fulfillment model, the respect for traditional authority of the Scholarly Discipline model, the reality and power of positive reinforcement in the Educational Technology model, and the reflective participation in society of the Social Reconstruction model. An adequate theory of discipline should attempt to draw on each of these insights.

At the same time, I would argue that it is important that the administration/faculty of a school place predominate emphasis on one of these models. In the end, they are contradictory and competing approaches to discipline. Without a definite option for one of these models as the framework to guide the principles and practices of discipline, a disciplinary policy will likely lack firm and coherent direction. The most frequent problem in discipline is a failure of the faculty to adopt a consistent, generally agreed upon approach to discipline. Competing, inarticulated philosophies of discipline, held by teachers and administrators working in the same school, create chaos in the school environment. Given clearly defined expectations, students are capable of adjusting themselves to any of these systems. A disciplinary policy which firmly establishes a predominate direction along the lines of one of these models and which then searches for ways to weave in the insights of the other approaches is reaching for the most productive and effective model of discipline.

Notes

[1] The application of the four models of schooling to the area of discipline was suggested to the author by Thomas R. Schadelback, S.J.

[2] The following sources might be taken as typical statements of the Individual Fulfillment or humanistic approach: Abraham H. Maslow, *Toward a Psychology of Being* (rev. ed.), (Princeton: Van Nostrand, 1968); Carl R. Rogers, *Freedom to Learn*, (New York: Merrill, 1969); Roland S. Barth, *Open Education and the American School*, (New York: Agathon Press, 1972).

[3] Typical descriptions of the Scholarly Discipline model might be: Jerome S. Bruner, *The Process of Education*, (New York: Vintage, 1960); Philip H. Phenix, *Realms of Meaning: A Philosophy of the Curriculum for General Education*, (New York: McGraw-Hill, 1964).

[4] Representative discussions of this approach might be: B. F. Skinner, *The Technology of Teaching*, (New York: Appleton-Century-Crofts, 1968); Benjamin S. Bloom *et al.*, *Handbook of Formative and Summative Evaluation of Student Learning*, (New York: McGraw-Hill, 1971).

[5] Summary statements of the contemporary version of this trend can be found in the following: Elliott W. Eisner and Elizabeth Vallance (eds.), *Conflicting Conceptions of the Curriculum*, (Berkeley, CA: McCutchan, 1974); "The Social Reconstructionist Curriculum," in John D. McNeil, *Curriculum: A Comprehensive Introduction*, (Boston: Little, Brown and Co., 1977).

Examine the four models presented by Newton. Which model is most compatible with your developing philosophy? Find a classmate whose philosophy is similar to yours and discuss how you would carry out discipline in the classroom. Then discuss it with one whose philosophy is different from yours. During this discussion, challenge each other to defend your reasons for your beliefs about the goals of discipline, its basic principle, the type of rules that are appropriate and the source of rules.

There is a great deal of discussion between educators in Europe and those in the United States about common educational problems and issues. Often educators from one country will travel to another country in order to see how things are done. The following article by Brian Oakley-Smith from England contains his reflections on good teaching. It was written after he had spent time touring our schools.

A British Perspective

Brian Oakley-Smith, M.A.
Cambridgeshire School District, England

Why should you wish to read what I have to say about becoming a teacher? First, I was a teacher for seven years in secondary schools in England teaching youngsters between the ages of 11 and 18 mainly history but also some French and English. I not only taught these subjects in the formal sense for public examinations but I also took on a wide range of extra-curricular subjects like swimming and other sporting activities. I also took groups of students to Europe and entertained others in the evenings when we talked about a wide range of issues.

The second reason is that I left teaching when I could no longer enjoy it because I had exhausted my fund of knowledge and my ability to "give out." At that stage I became an education officer with responsibility for hiring teachers in primary and special schools in a large city. I had to judge the suitability of young teachers for posts in highly demanding situations and to help select teachers for promotion to posts of responsibility.

In due course I became the deputy chief education officer of a large school system with 100,000 school students and had the privilege of visiting many of the 350 schools in the county and witnessing teachers at work in dozens of classrooms. Advising the County Council on staff development, inservice training and policy are now my major responsibilities. Recently I have had the good fortune to travel extensively in the United States. I have talked to many teachers, watched them teach, talked to their professors, and questioned administrators and legislators

Written expressly for *Preparing for Reflective Teaching.*

about their hopes and fears for the future education of children in American public schools.

What can I tell you as you contemplate joining the teaching profession? In the first place, becoming a teacher is like obtaining a license to form a vital relationship with a group of children. It is both an exciting challenge and an awesome responsibility. It will test you to the full. Everything that you and all that you are will be engaged in the task. There will be no possibility of holding back. Every facet of your personality will be exposed in your relationship with the students in your care. It will not be possible to engage only part of yourself. You cannot leave some other part of yourself at home when you enter the classroom. Children of all ages are very responsive. They may not be able to explain your behavior, but they will be well aware of your changing moods and attitudes.

What will you need to discharge your responsibility to the children in your care? First, of course, you will need to be trained in your profession. You will have to have an understanding of the way children develop and learn; you will need to have the knowledge of what you are to teach and how you are to teach it. You will need a school which is organized around the needs of the student, where the teachers work together as a team, where the principal leads the whole school community and is as concerned about staff development as he is about the welfare of students. You will need support and advice, an opportunity to learn from more experienced teachers, an opportunity to devise your own teaching strategy and choose the appropriate materials, and a feeling that what you are doing is part of a coherent program that is being constantly reviewed and evaluated. You will be very lucky to get these optimum conditions; nevertheless they should be your standard. Anything that does not minister to the needs of your students should be mistrusted and its purpose questioned. If teachers have this vision it will be more likely to become a reality. In this regard John Dewey once wrote: "What the best and wisest parent desires for his own child that must the community want for all its children. Any other ideal is narrow and unlovely; acted upon it will destroy democracy."

You will need to be constantly aware that you share with the parents of your students their concern for their children's happiness and future progress. The parents may seem to you wrongheaded, neglectful, overly protective, or absent altogether, but the children still carry our hopes for the future. The society that has lost its hopes for its children is in a parlous state indeed. If you are fortunate, your school will want to share its mission with the parents and the local community, and that should always be the aim.

Now let me tell you about some of the really good teachers I have met during my trip to the United States. The first was teaching first grade in an elementary school in Ohio. She had a manner that I can only describe as graceful; everything she did was unhurried and deliberate. Her calmness affected the children, who went about their tasks happily with a sense of purpose. Her own obvious interest in and equal treatment of all the children affected the attitude of her pupils. She was patient but firm. She smiled a lot. She was very well organized.

The second teacher was teaching a combined third and fourth grade class in a school in Illinois where the parents were given a choice of teaching styles. This teacher's class was based on an integrated day with work stations and children following their own individual programs. She carefully recorded the children's progress, giving more structure to those who needed it and encouraging those who could to take more control of their time and the tasks they had to perform. She knew she had great energy and was enjoying using it for the benefit of the children. She loved to do projects with them and to go on trips to places of interest but she sometimes worried whether these would interfere with their programs in the basic skills. She knew her success depended on a principal of real vision and a well thought out strategy for the curriculum of the whole school.

My third teacher is in special education in a high school in Wisconsin. He has responsibility for a group of children with learning disabilities. Not only does he teach them but he follows their whole school career, briefing the other teachers about them, talking to their parents, consulting the school psychologist, advising them on their careers and trying to get money from various sources for additional programs. These children were even more obviously in his care than those who are less vulnerable.

There are many different ages and stages of children that a teacher can be responsible for, but you need to find those children with whom you feel most comfortable and to whom you relate most easily. Most aspects of teaching can be learned, but an initial understanding of the way children of a particular age group react is probably one of the things you cannot be taught. Without it you will be flying blind. If you have it you will always be one step ahead of the children.

If it is for you, enjoy your career as a teacher. It need not be a lifetime career, but while your enthusiasm lasts there is nothing more rewarding.

Chapter 5

Kids

What would kids say about teaching if they were asked? Kids do have their own opinions and ideas, which often diverge from what teachers think kids are thinking. The following three articles explore teaching from kids' perspectives. The first article by the Children's Express contains students' replies to questions about teachers and teaching. The second article, by Boyle, discusses the importance of remembering that kids are all thinking human beings, not standardized "students." The third article, by Gordon, presents the stories of kids whom the schools have failed and emphasizes the tragedy that can occur when people do not listen to kids.

"I Like It When Teachers Are . . ."

Dorriet Kavanaugh

Listen to Us, The Children's Express Report, from which this article is excerpted, is a unique report—not only because it consists entirely of the words of children, mostly 13 and under, but because the questions that elicited those words also came from children—completely free of the adult world.

Most of the report is edited from round tables. A round table consisted of four or five people sitting around a tape recorder discussing an interesting subject. The 30 teenage assistant editors who conducted these round tables were required to think through their own experiences on a given topic and come up with a list of questions. These questions were used as a starting point. The assistant editors had sole responsibility for the way the topic was covered and were required to include a full age range of children 7 to 13 as participants in these round tables—*with no adults present.*

Teachers

JILL (12): I like it when teachers are funny. Last year I had a teacher who cracked a joke every ten minutes. She was my favorite teacher.

If I was a teacher, at the beginning of the year I'd be pretty strict. Then if my class really paid attention, I'd just get nice. I think it's good to incorporate fun with learning. Instead of just studying verbs or nouns, you can play Scrabble or Hangman—it's more challenging and fun.

I hate it when teachers never admit their mistakes. Teachers should be careful about giving their opinions about a subject, because kids are going to think teachers are *always* right.

LINDA (13): I think a teacher should try to identify with the students personally. He should try to put himself in the place of the child he's teaching and figure out how the child would feel. I had a teacher who gave me a bad grade 'cause he thought it would help me work harder . . .

I hate a teacher who has favorites. If the favorite gets a question wrong, "Well, it's natural." But if *you* get a question wrong, "Study it!"

IVAN (12): I like my teacher 'cause he knows I'm kind of shy and doesn't call on me a lot. When I have to ask him a question, I wait until the bell rings and then I go up and ask.

I hate teachers when they're too strict. A little is all right, but I don't like it when they yell at you. Once I yawned and I had to go out into the hallway just because I was Black.

DONNAROSE (12): I like easygoing teachers better. They joke around and they can take it if you make a crack. But strick teachers don't like it—they'll send you down to the principal just for making a little joke. I think you learn more from easygoing teachers—they wanna teach right and want you to learn.

I have a math teacher who doesn't really want to help. She's been there a long time and she never wants to explain anything to you. Almost everybody in the school fails math because she doesn't care. I asked her in a nice way if she could please explain it to me and she just says, "You should know it," or "Sit down. Not now, come after school." If I were a teacher, I'd want my students to learn the things that they had to learn that year. I'd try to get them interested in the subject, and I'd call on them to see if they knew the answers. That's the best way.

A Good Teacher Is . . .

MAXINE (11): A teacher who always knows what's going on, 'cause I can't stand teachers who are confused. They get *me* confused!

KLAUS (9): A teacher that sits down and talks with me.

MIKE (10): One who doesn't give lots and lots of homework.

LORI (10): She wouldn't treat us like a whole class. She treats everyone individually.

KEVIN (13): Easygoing, she wouldn't yell at nobody.

ELLIOTT (12): When I put up my hand, she would always answer me.

MARIE (12): A good teacher thinks you're capable of doing things and doesn't just have a certain way or an impossible way to do something quickly.

CAROLINE (13): A teacher who can joke around and can take it if *you* make a joke.

RAJAH (11): The kind of teacher who won't let me get away with anything. She'd do what she had to do to teach us. She would seem very strict. But when you were very good, you know, she'd be really great.

JASON (10): He just treats everybody fairly. He's not too hard on you, he's not too soft, he just treats everybody equal.

KATHLEEN (12): Someone who takes the time to teach you something when you don't understand it and who'll keep on teaching you till you understand it.

SUSAN (11): Someone who tries to put himself in our places, who tries to see what we would be seeing.

RAJAH (11): A perfect teacher would be gentle, like my favorite teacher was.

What Do You Hate About Teachers?

SUSAN (13): Teachers are always expressing their opinions. They should explain to the class that this is my opinion and you don't have to follow it. If they just go and teach it, it's not right. Even if it might be true, it could damage you.

JASON (10): I hate it when you're made to be perfect. When the teacher says, "Try a little harder," and you try much, much harder and think you did very good, and he says, "That's not hard enough, you gotta do even harder, harder till it's perfect." And you can't be perfect.

LINDA (13): I don't like teachers who have favorites.

CAROLINE (13): I don't like teachers who have trouble organizing us, who don't know how to make us stop being bad.

MARIE (12): I hate when you get in trouble for something someone else did. The teacher has to see the person do it before he can accuse somebody.

DONNAROSE (12): I hate teachers who don't listen to you. I hate teachers who be hitting on you or be cursing at you.

KEVIN (13): I hate teachers who'll be saying things that will be putting the kids down, that they'll feel bad about. Some teachers you can't have feelings for.

ROBERT (10): When teachers tell you to do something and you can't do it, they keep on yelling at you 'cause you're not doing it. You're not doing it because you *can't* do it, and you can't get them to give you help.

Schools and Teachers:
What To Do About Them?

AMY (13): I think we've got to get rid of this attitude about school that the teachers are there to teach you, and the kids just go to school and sit in there, get directed and taught by one point of view, and they don't really get any say in it. We need more of a group learning experience instead of one person trying to teach everybody.

JOHN (13): Teachers in general seem to think you're in the military. You speak when you raise your hand and you go to the bathroom when you're allowed to. You have to ask to do everything. The teachers have all the control. They treat you like you're a piece of—like you're nothing at all.

JULIE (10): In my school lots of kids just can't wait till recess, and then at recess they charge outside, like that's the best thing of the day. If the children have more say about what they do in class, I think they'd be happier with what they do.

LEAH (12): And people wouldn't dislike school so much, or skip classes as much.

LAUREL (11): School teaches you to expect decisions to be made for you.

JOHN (13): That's why a lot of young people right now wouldn't be able to make decisions like voting. In school you're taught to let the teacher or the principal make all the decisions. You have no control over it. I used to get in trouble for contradicting the teacher. I had some really dumb teachers. They were often wrong about everything they said. I'd say, "That's wrong," and they'd say, "I'm the teacher, you're the student."

LAUREL (11): Often you can correct the teacher, but they're going to carry out the arguments to the finish so you'll give up first. But they treat you differently when you're smart. When my brother was in kindergarten they thought he was a real imbecile because he would crawl under the tables and things like that. But they handed out this test and none of the other kids got any right and he got all of it right. *Then* they treated him great.

JOHN (13): A lot more attention should be paid to the individual. Now they give you a test and they say, you're in the fast group and you're in the slow group; the slow group gets this and the fast group gets this.

LEAH (12): At our school we have student-taught courses. If you know a lot about something, you can teach it. You have to get it approved by the teachers, but they let you do almost anything you want.

JOHN (13): Most of what is taught in school right now is totally irrelevant to what you're going to do when you get out. After you get out of school, you're not really prepared for any kind of career. They force you to go to school, and then they act like it's your privilege. You're in the U.S., you got a free education. Of course, you have to come every day, whether you like it or not.

LAUREL (11): I think it would be better if they made school more interesting so that people would want to go. They should *really* make it a privilege.

JOHN (13): With the type of schools that you have now, if schools weren't compulsory, people wouldn't go.

LAUREL (11): Even the way schools are now, kids would still probably go because kids want to learn and it's the only way there is.

Teaching Kids: Do You Dare to Be Different?

Marilynne Boyle
University of Wisconsin

Kids, educating kids. That's what teaching is all about. You've been reading some articles that have raised questions about the ways teachers and schools are educating kids—all different kinds of kids. Stop and think about what educating kids really means to you. What it seems to mean to a lot of kids right now is "another brick in the wall." Will you

Written expressly for *Preparing for Reflective Teaching.*

be another brick in the wall enclosing kids' minds, strangling their creativity, enforcing conformity to the rules of schooling that keep schools the same year after year?

"No," you say. "That's why I went into teaching: to help kids, to give them a better education than I got, to turn on their interests, to prepare them for society as it is now." These are some of the answers a group of student teachers I supervised gave me when I asked them recently about their goals for their student teaching practica. They were worried: "How can I interest kids, how can I be creative enough?" My students were sincere. They remembered being students—the hurts, the joys, the boredom. They wanted to offer their students only the best.

And yet, on the first day in the classroom the students saw a sea of faces looking at them as teachers. They started forgetting those faces belonged to kids and began to think of them as students: students they were expected to control; students who achievement scores they were responsible for; students who were expected to learn certain amounts of curriculum material. With these expectations in mind, for themselves and for their students, many of my student teachers said something like this: "Please get out your spelling books quietly and turn to page one."

Have you ever thought about how surprising it is that all of us remember our teachers saying something like this? That no matter where we grew up, what kind of neighborhood we lived in, our race, or our sex, we all remember schooling in pretty much the same terms. We remember classrooms full of about twenty-five kids and one adult— the teacher. The teacher directed the kids' learning using textbooks as the major source of information. As kids, we were expected to sit quietly and either listen to the teacher and answer questions raised by the teacher or do work assigned by the teacher. Our work was graded, usually according to the number of right answers, and those who got the most knew the most—they were "bright." Others may have had trouble coming up with just the right answer—they were called "slow." These experiences were so usual that for us the words "education" or "schooling" were synonymous with this description. In fact, it was so usual we might call schooling in this way "business-as-usual."

Ah, but you say times have changed, now there are individualized learning packets, learning centers, small group cooperative tasks—the things we learn about in methods classes. Yes, you will be learning about alternative methods of teaching. But, there is overwhelming research evidence that business-as-usual is still what is most common in schools.

Let us think about what this means for the many different kinds of kids who are being educated in classrooms right now. First, let us consider what I mean when I mention many different kinds of kids. Our schools serve a vast and differentiated public: kids of different social classes, races, sexes and handicapping conditions; kids with different talents, abilities, interests and needs; kids who speak standard English as their primary language and those who do not. For these many different kinds of kids we offer one standard fare—business-as-usual.

In the business-as-usual approach to education all kids are expected to learn the same things and often are instructed in the same ways. We might argue, and with credence, that there are some things all kids need to learn. For example, mastery of basic skills like reading, writing and computing is considered a necessary pre-requisite for becoming educated. Also, being informed about literature, history, and geography is taken-for-granted as a necessary requirement for the educated person. I am not faulting what has been said about the criteria for being considered "educated." I am encouraging you to think about what has *not* been said. The idea of "sameness" can help you get started. Try thinking about sameness in the following way: the same things are defined as important to learn, the same perspective is described within these priority areas, the same strategies are used to teach priority information, and the same standards are used to evaluate student mastery of valued content. Let me explain what I am referring to in this litany of sameness.

Do you remember what courses you took while you were in school? If you were like most of us you were required to take some history, geography, English, mathematics, and science. Most of your course work centered on learning the "golden nuggets" or most important facts about a particular topic. For example, you might have learned about famous battles of the Civil War or celebrated heroes of an era or significant pieces of legislation. Let us consider what you were and were not learning as you hurried to memorize these "nuggets" of information.

You were learning general information within traditional subject matter areas. You were learning what you were told was important to learn—it would be on the test. This information could be called "need to know" knowledge. In comparison, things that were "nice to know" were given secondary status—they were not on the test. Nice to know knowledge was information or skills that were not considered fundamental for kids to know. Nice to know knowledge was beyond the basics. For example, everyone needed to know what the stock market was and when the stock market crashed. It was nice to know how the stock market worked and why the stock market crashed. As another example, everyone needed to know what the major political parties were and what platforms they endorsed. It was nice to know why the parties endorsed their selective platforms and why certain groups supported the platforms. Have you ever realized that most of the "need to know" knowledge centered on questions asking *what* rather than why? Have you ever wondered about the impact of the focus on "whats" on the way we approach information as adults? We wait to hear *what* happened on the daily news, but do we question what we hear asking why it happened or why certain news was highlighted? Also, many of us make up what is called the silent majority. Have you ever wondered how our schooling prepared us for silence?

Ask yourself what this discussion means for the kids you will teach. What will you decide is "need to know" as opposed to "nice to know" information? What criteria will you use to determine what is most important to know?

Are the same things you were taught relevant and important for your students to learn? Are there things *all* students should or need to learn and/or are there certain kinds of information particular students need to focus on? For example, what do nonwhite kids or girls need to know about the history, present, and future of political leadership in our country? Should your students influence decisions about what will be taught? As you reflect upon these questions, think about your task as a teacher to serve kids, all different kinds of kids. To acknowledge the diversity of the kids you will teach and the world you are preparing them for, do you think it is necessary to reconsider the standard categorization of necessities rather than niceties in regard to what should be taught?

Let us look at what you were taught in another way. Whose story was told in your history, English, and geography books? Consider this proposition: Most of what you were taught was biased toward the story of the white middle class and really leaned toward the story of just half of this group, white males. To fully appreciate this, ask yourself the following questions: How many of you know about the contributions and struggles of minority and majority women in this country? Do you know about the struggle of women to be admitted to colleges? Have you heard of the song "Bread and Roses," and do you know about the occasion on which it was sung? How many of you know about the black pioneers who homesteaded in the midwest or the black regiments who fought in World War I? What do you know about the Depression era? Most likely you remember memorizing different laws passed as part of the New Deal. But did you learn about how these laws affected poor people, from the point of view of those who were poor?

While you probably answered "no" to most of the above questions, you most likely remember learning about the history, traditions and contributions of white, male, middle and upper class people in our country. For example, you learned about inventions by males, elections of males, and wars fought by males. The names of the males you remember were most likely middle or upper class males: military, industrial, or political giants.

Now ask yourself what teaching this particular brand of sameness means for the kids you will teach. Is this content relevant in the same way for different kids? Does this content acknowledge and affirm the diversity of students? For example, think about the physically-impaired student who might be in your classroom. Curriculum content that does not include information about the strengths, concerns, and contributions of physically-impaired people fails to convey to this kid that he or she is an important person in the fabric of our country. At the same time this curriculum fails to provide non-physically impaired students with the opportunity to learn about and to respect physically-impaired people. As another example, consider the relevance to nonwhite kids of curriculum content that concentrates on whites. How are nonwhite kids to learn that the history and contributions of nonwhite people is a vital part of our country's past and present? Also, white kids are only learning a portion of our country's legacy when they are acquainted with white, male history. Let us think about one more group of kids whom you will teach—girls. The curriculum usually taught in schools omits or glosses over women's history. Neglecting to teach this history leaves girls without heroines for role models. Also, boys fail to learn about the many things women have done and can do. When you really think about kids—different kids—teaching kids about the same one group of people seems very inadequate.

Sameness describes not only what we teach but how we teach. Think about your experience as a student and how you have been instructed. This will give you an idea of what I mean by sameness in instruction. Quite likely, the teacher required you to read something, then he or she asked you questions about it, praised you for right answers, and later tested your recall of these answers. Most topics usually were presented through reading, writing, or lecture. Also, most topics were presented to the class as a whole. The whole class proceeded at the same rate in learning the same things.

Now, think about what teaching in the same way means for the kids you will teach. Most kids will learn that valued knowledge comes from the teacher, and that being a "good" student means paying close attention to and trying to remember what the teacher had to say. Many of you learned this definition, followed it, and were labeled "good students." Perhaps, however, you remember an occasion when your status as a good student was challenged. Did it have anything to do with your first research assignment? Did you find yourself complaining that your teacher or professor never told you exactly what you were supposed to do? If you are ruefully nodding yes, think about why undertaking independent research was frustrating. One reason could have been that you had had little prior research experience. Have you ever considered that most of your efforts toward being a good student went into receiving and memorizing rather than searching for and evaluating information?

Consider the sameness in instruction in another way. In the business-as-usual approach to teaching most instruction centers on learning through reading and writing. Some kids prefer to learn by reading and writing; they will be served well by the sameness we have been talking about. Other kids do not and will not learn this way. Think of yourself and your friends: how many of you prefer to learn by doing, by talking about something, by listening to someone or by watching a film or videotape? This might be a hard question for you to answer. Maybe this is because our preferences were never acknowledged; we were trained to learn in only one way, and now it is hard for us to consider alternatives.

In addition, think about what teaching kids at the same pace means for the different students you will teach. Some learn faster than others. Some already know the material presented to the group as a whole. In contrast, some may be totally unfamiliar with it. Teachers usually say that they try to teach to the "middle," which means that they try to teach at a rate that is not too fast for some or too slow for others, and to present information at a level that is not too difficult for some or too easy for others. Have you ever thought about what focusing on the "middle" misses? What alternative ways of teaching can you think of? Are you having trouble again? That's the worst part of business-as-usual: it is so usual we are hard pressed when we try to generate alternatives.

Let us begin the difficult process of considering alternatives to business-as-usual that acknowledge kids' diversity. First, we could expand what is usually taught to include topics and skills relevant to being "educated" for living in a pluralistic society. Second, we could modify curriculum content to include information about nonwhites, working class people, people with handicapping conditions, and women. We could also modify it to acknowledge student interests and prior learning. Third, we could diversify instruction to include teaching by reading, writing, and doing, and for researching information. Fourth, we could tailor curriculum and instruction to kids' needs and abilities.

To do any of these requires readjustments in your thinking about teaching. You will need to focus on the students you will be teaching rather than the subject matter that usually gets taught. You will need to learn about what kids' already know, their interests, talents, strengths, and weaknesses. You will need to recognize that kids are members of groups—groups that may have been omitted from what is usually taught in schools. And, you will need to let your teaching be guided by the kids you teach in order to respond to their uniqueness. Let me give you some ideas for getting started.

On the first day of school, rather than orienting the kids to your rules and routines, use the day to orient yourself to them. Interview each kid personally to find out his or her interests, hobbies, goals, and views about school. Brainstorm with the class about things they want to learn or experience during the year. Spend the better part of the day watching and listening, rather than telling and directing. After school, study the information you've collected. Group kids who have the same interests. Plan ways to include things kids want to know in what you will teach.

Quite likely, you may not be an expert concerning the many things kids would like to learn. Instead of ignoring these interests or scrambling to learn something about them that you can present, consider helping your students find information independently. Helping students do research may mean teaching them how to locate various books, tapes or films in the library; to identify resource people to contact for information; to take or dictate notes to recall information; or to discover ways to share information. Organize a teaching unit around these research skills.

During the first weeks of school try different instructional strategies. Watch to see which kids seem to prefer learning in certain ways. Interview each kid about the easiest ways for them to learn. Then, use this information to group kids who learn in the same and different ways and to plan for variety in your instruction.

Whenever you are considering teaching about a particular topic, develop ways to test kids for what they may already know. Plan your teaching in light of the information you gather from this testing. You may decide to eliminate some material because they have already mastered it. You may decide to group some students with others who have a similar level of knowledge about an area. Or, you may pair someone who knows something about an area with someone else who knows little and have one teach the other.

As another strategy, you may want to carry a notebook with you at all times to jot down things you observe about kids' abilities, what they seem to know, what they are interested in and how they prefer to learn. I have encouraged my student teachers to do this. Most of them were very surprised to discover how much they were missing by staying in the front of the room, behind the teacher's desk, acting as teacher. They tell me their observations generated many ideas about what to teach and how to teach different kids.

As you observe kids also note their group membership. Start looking for and collecting artifacts and information to acknowledge and teach kids about different groups. Collecting pictures and newspaper articles is a good place to start. These can be displayed and used to initiate discussions about human diversity. You may be pleasantly surprised by the kids' response if you ask them to help you collect artifacts and information about different groups.

Educating kids is not easy, but it can be exciting. If you center your teaching on the kids you teach, no two years will ever be the same because no two kids are the same. And, because they are not the same, business-as-usual won't do if you are sincerely interested in helping all kids learn—about themselves and about others. To really educate kids you need to work at making business-as-usual unusual.

As I encourage you to reflect upon educating different kinds of kids, I am asking you to consider what good teaching really means, from the kids' point of view. I am asking you to leave the front of the room and go sit in a student's seat as you ponder what you, as a teacher, will do to serve the many different kids in your classroom. In light of the pervasiveness of business-as-usual, what I really want to know is this: do you dare to be different?

Visions of Classrooms from the Other Side of the Desk: Notes to Prospective Teachers

Beverly M. Gordon
Ohio State University

On the way to adulthood, all of us experienced some type of schooling. Think back: your third grade reader, the field trip to the county seat when you studied state history, those nerve-wraching, timed arithmetic tests, or the poem on the door about Charley the chipmunk (who was chatty) that ended by asking, "Are you a Charley Chipmunk?" Such experiences are easily remembered, but it is not so easy to remember how these cumulative experiences influenced your perceptions of the world.

Seldom do we realize that during our prerequisite schooling, we were also acquiring a way of viewing the world. You learned, although you might not have realized it, a view of the American ethos, or middle

Written expressly for *Preparing for Reflective Teaching*.

class culture, in part through the academic and implicit knowledge disseminated in school. You also learned that if a child's cultural ethos differed from what was sanctioned by the school, a clash usually occurred. Being different in schools unfortunately has implied deviance. Since no one usually wants to be considered different because of real social consequences, most strive to be "normal," and the label of "different" or "deviant" becomes a controlling mechanism used by the school. Moreover, it also makes legitimate the need to prescribe certain treatment to remediate or correct the problem. Unfortunately for the child and his or her family, whether or not they agree with this assumption is irrelevant. Schools carry the ultimate control and power: by perceiving an incident, experience, or a test score and interpreting the meaning, based in its "legitimated" view of the world, the school makes decisions about a child's career as student.

As aspiring teachers, you must realize that your perceptions of the world (which reflect your experiences, values, beliefs, and accumulated knowledge) will affect how you view the vocation of teaching and the individuals you teach. Teacher training programs are not too much different from your own elementary and secondary schooling. Regardless of the student's grade (primary school or college) the knowledge that is given to you by your school is laden with social values and beliefs and provides you with a particular frame of reference through which you view the world. As part of your preservice program, I invite you to reflect on the language and labels you have learned during your teacher training program, and on how labels categorize children and affect the way they are perceived and subsequently treated in school.

A Dominant School Rationale:
Theories About Those Who Fail

Throughout the educational community, it is widely believed that students who drop out of school do so because of academic failure and/or behavioral conflicts. It is further believed that such conflicts and failure occur as the result of the culminating effects of deprivation and remediation problems. The prevailing belief is that although schools provide quality education, especially in light of the back to basics movement, some children are more predisposed to experiencing problems and failure, especially those from socioeconomically poor families.[1] Several deprivation theories—primarily the theory of cultural deprivation—have been devised to "explain" why these children are not likely to succeed.

The cultural deprivation theory proposes that children from low socioeconomic homes do not acquire the cultural values and belief systems that are condoned by the school and society at large. Moreover, these children are considered to be environmentally deprived because their homes are structually inadequate (in both rural and urban areas) and lack stimulating preschool educational experiences. Compared to other youngsters, these children come to school with "cognitive deficiencies and a poor attitude to learning."[2] Cultural deprivation was used to explain student animosity that resulted in hostile relationships with the staff, rejection of the social values and beliefs transmitted by the school, and eventually academic failure.

The problem with this explanation is that it assumes the labels and categories describing a child's "deviance" are justified and appropriate when in fact there are persisting questions and misgivings about the validity and consequences of these labels on the educational attainment and social futures of the children to whom they are given. Identifying a child as an educational deviant has longitudinal and grave consequences because the label of deviance attached to the child by institutional classifications makes how the child is viewed and treated by the school legitimate.

What is needed by you, the teacher, is an awareness of how labels affect the way you view and treat your students. Furthermore, you must not make naive assumptions about the allegedly neutral stance poised by this schooling language. Language that identifies academic deviancy in children also creates categories that are political in nature, justifies both an unfavorable view of the students and imposes restrictions on them in the name of helping. Murry Edelman in his book, *The Political Language of the Helping Profession*, comments:

> The teacher who defines a student as a slow learner . . . creates a relationship that is far more fundamental and influential for both professional and client. It tells them both who they are and so fundamentally creates their social worlds that they resist evidence that the professional competence of the one or the stigmatizing or exalting label of the other may be unwarranted. For both, the label tends to become a self-fulfilling prophecy and is sometimes immune to falsifying evidence.[3]

The specialized vocabulary (such as, low motivation, low academic ability, defiant, delinquent) used to define children makes social and political biases others have of them legitimate. Moreover, such labels, more often than not, provide a set of expectations leading to student failure. The language used to characterize children stigmatizes them from the time they are first identified as problem children or underachievers. Once so labelled, children are hard pressed to change these impressions others have of them.

The overall vexing problem for these children is that while they do not perceive of themselves the way the school does, they have few options concerning what happens to them in the name of education. They can accept the school's view of themselves, or they can rebel against it. In either case, they are in conflict with a system that has the power to track them into future adult roles in society. Often we think of children as not knowing what is occurring around them. Although they might not have the vocabulary to express themselves, research indicates that they do have an awareness of their own histories and the social contradictions in the world around them.[4] Moreover, although their parents send them to school with values, attitudes, and aspirations (contrary to dominant thinking), when they arrive they are confronted with attitudes of apathy, discouragement, failure, hopelessness, and even hostility, due in part to the preconceived notions and fears staff and other students have of them. The cultural capital (skills, knowledge, language) they bring with them[5] is assumed to be of little worth and can actually cause conflict when their vibrancy explodes into movement and action in a classroom where the teacher has mandated a certain "order," "stillness," and "silence."

What you decide about deficiency theories will be important to your classroom pedagogy. Part of your decisions should take into account how children feel about their schooling. The next section will present the reflections of several students on the schooling they did and did not receive.

Students on Schooling:
A View of Classrooms From the Other Side of the Desk

The law says children must go to school. It does not, however, guarantee a positive experience nor success in acquiring socio-academic skills for a promising future. Many students approach school hopeful but find they are either given limited access to academic knowledge or they are provided with help that hurts their self-esteem. At first, they believe in the benevolent power and benefits of education to enrich their lives, giving them literacy, career opportunity, and a way up from their lower socio-economic status. What they find is that learning, even accessibility to knowledge, is predicated on how they act and the perceptions teachers have of their abilities. Such obstructions to learning are threatening, and while some students suffer the consequences and say nothing, others rebel and fight back.

Listening to these youths helps us perceive schooling from the opposite side of the desk. The means by which we will listen is through the educational life histories of several students. The social biography or life history document has consistently given social researchers important insights but only recently has it been used for inquiry into the lives of students.[6] The next section presents the recollections of several students of what life in school was like. Some students were given special education labels, others were simply labeled as slow or unmotivated. Some saw the contradictions in schooling life. All of these students, however, refused to accept their school appointed status. Instead of acquiescing, they rebelled against the bigotry and apprehension that confronted them. These excerpts of educational histories will illuminate two points: first, students are aware of what happens to them; and second, within the cultural capital students use to understand their position in school there is the antecedent for positive and meaningful educational experience.[7]

Schooling and the Dream Deferred: Limitations, Pain, and Futility

Some students are systematically ignored in their classes. Even at the elementary level, students learn that knowledge dissemination is conditional—teachers dole it out on a selective basis.

Jackie: The ABC's, I never learned mine.

BG: How come?

Jackie: Because she never taught them to me. I used to tell my Mom, but Mom used to think I was crazy. Them teachers . . . didn't take no time to teach you nothing, they didn't with me. I would sit there all day with my paper and stuff.

BG: Did other students learn because they were white?

Jackie: No, [they learned because] the teacher *taught it to them.*

By the intermediate grades, Jackie recalled that because she had not learned basic reading and computation skills, teachers avoided her because they thought she was "slow." She suspected that she received little help, not because she was slow, but because the staff did not know how to teach her.

Another student offered his own ideas on the kind of help some students receive in school:

Robert: [The teachers] tried to stress the fact about education, but, you know, the white kids they was always gettin' it [but] the black kids they really didn't get that much . . . . I think we really never asked for nothing . . . [that] is one reason why we never got nothing . . . . [As] far as help and what not . . . if you didn't ask for it they [the teachers] didn't come and offer it to you.

Both Robert and Jackie learned that knowledge acquisition is controlled by the classroom teacher, and there are certain postures a student must demonstrate in order to ask for and receive it.

In other instances, the "help" teachers provided was neither useful or practical for classroom learning.

> Juan: I recall there was a Spanish teacher that tried to help us. But the way he spoke Spanish was a very different dialect than Chicano Spanish dialect ... more like a Spain [Castilian dialect] .... In Mexico and United States, the Spanish is more like a slang way, than an upper lip class. Sometimes there were words that I could understand in his conversation but when I talked, he couldn't know what I was talking about .... He didn't get the actual meaning.

> Sarah: I cannot spell at all. I can read and everything else, but I can't spell. Then a teacher I had here said you don't have to spell to make it. She said spell it the best way you can. But I still didn't like it. I wanted to be able to jot stuff down like everybody else .... They tell me to spell the word the way I hear it ... it's still not right. I said, "Now what do you want me to do?" ... They told me when I didn't know how to spell the word, look the word up.

If you smile at these scenarios, it might be because you recognize and perhaps have heard the words or used them yourself. To say this kind of help is not helpful is obvious but does not clarify why students would encounter these kinds of situations in learning institutions. What we begin to realize is that the acquisition of knowledge transmitted by the school is possible and most assured for those who can decipher the transmission code. Interestingly enough, schools do not readily teach this code (for example the mannerisms, interpretations, beliefs, and values) to those who do not already possess it.[8]

Perhaps the students believed that they should not have had to ask for knowledge—that knowledge should have been forthcoming without stipulations. These students learned, however, that what they received impeded the development of their knowledge base. Such incidents remind us that teaching should facilitate knowledge acquisition, not limit access to it.

Help That Hurts:
The Futility of Remediation

Learning the role of student is a complex and sometimes vexing activity, especially if you are classified as a remedial student. The classroom a child is assigned to, his peers within the room, and the curricula imparted has critical import for his future life in school. The term "remedial education" fosters innuendos of cognitive or behavioral deficiencies.

Thus, such "help" becomes a lesson in humiliation and limits the kind of advancing academic knowledge available to students.

> BG: You mentioned you were in a special education class. How did you know you were?
>
> Virginia: Well, it was kind of a class for . . bad kids.
>
> BG: Were you bad?
>
> Virginia: I wasn't bad. I just wouldn't do my work, I guess. I knew that I was in a special class because everybody else that was dumb was in the same class with me . . . . They would give us the easy work and the other kids would get the harder work . . . . She [the teacher] used to make me stay after school . . . because I wouldn't finish my work . . . . I did do my work, I just didn't get it done all the time . . . . And . . . if I did it . . . but I just got some stuff wrong on it, she'd made you [me] stay after and get it corrected.
>
> BG: Do you remember the other kids in your class? What were they like?
>
> Virginia: They were bad. They were all bad. Some of them did their work, and some didn't; and some of them did their work but didn't get it right, because they just didn't know. They were in the same situation as I was . . . the whole class . . . would be after school . . . . From what I remember a lot of the students were in my classes for a couple of years. Like every year . . . they would be in my class. That's why I always thought it was the dumb class, and the class where all the bad kids were . . . . I didn't like [the teacher]; nobody liked her . . . I'm sure she didn't particularly care for us either. We didn't like her because of the way that she would help us, like make us stay after school . . . and once in awhile she'd hit the kids . . . . [The teacher] didn't know me as a person at all . . . . You could tell the only reason she was there was because she was getting paid to be there . . . . It wasn't really nothing that she was crazy about doing.

The belief in the existence of classes for "bad kids," the distinction between hard and easy work, how students know if they are in the "dumb class," and the dislike of the teacher because of "the kind of help" she or he gives to students sheds light on how children determine their position in the school's academic hierarchy. It is also an indication to them of how they are perceived by the school and teacher.

Care needs to be taken with labels that describe children in order to help them. In the previous conversation we realize that the "help" the student received seemed to do little except exacerbate the situation. Moreover, once an individual is labelled rarely is there an end to such remediation. The tacit promise of catching up with peers eventually fades and students find that they are remediated for the duration of their educational careers.

Students trust teachers to impart the information needed to live successfully in the adult world. They want to receive help when it is needed and then return to the path to success. But some find that they never get back on the right road. In one case, being classified as a special education student, from elementary to high school, resulted in little program continuity or academic advancement due to numerous changes in the teaching staff and limited access to advanced materials.

> Jackie: Everytime I get a new teacher, I'd take a little reading quality test and here we come with this Jane and Jack's and Jump Skip Jump books again . . . . I didn't like that . . . it was so far behind. They usually start me way back in first or second grade level. And we could work up, but we never worked up to the level I was supposed to be at.

While the schooling labels used to describe and categorize may seem to be a reasonable way of talking about students, as a teacher you must be aware that language reinforces beliefs about a child that are difficult to change once teachers and significant others adopt a certain impression of him or her. Therefore, you must attempt to view each child as an individual and judge him or her on his or her own merits and accomplishments and not rely on previous school files or conversations in the teacher's lounge for an accurate interpretation.

Schooling, Students, and Their Notion of Justice

School justice, as reflected in academic and behavioral rules and disciplinary procedures meted out by the faculty, was another point of contention for student. Children (regardless of color or social status) possess a tacit understanding of their world and have a sense of what is and is not right and how people feel about them. In certain instances school rules and teachers are justifiably perceived as adversaries. As a new teacher, it is important that you become attuned not only to your own sense of justice and ethics in your classroom but also to the sensibilities of your students.

One of the more common criticisms students have of school is that they never acquired proficiency in the basic reading and computation skills school is supposed to teach. As we learned earlier, students designated as remedial seldom became proficient, which they felt was unjust. Grades were also a source of contention for some students. One student, for example, criticized a teacher for giving As indiscriminantly without requiring effort and academic excellence. Still other teachers are criticized because of their negative attitudes and behavior towards students.

> Kevin: It wasn't this way with all the teachers . . . . A few of the teachers [were] cool and you could talk to them, but they wasn't going to let you get over 'em or nothing like that . . . . A few of them was funny [prejudice] that's all . . . . I had this home economics teacher, and she was funny . . . .

I believe she came down on a lot of people. She was prejudice if you ask me,
anyway . . . . One day we was cookin' something. I don't remember what it
was . . . . some ole slop. And like she came over there . . . . "Wow, whatcha'
all going' do with this? This ain't done right and everythin," you know. I
don't know. It was she came down funny. She didn't have to come down the
way she did—all smart and stuff.

What these students wanted was basic educational rights, equity, and
accessibility to worthwhile knowledge and positive pedagogical experiences. What they received did not meet their educational expectations.
Not surprisingly, teachers are ultimately responsible for and control
those pedagogical experiences which determine classroom life, and for
some students, it was easy to determine the teacher's feelings towards
them. The assertion that the way teachers treated students indicated
their feelings towards them is a common theme in the educational
histories of students. As one stated succinctly: "The way teacher talked
to me, you know . . . you can feel their reactions or emotions. You can
tell if you are appreciated or not."

Social justice in school seemed questionable not only with regard
to academic rights, but was also an issue regarding peer confrontation.
School rules are not designed to protect students from social ridicule
and scorn. Students, especially those known as being academically
behind their peers, have little faith in school rules as a buffer against
laughter. Such actions by peers, as most teachers know, are a painful
part of school life children experience. While students know there are
rules, many of those that fail seldom believe school rules work for
them and with good reason: they tried to obey them but received
unsatisfactory results.

Jackie: Then kids used to walk past the office and laugh at you. You're in a
special class, you dummy. You can't read. I'd get up and kick their ass.
Nobody's going to call me dummy and get away with it.

BG: What happened?

Jackie: I get suspended—for three days.

BG: Did you ever say to anybody, listen these kids are messing with me?

Jackie: Yes. I use to tell them all the time. Just tell the teacher and we'll take
care of it. I'm going to tell a white teacher on a white kid? What the hell is
they gonna' do about that? Can't you take teasing? No! No, I'm no dummy—
even though I couldn't read. I'm no dummy.

Because of the complexities and mitigating circumstances of interaction
between individuals in institutions, rules can be ineffective in protecting
students from verbal abuse.

Physically violent confrontations with school staff were also not
uncommon, and the overwhelming but not surprising fact is that physi-

cal discipline triggered students' violent retaliations. While violence and fighting cannot be condoned, and students realize this, there are occasions when both teacher and student are equally guilty of inciting violent confrontations. For example: during the lunch hour in a middle school, as in many other schools, students were required to remain outside the building until the afternoon bell. One student recalled holding the door ajar so that he could get back into the building prior to the bell. A teacher, realizing what the student had in mind, pushed the door open on him, knocking him to the ground.

> Michael: I jumped up and said what did you do that for, and he slapped me and turned around to go back in the building and I hit him back. I got suspended for two weeks.

Michael stated that no action was brought against the teacher for hitting him because, "that's just the way it is."

> Michael: We ain't go' no say so. Okay, just say you slap me, pow, pow. I slap you back. Okay, you run into the main office and get [the school policeman] you know. He comes in here and slaps me around for a few. There ain't nothing I can do about it . . . . and all the time you fired on me first . . . . There's a lot of teachers that pull that.

Students have their own sense of justice. Although they would attempt to resolve their disputes through the school's procedural channels, if they were treated unfairly and got no satisfaction from school officials, they would resort to their own means of obtaining what they were denied.

The schools did not succeed in socializing these students into accepting life under perceived inequitable rules with few questions and no breech of school laws. Instead of being submissive, these students protested and rebelled against what they believed to be unjust treatment, accepting the repercussions as part of the price they would pay for justice in school.

Discussion

Even from this truncated view into educational biographies of students, we are able to understand how students perceive what schooling is and how it affects them. We realize that students think and question and have the ability to develop a healthy skepticism of what they perceive to be academic and/or social injustice. We also come to realize that compliance and not skepticism is condoned in public schools. This is not to suggest that everytime a child objects to something he is right and the school is wrong. Children, when reprimanded for a transgression, know what they did to warrant disciplinary action. Those (similar to the students in the discussion) who believe that they have been wronged will be vocal in their protests. As a teacher, you must be mindful of this when resolving a conflict. You might also consider incorporating the ability of students to delineate unjust situations and contradictions that are specific to their own interests and concerns into your classroom pedagogy.

The analytic sensibilities of students to understand and decipher what was happening to them demonstrate their potential abilities to acquire, analyze, and manipulate knowledge. This suggests conditions in academic schooling that make it possible for alternative educational paradigms such as emancipatory and ethnic science to be incorporated into classroom curricula as opposed to those failure theories that sort, categorize, and socially stratify children.

Accomplishing such a task requires a socio-political and humanistic view of what "education for all the people" really means and of the implications of such education for contemporary and future society. For a preservice (and inservice) teacher there is a need to conceptualize alternative educational paradigms[9] by initiating critical thinking, research, and practical classroom application.

Ethnic Science

The ethnic science paradigm, for example, offers an alternative to the theory and practice of educating minority children. Usually when black and other ethnic-racial groups of students are observed and measured by the criteria established for the dominant white middle class values system, their actions and behavior are judged as "deviant." The ethnic science paradigm rejects such analysis and prognostication based on measurements and abnormalistic-medical models dealing with behavioral attitudes and corrections, such as remediation, medication, or incarceration. Instead the ethnic-science paradigm is based on the assumption that cultural traditions, physical activity levels, behavior, knowledge acquisition patterns, and so forth, of blacks and other ethnic racial groups are neither deviant nor inferior but simply different from those of the dominant social structure.[10] Therefore, such phenomena must be studied within their own contexts and frames of reference and not by alien standards. Your daily classroom practice should reflect an appreciation and respect for the legitimacy of minority cultures.

Harry Morgan's work is an example of research that reflects a conceptual switch from a pathological to a more humanistic model. Morgan believes that some children acquire and process knowledge differently than their peers. Morgan's work argues that the active, violent behavior of black children reflects a unique, early, and advance sensory motor development that is perceived by school staff as chaotic and disruptive. He believes that there is a need for a theory of knowledge acquisitions patterns among black children as a positive resource that can be used constructively to enhance their education.[11] This is one example of an educational paradigm that provides alternative ways of viewing educative activity.

Education as Emancipation:
Pedagogical Implications

Education that emancipates individuals from technological ignorance and social subordination is an ethical act. Teachers, therefore, find themselves caught in a paradox, which can only be resolved on an individual basis. On the one hand, schools as a part of the larger social power structure have a mandate to maintain the societal status quo. On the other hand, teacher education programs realize the need of "all socio-economic classes to learn about and to transform the nature of their existence."[12] The emancipatory paradigm assists teachers in demystifying and disseminating such knowledge to children. It is a pedagogy in which you as an individual can actively and promptly engage. At this state of your preservice training program, you should carefully think about the "stuff" of curriculum content—that is, what you present to children as worthwhile knowledge and learning, what you actually teach day-to-day, as well as what is in your textbooks. You should begin to reflect on your own activities (why you select and distribute certain knowledge in your class to your students) in terms of the wider patterning of social and economic relationships of the community in which you teach and in terms of the social economic structure of the community at large of which you and the school itself are a part.[13] You will not only develop an awareness of what influences your decisions about teaching, but you will also be in a better position to provide education that emancipates rather than confines. Moreover, you as a teacher must ask yourself whether the curricular knowledge you distribute assists the learning process by demystifying knowledge and teaching children that the world around them is not objectively constructed but is the product of human imagination and creativity. Not only would your students profit, but you as the teacher would also be more cognizant of what you teach and why.

The educational biographies provide examples of the students' cultural capital—a prerequisite for facilitating emancipatory education. A teacher using the emancipatory strategy would incorporate this analytical awareness and understanding of the world with academic preparation and socio-political consciousness. By teaching children to raise questions about the legitimacy, credibility, or equity of what they see, you the teacher can help them understand what is happening in the world around them. As informed adults, these students will be able to make knowledgeable and humane decisions about bettering their society.

There are alternative schools[14] in existance today that are based on this kind of emancipatory curriculum design that focus on "institutional reality." Classroom learning, for example, is organized around institutions that interpret knowledge, such as the media and museums. Here is one view:

> The children were urged to question the structure of these institutions and to organize alternative structures for presenting the same type of material. The schools['s] . . . purpose was to demystify that which is really subjective, and to show children that institutional organization and purpose is not derived from 'natural order' but from people's minds.[15]

Obviously this vision of the role of education in the perpetuation of society is controversial and difficult. Alternative pedagogies do not have a raft of "cookbook" ideas and workbooks for classroom use. Much of what you will need to incorporate in the daily curriculum will have to be found, initially at least, on your own. You might also be pressured by other teachers and administrators to conform to the "tried and true" teaching strategies. So how do you start? Cynthia Brown,[16] Chris Searle,[17] and Sylvia Ashton-Warner[18] provide examples of classroom techniques that may prove helpful for your initial emersion into emancipatory education. Brown discusses Paulo Friere's literary pedagogy, its adaptation in American schools, and the implications of expanding children's awareness and consciousness. Based on conversations with Brenda Bay and Herbert Kohl, Brown also discusses how to bridge the child's knowledge with academic learning and social awareness. She shows how to give children concrete examples for understanding and how to incorporate in teaching what children bring with them to the classroom.

Ashton-Warner provides examples of pedagogy in action and the pulse of daily classroom life. She believes that through teaching, reflecting, and adapting, education is a continually dynamic and dialectical process between teacher and pupil. Her idea of organic vocabulary (similar to Friere's generative vocabulary) offers more examples of how the cultural capital of children can be used as a bridge to understanding and using the knowledge children learn. Warner's critique of a middle-class, suburban, open school should also be carefully read: she wonders about the affects of American advancing technological society on how we teach and raise our young.

Searle's work is an intensely provocative collection of poems, prose, drawings, plays, and stories created by his classroom children—youngsters from the poor, ethnic, and working classes of England. This book dramatically presents what children can do and how they see the world. Their written explorations of their neighborhoods, community, country, and the international scene show without a doubt that given the appropriate pedagogical tools, they can think beyond the superficial world schools try to present. Searle's book proves that what children see in the world is subjectively constructed and comes from the minds of individuals. Moreover, in creating this literary work, they as individuals created a valid piece of culture.

Encountering works such as these, which are concerned with the struggle for emancipation as a literary genre, will help you to focus on how you view what you do and to begin to pose critical questions about your actions. As Greene expresses it,

> Without the awareness . . . teachers find it unimaginably difficult to cope with the demands of children in these days. They may become drifters as a result, or authoritarians. If they undergo purely technical training or a simplified "competency-based" approach, they are likely to see themselves as mere transmission belts—or clerks. The question of the freedom of those they try to teach . . . recede before a tide of demands for "basics," "discipline," and preparation for the "world of work." Teachers (artlessly, wearily) become accomplices in mystification. They have neither the time, nor energy, nor inclination to urge their students to critical reflection: they, themselves, have suppressed questions and avoided backward looks.[19]

Teaching is not an easy vocation. But there can be no excuse for naivete. With the knowledge gained from alternative perspectives on the role of schooling, what schools do, and what ethical responsibilities teachers have, you are on your way. Moreover, now that you have acquired knowledge, you have the responsibility to act.

Notes

[1] Beverly M. Gordon, "The Educational Life Histories of Nine High School Dropouts" (Dissertation: University of Wisconsin, 1979).

[2] Nell Keddie, ed., *The Myth of Cultural Deprivation* (Harmondsworth, Middlesex, England: Cox & Wyman Ltd., 1973).

[3] Murry Edelman, *The Political Language of the Helping Profession* (Madison, Wisconsin: Institute for Research on Poverty-Discussion Papers, University of Wisconsin, 1974).

[4] R. C. Connell, *Ruling Class, Ruling Culture* (Cambridge, England: Cambridge University Press, 1977).

[5] Cultural capital is defined as the knowledge and skills the student brings into the schooling situation.

[6] For further discussions, see Connell, *Ruling Class, Ruling Culture*, and Gordon, "The Educational Life Histories of Nine High School Dropouts."

[7] This small sampling was taken from an extensive study of the educational biographies of high school dropouts. See Gordon, "The Education Life Histories of Nine High School Dropouts."

[8] Pierre Bourdieu, "Cultural Reproduction and Social Reproduction," in *Power and Ideology in Education*, ed. Jerome Karabel and A. H. Halsey (New York: Oxford University Press, 1977).

[9] Tom Alan, "The Reform of Teacher Education through Research: A Futile Quest," *Teacher's College Record* 83 (Fall, 1980).

[10] Edward T. Hall, *Beyond Culture* (Garden City, New York: Anchor Press, 1977). Hall's discussion in chapter five of the rhythm and body movements among cultural groups gives an example of how individuals are, in his words, "habituated to the rhythms of their own language and culture."

[11] Harry Morgan, "Towards a Theory of Selected Knowledge Acquisition Patterns Among Black Children," *Journal of American Ethnic Science Society* 1 (December, 1976).

[12] Henry Giroux, "Teacher Education and the Ideology of Social Control," *Journal of Education* 162: 1 (Winter, 1980) 5.

[13] Michael W. Apple, *Ideology and Curriculum* (London: Routledge and Kegan Paul, 1979). See chapter 3, "Economics and Control in Everyday School Life," written with Nancy King.

[14] Other alternative schools such as the Patterson School in New York, The Westside Academy, and Providence St. Mels School in Chicago, are successful urban schools, sympathetic to the ethnic-science paradigm, that defies current thinking about the intellectual potential of minority and poor children by producing young scholars in a variety of academic disciplines.

[15] Martin Carnoy, *Education as Cultural Imperialism* (New York: David McKay, 1974), p. 367.

[16] Cynthia Brown, *Literacy in Thirty Hours: Paulo Friere's Process in North East Brazil* (Chicago, Illinois: Alternative School Network, 1978).

[17] Chris Searle, ed., *Classrooms of Resistance* (London: Writers and Readers Publishing Cooperative, 1975).

[18] See Sylvia Ashton-Warner, *Teacher* (New York: Bantam Books, 1963), and *Spearpoint: Teacher in America* (New York: Vintage Books, 1976).

[19] Maxine Greene, *Landscapes of Learning* (New York: Teachers' College Press, 1978), p. 38.

I am sure you know that kids going to school are not empty vessels waiting to be filled; they are people with their own individual needs, concerns, hopes and experiences, and each one is different. If I had my way, I would have all teachers repeat this statement each and every morning before they start teaching. Too often we forget this fact. The articles by Shaw and Robbins serve to remind us further.

Busing: Journey Away from Self-Esteem

Valerie Shaw

Each September, at the start of the new school year, I solemnly observe the procession of black youngsters boarding the yellow school buses that will be their vehicle to another world.

Out of their "deteriorating" neighborhoods and "economically depressed" inner-city communities, out from under the dust of their "disadvantaged" backgrounds and racially isolated schools, their destination is a white suburb where they can receive a "quality" education.

I look at them, all starched and scrubbed and expectant, and I wonder whether, inside, they are mystified, bitter, angry, and hurt by the negative image we impose on them and their neighborhoods. I wonder about the harm we are doing with such sociological labeling.

I have a great affinity for these youngsters. I know their pain, hurt, and anger, for I was a black child who grew up during the dawn of school desegregation in Los Angeles.

The only child of a respected, middle-class minister and schoolteacher, I was 10 and in the fifth grade when I forfeited my childhood.

Parents Praised Ruling

It was 1955, the year following the landmark Supreme Court decision, *Brown v. Board of Education*, which my parents applauded. "It will hasten integration efforts in housing, jobs and schools," prophesied my father. My mother pointed with pride to our own multiracial, model neighborhood, where integration had been achieved without the courts.

No one warned me—probably no one wanted to suspect—that the Brown ruling would introduce a phenomenon called white flight, and that it would hasten the departure of my best friends and classmates, whom I had always regarded as my equals.

Eileen—my plump, rosy-cheeked confidante for five years—was the first of my white friends to tell me that her family was moving to the San Fernando Valley district of Los Angeles, where she could get a "better education." That gave me the first inkling that there was a difference, for I had believed that our school was as good as any. Eileen

Los Angeles Times, September 21, 1980. Reprinted by permission from the author.

and I had been like sisters, sharing homework and girlish secrets, and on moving day we cried and clung to each other. A moment later, she vanished from my life.

The following spring, the loss of my best friend was numbed by the anticipation of being a sixth grader with lots of friends. And then Karen, Sally, and Diane announced that they would not be returning to school in the fall. When each told me, independently of the others, that she wouldn't be graduating from our school because it was "not a good school," I was sure that I somehow had personally affected her parents' decision to move.

Until recently, I was frequently haunted by the image of myself—a 10-year-old blessed with love and a promising future—bent in tears, looking out from my roof garden at the gray and distant hills to the north, praying to join my friends. Where were these strange lands called Glendale, Sherman Oaks, San Gabriel? Why couldn't my family move there, too?

Heidi left late that summer, before school started. I feigned indifference, although I knew that the love I had felt for this friend had been replaced with hurt and bitterness.

That same month, Richard moved to another suburb. It was a "safer neighborhood," he had confided to me in Sunday school. That was the precise moment of my discovery that I could no longer afford to hold on to those childish dreams of becoming a Mouseketeer or wearing my hair in a saucy pony tail or going to a "better school." Such dreams were reserved for white kids, those white kids who moved away.

Self-Esteem Was Lost

It came as a surprise to everyone when my grades fell—to everyone but me. I turned inward and grew solemn. My parents worried but could do nothing to bring back their bright and sunny little girl.

Educators and psychologists now recognize the devastating effects of lost self-esteem and a negative self-image. But in 1955, my withdrawal was as mysterious as outer space.

Perhaps I was fortunate that the issue of desegregation was not in the daily news when I was a youngster. Not being constantly reminded of my "difference," I was able to survive and let the superficial scars heal. It took only another 20 years to forgive the white ghosts of my childhood and to understand my full value to our community and to the human race.

But my long-ago experience gives me cause for great alarm today. With the constant bombardment of news about the busing controversy— the white flight and lawsuits and the other fierce issues in the fight against desegregation—what are black youngsters feeling? And how long will it take them to learn to forgive?

Student's Suicide
Stirs New Interest In Gifted

William Robbins
The New York Times

Detroit, Mich.—After the death of James Dallas Egbert III, the brilliant student from Dayton who shot himself last month, one of the first expressions of sympathy for his parents came from a woman who had experienced both the problems and the joys of rearing talented children seven times over.

She is Mary Connelly of Birmingham, Mich., mother of seven children with IQs ranging from 130 to 150. Five of those children, like Dallas Egbert, had contemplated suicide, Connelly said in an interview.

Because of the experiences in her own family, Connelly long ago recognized what many experts regard as one of the most serious wastes of a national resource—the neglect of the country's gifted children.

The Egberts got other calls. One mother told of a 6-year-old son who felt as if he was "in an iron cage" because his mind had developed so much faster than his body. Another told of a son who said he was so alienated from his peers that "he could understand just how Dallas Egbert felt." Still another spoke of a son so troubled by his failure to communicate, even with his own family, that he killed himself four days before Dallas did.

New Attention

But Dallas, 17 years old when he died, focused new attention on the problems of the gifted. A boy who knew the alphabet at the age of 2, could read at 3, finished high school at 14 and entered Michigan State University at 15, he was frequently described by schoolmates and teachers as "a loner," isolated from his peers by his brilliance coupled with his immaturity. He had an IQ listed at 145, which teachers whom he outdistanced in computer science said did not accurately reflect his intelligence.

After his death last month, Dallas' parents, James D. Egbert II and his wife, Anna, established the Dallas Egbert Memorial Fund to be administered by the Wright State University Foundation. The fund is intended to create a clinic to help other gifted but troubled young people.

"If there is anything else like it available, I don't know about it," said E. Paul Torrance, author of *Guiding Creative Talent* and other works dealing with problems of educating the gifted, who is now a professor at the University of Georgia. "But there is a growing awareness of the need. There is a large enough number who need that kind of help to be concerned about."

"That is one of the areas where we hope to increase our knowledge," said James T. Webb, assistant dean for special programs and professor at the school of professional psychology at Wright State University, who will direct the work of the Egbert Fund. "When we have developed our clinical services we hope to use that as a springboard for research."

70 Percent Not Identified

In the schools, the gifted are generally regarded as those with IQs ranging upward from a level of 125 to 130, but Harold C. Lyon, director of the Office of the Gifted and Talented in the Federal Department of Education, believes that, when only IQ tests are used as a guide, as many as 70% of creative students will be missed by educational enrichment programs.

A generally accepted belief that, as a group, gifted children are better adjusted than their peers, is based on the work of Lewis M. Terman, who was a leading educational psychologist. He conducted studies on 1,000 gifted children in the first half of the century, work that is still widely regarded as the best evidence available.

Several experts noted that problems persisted in identifying the gifted, even though techniques were available. But they require a large degree of interest and attention, often from overworked teachers.

In many instances, experts say, teachers who must devote most of their attention to their average students sometimes tend to resent the inquiring minds and challenging questions of the gifted. And when talented students are neglected, the experts say, severe emotional problems can develop.

"The fact is that a very high percentage of our dropouts are the gifted," said Lyon, the federal official.

"In the inner city," said Lyon, "where the gifted youth isn't challenged, he's likely to become a gang leader. And today, a lot of the cells in our prisons are filled with the gifted who were never identified and given appropriate educational challenges."

Lyon's Federal Office of the Gifted has a budget of $6.7 million for the fiscal year 1981, a big increase over 1979, when his budget was $3.28 million, the director noted.

What is needed in addition to special enrichment programs, said Torrance, is a mentor for the gifted child, "some distinguished person" for him to talk to and to challenge him.

Morrison Wong conducted research on teachers' perceptions and expectations of their Asian and white students. Wong's article is included for two important reasons. First, it is important that you as a beginning professional read and understand the research that is conducted in your field. Second, this article can help you examine the following questions: Are there model students? If you believe there are model students, how does that affect the way you teach students, your attitudes about students, and the students themselves? Can you justifiably formulate expectations for students on the basis of their ethnicity and their fathers' occupation?

Asian Students as Model Students?

Morrison G. Wong

Texas Christian University

A 1970 *New York Times* article noted a change in the perception of the Chinese in America: "the pig-tailed coolie has been replaced in the imagination of many Americans by the earnest, bespectacled young scholar." Asian-Americans have been referred to by some policy makers as "model minorities." Inheriting part of this "model minority" legacy, Asian students have been depicted, and to some extent perceive themselves, as "model students." In this same article a student commented, "My teachers have always helped me because they had such a good image of Chinese students . . . good little Chinese kid, they said, so bright and so well behaved and hard-working."[1] And an article in *U.S. News and World Report* noted: "Even in the age of television and fast automobiles, Chinese-American children are expected to attend school faithfully, work hard at their studies—and stay out of trouble . . . . A study of San Francisco's Chinatown noted that "if school performance is poor and the parents are told, there is an immediate improvement." And in New York City, school teachers reportedly

Revised from an article that first appeared in *Sociology of Education*, October 1981. Reprinted with permission from the author.

are competing for posts in schools with large numbers of Chinese-American children."[2]

Asian-American educational achievements have been spectacular—far surpassing the educational achievements of whites. In 1970, for all three traditional measures of educational achievement—median school year completed, percentage with four years of high school or more, and percentage with four years of college or more—both foreign-born and native-born Chinese males surpassed the educational attainments of the white population. Most interesting was the fact that 30.8% of the total Chinese male population as opposed to 14.4% of the white population had completed four years of college or more (Wong, 1980).[3] The Japanese have also exceeded the educational achievements of the white population on all three educational measures (Kitano, 1969; Schmid and Nobbe, 1965).[4] A recent study by Levine and Montero (1973) indicated that almost 90% of the *sansei* (third generation Japanese) have attended college.[5]

The purpose of this paper is two-fold. First, it examines the various components of the "model student" concept, in particular teachers' perceptions of the social, emotional, and academic characteristics of Asian students at both the elementary and secondary level and then compares these perceptions with the white student population. It is hypothesized that in a comparison of Asian and white students at both levels of education there will be significant differences in favor of Asian students in the teacher's perceptions of behavioral and emotional characteristics and that these favorable characteristics may be considered components of a "model student" syndrome. Second, it analyzes the relationship of ethnicity, the student's father's socioeconomic status, and the teachers' perceptions of the academic competence, sociability, and emotional stability of the student, as well as teachers' expectations regarding the student's achievement.

Theoretical Background

Empirical studies of the behavioral and emotional differences between Asians and whites may shed some light on the possible bases of teachers' perceptions of ethnic differences in behavioral and emotional characteristics and their relationship to teachers' educational expectations of students. Figure 1 illustrates a hypothetical model of the variables which may influence teachers' educational expectations of students.

A possible basis of teachers' perceptions of ethnic differences between Asians and whites in behavioral and emotional characteristics may be the actual ethnic differences. Among some students of race relations, Asian-Americans have been referred to as "the quiet Ameri-

Figure 1. Hypothetical Model of the Relationship of Ethnicity
and Educational Attainment

ACADEMIC
COMPETENCE

ETHINICITY

EMOTIONAL   TEACHER'S
STABILITY   EXPECTED
               EDUCATION

FATHER'S
SOCIOECONOMIC
STATUS

SOCIABILITY

cans." Is there a kernel of truth in this stereotype? Or is it that many
Asian students feel uncomfortable conversing in a foreign language—
English—and, therefore, are less likely to speak up? Or is it that they
are raised to respect authority and thus never question the instructor?

Empirical studies on the behavioral and emotional characteristics
of Asians and whites in the United States suggest that actual ethnic
differences do exist. Using the Edwards Personal Preference Schedule,
Fenz and Arkoff (1962) found that both Chinese and Japanese males
scored significantly lower than their white counterparts in dominance,
autonomy, aggression, exhibitionism, and heterosexuality.[6] Other
studies have suggested that Japanese-Americans exhibit a higher degree
of introversion (Meredith and Meredith, 1966),[7] passivity (Kitano,
1969),[8] and quietness (Ayabe, 1971)[9] than whites. Similarily, Sue and
Kirk[10] (1972) found Chinese-Americans more introverted and con-
formist than their white counterparts. Thus, it seems quite plausible
that some of the differences between Asian-American and white students in various social, emotional, and academic characteristics that
are perceived by teachers may be due to actual ethnic differences.

The question can be posed: what effect will these ethnic differences have on teachers' educational expectations for the students?
Research by Williams[11] (1976) suggests that teachers' expectations
concerning students' performances are influenced by two categories
of student behaviors: ascribed characteristics of the students (such as
ethnicity) and characteristics that students take on as a result of their
achievement within school (academic potential, behavioral conformity, etc.). The landmark study, *Equality of Educational Opportunity*, found substantial differences among the various racial-ethnic
groups in the scores on a set of standard tests. The study notes, "With
some exceptions—notably Oriental Americans—the average minority
pupil scores distinctly lower on these tests at every level than the
average white pupil" (Coleman et al., 1966).[12] Regarding virtually
every variable of intellectual value, aspiration, or achievement, Asian-

American children were equal to or even outperformed their white majority group peers. Caudill and De Vos (1973) argue that the source of the phenomenal rise of the Japanese is the "significant compatibility (but by no means identity) between the value system found in the culture of Japan and the value system found in American middle class structure . . . . What has happened here is that the peers, teachers, employers, and fellow workers of the *Nisei* have projected their own values onto the neat, well-dressed, and efficient *Nisei* [second generation Japanese-Americans] in whom they see mirrored many of their ideals.[13] Boocock (1972) arrives at the same conclusion, stating that teachers expect Japanese-Americans to achieve high levels of performance.[14] The Japanese, in turn, fulfill these expectations by actually obtaining relatively high-level jobs. This, in turn, reinforces the expectations of those around them. Similar arguments have been presented regarding the Chinese (Hsu, 1971).[15]

The exact extent of the purely racial or ethnic effect on teachers' expected educational attainment is difficult to specify because race or ethnicity is itself related to other family background characteristics. Probably the strongest relationship is between race and socioeconomic status. Numerous studies have noted a strong positive relationship between the students' socioeconomic status, their teachers' expectations, and the students' later achievements; that is, the higher the socioeconomic status of the student's family, the higher his or her academic achievement (Hsu, 1971; Clark, 1962; Sewell et al., 1957; Hieronymus, 1951).[16] Reexamination of these studies, however, suggests that the relationship may be complicated by the fact that socioeconomic status is related to other characteristics of the family that are independently related to achievement. Berstein (1961) concludes that middle-class children are exposed to a richer, more varied and more grammatically correct verbal communication, which gives them a headstart in school.[17] Rosen (1956) characterizes the typical middle-class family value system and child-rearing patterns as an "achievement syndrome," with all efforts bent toward success in school and later life.[18] Using as a point of departure Jackson and Lahaderne's[19] (1967) assertion that instruction and social control are the two basic tasks that teachers face in teaching, Williams[20] (1976) points out that because teachers tend to come from middle-class socioeconomic backgrounds and "because the social control facet of classroom life is so important to teachers, their expectations for students' normative behaviors may substantially affect their cognitive expectations. Students whose behaviors fit the expected model (that is, the middle-class model) benefit in terms of teachers' prophecies for their cognitive performance. On the other hand, the disjunction between the behaviors of working-class students and the middle-class norms of classrooms may affect teachers' cognitive expectations of these children adversely."

Although actual social class differences exist between Asians and whites (Asians tend to be less middle-class than whites), many of the ethnic differences in behavioral and emotional characteristics cited above show them as adhering more to middle-class norms than whites do. Therefore, because Asians are more "middle-class" in terms of normative behavior (although not necessarily in actual social class) than white middle-class students, the teacher's educational expectations of Asian students should be higher than their white counterparts.

Methods

A. The Sample

This study deals primarily with teachers' perceptions of their Asian and white elementary and secondary students. The teachers were given a questionnaire consisting of a series of semantic differential ratings to measure their perceptions of the social, emotional, and academic characteristics of their students. They also estimated the educational level they expected each student would probably achieve. This questionnaire was supplemented by some factual information obtained from the students.

The sample used in this study was selected by the Program Research in Integrated Multi-Ethnic Education (PRIME) of the University of California, Riverside. The data were obtained from a sample of students and teachers using a stratified random sampling procedure of 144 elementary and secondary schools. The two parameters of stratification were grade level (3rd, 6th, 8th, and 11th grades) and ethnic groups (white, black, Chicano, native American, and Asian). Prospective participants were selected from those eligible by a systematic random sampling process from the school roster. For the purposes of this study, only the Asian and white elementary and secondary school student populations of San Francisco were analyzed. This selection process resulted in 852 elementary students (466 whites and 386 Asians) and 311 secondary students (150 whites and 161 Asians). Because the data did not differentiate among Chinese, Japanese, Filipino, Korean or Vietnamese, the term "Asian" will be used to denote these five major groups.

B. Variables

Although different questionnaires were used for the elementary and secondary student population, the variables that were analyzed were compatible.

Ethnicity. At the elementary school level, the teacher coded the ethnic group for each child in the class using the following categories: Anglo (Caucasian, white); Mexican American; black; Oriental; American Indian; other. Thus, the ethnic group of the elementary school children was measured as perceived by the teacher. The ethnic groups of the secondary school students were reported by the students themselves. Only the white and Asian populations were selected for analysis.

Sociability, Emotional Stability, and Academic Competence. The three measures of sociability, emotional stability, and academic competence were derived from a series of eighteen, five-point differential ratings, six ratings for each scale. The teacher completed these ratings for each student.

Sociability consists of the following adjective pairs: extroverted-introverted, sociable-unsociable, warm-cold, colorful-colorless, friendly-aloof, and cheerful-morose. High scores indicate high sociability, that is, ratings toward the extroverted, sociable, warm, colorful, friendly, and cheerful ends of the six rating scales.

Emotional stability consists of the following adjective pairs: kind-cruel, obedient-disobedient, even tempered-quick tempered, easily disciplined-not easily disciplined, cooperative-obstructive and patient-impatient. High scores indicate high emotional stability, that is, ratings toward the kind, obedient, even-tempered, easily disciplined, cooperative and patient poles of the six rating scales.

Academic competence consists of the following adjective pairs: intelligent-dullminded, quick-slow, able to concentrate-subject to distraction, organized-disorganized, good memory-poor memory, and persevering-quitting. High scores indicate high academic competence, that is, ratings toward the intelligent, quick, able to concentrate, organized, good memory, and persevering ends of the six rating scales. For ease of presentation, only the adjectives toward the high ends of the scales are presented.

Father's Occupation. The occupation of the father (or other head of household) of elementary school students was ascertained by asking the teacher: What is this student's father's (or head of the household's) level of occupation? The choices were as follows: (1) Welfare or Unemployed; (2) Unskilled laborer; (3) Skilled laborer or trade; (4) Clerical-white collar; (5) Managerial-white collar supervising others; (6) Professional. The father's occupation was that which was perceived by the teacher as opposed to the student. The occupation of the father of secondary school students was ascertained by asking the student, "What type of work does your father do?" The description given was then recoded to conform to the scores of the Socioeconomic Index (Duncan, 1961).

Teacher's Educational Expectations. The elementary and secondary teachers' rating of the educational expectations for each child is based on a score from the teachers' responses to the following question: On the basis of your knowledge of this student's aptitudes and motivation for education, how many years of schooling do you expect he will probably complete? They were given the following choices: (1) Less than high school; (2) High school (12 years); (3) Some college or vocational training beyond high school; (4) B.A./B.S. degree (16 years); and (5) Graduate training in some field. Thus, all data are from the teachers except the measures of ethnicity and father's occupation for the secondary school pupils.

Findings

A. Ethnic Differences

Table 1 presents a comparison of the teachers' perceptions of white and Asian students by their educational level for the three different categories —sociability, emotional stability, and academic competence.

White elementary students score slightly higher in sociability than Asian elementary students. More specifically, they are perceived as being more extroverted and colorful than Asian students, whereas Asian elementary students are perceived as being more cheerful.

Asian elementary students are seen as significantly more emotionally stable than white elementary students; that is, Asian students are seen as more kind, obedient, disciplined, cooperative, patient, and less prone to anger than white elementary students.

Asian elementary students are also seen as significantly more academically competent than white elementary students. They are perceived as quicker, more able to concentrate, more organized, more persevering, and as having a better memory than white students. Asian students are also seen as more intelligent than white students although the difference is not statistically significant.

The secondary school population can be analyzed in similar fashion. The results indicate that the teachers' perceived differences in behavioral and emotional characteristics between Asian and white secondary school students are quite similar to those of the elementary school students. Although white secondary school students scored slightly higher than Asian students in terms of sociability, the difference is not significant. Asian secondary school students were seen as significantly more emotionally stable and more academically competent than white students. The differences on all six measures of emotional stability and academic competence are significantly different.

Table 1

Teachers' Perception of White and Asian Students by Their Educational Level

| | Elementary | | Secondary | |
	White N = 466	Asian N = 386	White N = 150	Asian N = 161
	Mean	Mean	Mean	Mean
Sociability	22.64	22.06	22.34	21.56
Extroverted	3.49	2.95*	3.34	2.95*
Sociable	3.91	3.85	3.91	3.81**
Warm	3.85	3.85	3.92	3.83
Colorful	3.61	3.43*	3.34	3.39**
Friendly	3.92	3.96	3.98	3.76
Cheerful	3.87	4.03**	3.92	3.81
Emotional Stability	22.69	25.99**	23.88	25.32**
Kind	3.86	4.21*	4.02	4.11*
Obedient	3.87	4.43*	4.11	4.30*
Not Prone to Anger	3.59	4.14*	3.83	3.94*
Disciplined	3.87	4.52*	4.15	4.47*
Cooperative	3.99	4.55*	4.11	4.44*
Patient	3.51	4.13*	3.61	4.02*
Academic Competence	21.94	24.66*	21.39	24.23*
Intelligent	4.01	4.12	3.75	4.09*
Quick	3.78	3.95**	3.57	3.91*
Concentrates	3.44	4.08*	3.39	4.09*
Organized	3.30	4.12*	3.37	4.02*
Retentive	3.86	4.18*	3.55	4.02*
Persevering	3.55	4.21*	3.59	4.11*

*Statistically significant at the .01 level.
**Statistically significant at the .05 level.

In summary, there were significant differences in the mean scores between the Asian and white elementary and secondary school students. Significant differences in favor of Asian students are particularly noted for the two general categories of academic competence and emotional stability. The hypothesis that there would be significant differences in the teachers' perceptions of the behavioral and emotional characteristics of their Asian and white students and that the rankings would be in favor of Asian students is confirmed. Although differences are not universal, they seem to be in the areas of perceived emotional stability and academic competence.

B. Ethnicity and the Teachers' Educational Expectations

After documenting the perceived ethnic differences between Asian and white students in behavioral and emotional characteristics, one can now address the question of the role these ethnic differences play in influencing the teachers' educational expectations of students.

Elementary School Students. Table 2 analyzes the effects of variables in the overall model for the elementary school population. In the first panel for academic competence, all coefficients are expressed as deviations from the grand mean of 23.17. The first model shows that white students scored an average of 1.23 points lower than the average of the total population while Asian students scored about 1.49 points higher than the average; that is, Asians score about 2.72 points higher than white students in terms of the teachers' perceptions of the academic competence of their elementary students.

One might ask how much of this ethnic gap in academic competence is due to the fact that the Asian and white populations have an unequal distribution of socioeconomic status? As noted previously, the higher the socioeconomic status of the student (or student's parents), the higher the educational expectations of the teacher for the student. The average father's occupational level is lower for the Asian than the white students in San Francisco. One can control statistically for any difference in occupational background; that is, through computational techniques, one can note what the differences would be in terms of academic competence if both the Asian and white students had the same socioeconomic status. When controlling for the effects of fathers occupations, the Asian-white gap increases to 3.09 points. In other words, if Asian and white students had the same socioeconomic background, the teacher would perceive Asian students as even more academically competent and white students as much less academically competent.

Emotional stability shows similar results. In the first model, Asian students are perceived about 3.32 points more emotionally stable than white students by their teachers. When controlling for father's occupation, Asian students are perceived as even more emotionally stable and white students as much less emotionally stable by their teachers.

White students are perceived by their teachers as slightly more sociable than Asian students, although the difference is not significant. Controlling for father's occupation reduces the ethnic gap even further. Much of the small difference in sociability can be explained by the occupation of the student's father.

The fourth panel looks at the role the various variables play in teachers' educational expectations of their students. The grand mean of

Table 2

Effects of Social and Social Psychological Variables on Ethnicity and the Teacher's Expected Education for the Elementary School Population

	Academic Competence Mean = 23.17		Emotional Stability Mean = 24.18		Sociability Mean = 22.39		Teacher's Expected Education Mean = 3.50		
	(1)*	(2)*	(1)*	(2)*	(1)	(2)*	(1)	(2)*	(3)*
Ethnicity									
White	-1.23	-1.40	-1.51	-1.59	.27	.11	-.06	-.14	-.01
Asian	1.49	1.69	1.81	1.90	-.33	-.14	.08	.17	.01
Eta/Beta	.23*	.27*	.29*	.30*	.06	.03	.06	.13*	.01
Father's Occupation									
Unemployed		-3.61		-3.18		-1.21		-.80	-.43
Unskilled		-1.33		-.54		-1.18		-.54	-.38
Skilled		-.49		-.52		-.60		-.27	-.23
White Collar		.14		.44		-.05		-.07	-.09
Manager		1.98		.57		1.28		.58	.36
Professional		2.33		1.45		1.59		.92	.67
Missing		-1.80		-.20		-.32		-.36	-.33
Eta/Beta		.29*		.19		.21*		.47*	.33*
Academic Competence									
Standardized Regression Coefficient									1.18*
Emotional Stability									
Standardized Regression Coefficient									-.90*
Sociability									
Standardized Regression Coefficient									.09
Multiple R²	.055	.136	.084	.121	.004	.047	.003	.218	.463

*Statistically significant at the .05 level.

the teachers' educational expectations of their students was 3.50, suggesting that the teachers felt that on the average their students would graduate from high school and probably receive some college education. Although not statistically significant, the first model shows that teachers felt Asian students would achieve slightly more education than their white counterparts. Controlling for father's occupation increased this gap, suggesting that if Asian and white students had the same socio-economic status, teachers would expect even higher educational achievements of their Asian students and even lower educational achievements of their white students than when just looking at ethnic differences. The addition of the variables academic competence, emotional stability, and sociability reduces the Asian-white gap to almost nothing, suggesting that although ethnic differences exist in the teachers' educational expectations, it is the teachers' perceptions of academic competence that are primarily responsible for the ethnic-socio-economic differentials. In other words, a student's ethnic background and socio-economic status affects the teacher's perceptions of that student, which in turn, affects the teacher's educational expectations of the student.

Secondary School Students. The secondary school student population can be analyzed in similar fashion. Table 3 presents the results of the analysis. In the first panel, one notes that teachers perceive Asian students as more academically competent than white students. Controlling for father's occupation did not have much impact on this differential, suggesting that ethnicity is a major factor in the teacher's perceived academic competence of the student.

Asian students are also perceived as more emotionally stable than white students by their teachers. Controlling for father's occupation had almost no impact on the teachers' perceptions of their student's emotional stability.

White secondary school students are perceived as being more sociable than Asian students, although the differences are not significant. Controlling for the social origins of a student's father increases the ethnic gap slightly, although again, this was not significant.

Secondary school teachers felt that, on the average, their students would receive at least some college education. The first model indicates that the teachers expected that their Asian students would receive more education than white students. Controlling for father's occupation slightly increases the white-Asian gap with teachers having higher educational expectations of their Asian students and lower educational expectations of their white students. Controlling for the academic competence, emotional stability, and sociability of the student results in a significant reduction of the Asian-white student differential. When all the variables are in the model, the teachers had higher educational

Table 3

Effects of Social and Social Psychological Variables on Ethnicity and the Teacher's Expected Education for the Secondary School Population

	Academic Competence Mean = 23.21		Emotional Stability Mean = 24.71		Sociability Mean = 21.91		Teacher's Expected Education Mean = 3.58		
	(1)*	(2)*	(1)*	(2)*	(1)	(2)	(1)	(2)*	(3)*
Ethnicity									
White	-1.49	-1.53	-.86	-.85	.46	.52	-.14	-.16	.07
Asian	1.21	1.24	.73	.73	-.38	-.42	.12	.14	-.06
Eta/Beta	.25*	.24*	.16*	.16*	.08	.10	.12a	.14*	.06
Father's Occupation									
Standardized Regression Coefficient		.05		-.00		.06		.00	.08*
Academic Competence									
Standardized Regression Coefficient									.81*
Emotional Stability									
Standardized Regression Coefficient									-.21*
Sociability									
Standardized Regression Coefficient									-.05
Multiple R^2	.055	.056	.025	.025	.008	.010	.015	.023	.550

*Statistically significant at the .05 level.
a Marginally significant at the .06 level.

expectations for their white students than their Asian students. Again, academic competence is the crucial variable in explaining the teachers' educational expectations of their students. The teachers' educational expectations of their students are not so much influenced by ethnicity or father's socioeconomic status, as they are by the teachers' perceived academic competence of their students. Put in another way, the ethnic background of the student affects the teacher's perception of the academic competence of the student, which in turn, affects the teacher's educational expectations of the student. As for the elementary school student population, a negative coefficient was noted for the variable emotional stability, suggesting that teachers have higher educational expectations of secondary school students who scored low on emotional stability than those who scored high. However, one should keep in mind that ethnicity influences the teacher's perceived academic competence of his or her student.

Discussion and Conclusions

The findings of this study indicate that there are significant differences in the teachers' perceptions of the behavioral and emotional characteristics of their Asian and white students at both the elementary and secondary level of education. Asian students were seen as significantly more emotionally stable and academically competent than white students. It is argued that it is the items in these two categories that form the bases of the "model student." This becomes clearer when one keeps in mind that the "model student" concept is viewed from the teacher's perspective, that it is a definition given by the teacher. Hence, the "model student" concept would probably entail those items or components that allow the teacher to exert the least amount of effort and incur a low degree of conflict and frustration. Seen in this light, it is probably safe to assert that the "model student" may be characterized as one who possesses a certain degree of intellectual ability (the ability to grasp instruction—academic competence) *and* one who does not cause trouble (emotional stability). In essence, it may be concluded that Asian students are perceived by their teachers as "model students" at both levels of education.

The second part of the study analyzes the relationship of ethnicity, father's socioeconomic status, teacher's perceptions of academic competence, sociability, and emotional stability with the teacher's expected education of the student. Although the study dealt with two different student populations, certain tentative conclusions can be presented. First, ethnicity is a good predictor of the teachers' perceptions of the academic competence and emotional stability of their students, with

Asian students being perceived as being more academically competent and more emotionally stable than white students at both levels of education.

Second, the teachers' educational expectations of their Asian students are slightly higher than of their white students at both levels of education. When controlling for the father's occupation, the ethnic gaps in teachers' educational expectations increases for both student populations. However, when the teachers' perceived academic competence, emotional stability, and sociability of the student are added to the model, the ethnic differences in the teachers' educational expectations virtually disappear for the elementary school student population and reverse for the secondary school student population. That is, teachers expect higher educational achievements from white secondary school students than from Asian students. It is concluded that the teachers' perceived academic competence of their students acts as the major intervening variable between ethnicity and the teachers' expected education of the student. Put in another way, teachers will expect "smart students" or students whom they perceive as academically competent to attain a high degree of education regardless of the student's ethnic background. On the other hand, for both student populations, the emotional stability of the student had a negative effect on the teacher's expected education of the student. The explanation for this negative effect is unknown.

Third, father's occupation had different effects on the teachers' perceptions and expectations of their students at both educational levels. For the elementary school student population, the father's occupation had a significant effect in explaining the ethnic differences in the teachers' perceptions and expectations of their Asian and white students. This, however was not the case for the secondary school student population. These differences may reflect real differences in the role the father's occupation plays on teachers' educational expectations of their students at the two different educational levels. That is, because elementary school students are quite young, the elementary school teacher may take into consideration, whether consciously or unconsciously, the occupation of the student's father in assessing the highest grade the student will probably complete. In contrast, because high school students are older and only a year or so away from high school graduation, the teacher is in a better position to accurately judge the academic capabilities and aspirations of the student, independent of the socioeconomic status of the student's father. Furthermore, it may be important to remember that the father's occupation variable is actually two different variables; for the elementary school student population, it is the teacher's perception of the father's occupation of the student, while for the secondary school student population, it is the student's own identification of their father's occupation. It may be reasonable to conclude that teachers' perceptions of socioeconomic status affect their expectations more than the actual occupational position of the father does.

In conclusion, it has been shown that Asian students at both the elementary and secondary educational levels are perceived by their teachers as "model students;" that they are seen as more academically competent and more emotionally stable than white students. Ethnic differences also exist in the teachers' educational expectations of their elementary and secondary students with Asian students being expected to receive slightly more education than white students. It is concluded that the teacher's perceived academic competence of the student plays a crucial role in accounting for the ethnic differential in educational expectations of the student by the teacher. Because Asian students are perceived by their teachers as "model students," particularly as more academically competent than their white counterparts, teachers have higher educational expectations of them, which in turn, probably influences the Asian student's later higher educational attainment.

Notes

[1] "Orientals Find Bias Down Sharply in U.S.", New York Times, December 12 1970, pp. 1, 70.

[2] "Success Story of One Minority Group," U.S. News and World Report, December 26 pp. 73-76.

[3] Morrison G. Wong, "Changes in socioeconomic status of the Chinese male population in the United States from 1960 to 1970." International Migration Review, 14:4 (1978) 511-524.

[4] Harry H. L. Kitano, Japanese Americans: The Evolution of a Subculture. (Englewood Cliffs, N.J.: Prentice Hall, 1969.) Calvin Schmid and Charles Nobbe, "Socioeconomic Differentials Among Non-white Races." American Sociological Review, 30 (1965) 909-922.

[5] Gene N. Levine and Darrel M. Montero, "Socioeconomic Mobility Among Three Generations of Japanese Americans." Journal of Social Issues, 29:2 (1973) 33-49.

[6] Walter D. Fenz and Abe Arkoff, "Comparative Need Patterns of Five Ancestry Groups in Hawaii." Journal of Abnormal and Social Psychology, 48 (1962) 311-313.

[7] Gerald M. Meredith and Connie G. Meredith, Acculturation and Personality Among Japanese-American College Students in Hawaii. Journal of Social Psychology, 68 (1966) 175-182.

[8] Harry H. L. Kitano, *Japanese Americans: The Evolution of a Subculture*. (Englewood Cliffs, N.J.: Prentice Hall, 1969.)

[9] H. L. Ayabe, "Deference and Ethnic Differences in Voice Levels." *Journal of Social Psychology*, 85 (1971) 181-185.

[10] Derald W. Sue and B. A. Kirk, "Psychological characteristics of Chinese-American students." *Journal of Counseling Psychology*, 19 (1973) 471-478.

[11] Trevor Williams, "Educational Ambition: Teachers and Students," *Sociology of Education*, 48 (Fall 1975) 432-456.

[12] Jane S. Coleman, Ernest Q. Campbell, et. al. *Equality of Educational Opportunity*. (U.S. Department of Health, Education, and Welfare, Office of Education. Washington, D.C.: U.S. Government Printing Office, 1966.)

[13] William Caudill and George DeVos. "Achievement, Culture, and Personality: The Case of the Japanese Americans," in N. R. Yetman and C. H. Steele eds., *Majority and Minority*. (Boston: Allyn and Bacon, Inc., 1973.) p. 299-305.

[14] Arance S. Boocock, *An Introduction to the Sociology of Learning*. (Houghton Mifflin Company, 1972.)

[15] Francis Hsu, *The Challenge of the American Dream: The Chinese in the United States*. (Belmont, California: Wadsworth, 1971.)

[16] Burton Clark, *Educating the Expert Society*. (San Francisco: Chandler, 1962); William H. Sewell, et al. "Social Status and Educational and Occupational Aspiration." *American Sociological Review*, 22 (1957) 67-73; A. N. Hieronymus, "A Study of Social Class Motivation: Relationships Between Anxiety for Education and Certain Socioeconomic and Intellectual Variables." *Journal of Educational Psychology*, 42 (1961) 192-205.

[17] B. Bernstein, "Social Class and Linguistic Development." in A. H. Halsey et al. *Education, Economy and Society*. (New York: Free Press, 1961.) p. 288-314.

[18] B. C. Rosen, "The Achievement Syndrome: A Psychcultural Dimension of Social Stratification." *American Sociological Review*, 21 (1956) 203-211.

[19] Philip W. Jackson, and Henrietta M. Lahaderne, "Inequalities of Teacher-Pupil Contacts. *Psychology in the Schools*, 4 (1967) 204-211.

[20] Trevor Williams, "Educational Ambition: Teachers and Students," *Sociology of Education*, 48 (Fall 1975) 432-456.

Throughout this book, we have had an opportunity to discuss many of the problems, issues, and concerns related to reflective teaching. Teachers, administrators, and other interested people have discussed teaching, schools and society, curriculum management, and kids. The two points that I have continually stressed are the importance of professional development and being knowledgable about and understanding the kids that you work with. Before the bell rings, there is one final piece that I would like you to read. To me it clearly illustrates the ability of kids to make it in spite of us. But imagine how great it would be if they always had us with them.

7th Graders Survive,
Despite It All

Ellen Goodman
Boston Globe

The girl has started seventh grade. This was to be expected. Nevertheless, her mother is of the confirmed opinion—based on experience—that seventh grade shouldn't happen to a dog.

If she were in charge, seventh grade would be eliminated like the 13th floor in hotels. Kids would go immediately from sixth to eighth grade, passing Go, without stopping to collect a set of teachers' scalps or social wounds.

The girl is not, praise the Lord and the local school board, going to something called junior high school. Just the name gives her mother hives. "Junior" high schools are the training bras of the educational world.

Once upon a time someone—probably the same person who invented "adolescence"—decided to isolate all the children between 12 and 14 in one institution, as if they had a social disease. Instead of finding a cure, they created an epidemic of precociousness, a generation of Jodie Fosters and Tatum O'Neals.

The mother remembers her own seventh grade, complete with terminal awkwardness, a math teacher who had deadly aim with erasers, and an English teacher who committed the ultimate mistake: she allowed herself to be vulnerable. Seventh graders go for vulnerability like ground-to-air missiles.

The funny part is that the mother loves this age, always has, loves the energy and wit and the devastating eye and appetites of the seventh graders who graze through her house.

But what is seen as energy in the world is often seen as unruliness in school. What is wit in twos or threes is often insolence in groups of 20. What is clarity to a parent or friend could be rebelliousness to a teacher.

Again the mother thought of the tension between family and school, between the two systems in which children live out their days. It was as loaded a relationship as any joint custody.

More often than not, families and schools, like divorced parents, hold different sets of expectations and goals, different views of one child, and of childhood.

When kids are young, families are the world they live in. Our power as parents is largely unshared. We are their environment, their standard, their reality, their value-tenders, and the people who interpret the outside to them.

If families work right, they are the place in which love is unconditional. If they work right, there is an assumption of love, even under discipline or anger. Good families don't flunk their children.

But on the first day of school—preschool, first grade, seventh grade, college—we give our children over to a system that doesn't love them. Give them over to be judged, to see if they can "measure up" to another standard. They enter a world in which they are only rewarded for how they perform.

I don't mean to present the schools as cold and teachers as uncaring. But parents see kids as special individuals, the school inevitably sees them as part of a group. School is the essential but scary halfway house between the home and the world.

I suppose we also give up our own teaching monopoly when we send them to school. There is nothing new in that. Since the beginning schools were the melting pots of a complex society. They taught immigrant children English and order; taught country people urban skills; taught everyone the "American" ways. We can only guess at how those lessons were at odds with family tutoring.

Even today the hottest issues at school are not about new math or phonetics but about conflicting values. A parent may encourage questioning, while the school has a bias toward passivity.

A parent may believe literally in the Bible, while the children are told that Jonah and the Whale is a story. A parent may abhor violence and the school enforces corporal punishment. A parent may praise order, while a school allows chaos. If sex education is the flash point, it is no surprise.

I don't know any parent who has not been aghast at some attitude or information lugged home with the school books. I don't know a teacher who hasn't felt that same flash of horror at some family opinion. We compete (as much as we cooperate) for influence, for space in the children's heads.

Eventually, I suppose it's the kids who make a kind of truce, even an uneasy one, by becoming their own people. Gradually they would pick and choose, find their own way through a thicket of teachers and parents and media.

Even now, in this miserable school year, they were becoming skeptical but dogmatic, unsure but stubborn, difficult but fascinating . . . self-made people. With any luck they would survive even seventh grade.